FARCRY PRIMAL

WELCOME TO THE HOSTILE TERRITORIES OF CENTRAL EUROPE IN 10,000 BCE

The Wenja tribe has always raised excellent hunter-gatherers. When resources started to dry up, they split into smaller groups in search of new hunting grounds around central Europe. One such group found a thriving ecosystem in Oros. The diverse selection of flora, fauna, and rock made the land ideal for settling and so they made it their home.

Unfortunately, two more tribes, the superior Izila and the brutish Udam, also consider the territory their own. As the Udam die out, they move out of the north in search of a better home—taking up arms against anyone who gets in their way. The Izila set up camp in the southern marshlands, enslaving members of the opposing tribes and putting them to work. This has scattered members of the Wenja tribe away from their village, and they now seek shelter wherever they can.

You are Takkar—a member of a Wenja hunting party—in search of food, fellow Wenja, and the legendary land of Oros. As you progress toward this bountiful land, your group is wiped out, leaving you isolated. It is now up to you to find Oros and rebuild the Wenja legacy. To do so, you must find several specialists and bring them back to the village so they can share their expertise and help bring peace to the land.

This official guide presents everything you need to reunite the Wenja and defeat the opposing tribes. Reference our world maps to find every important locale in the game. Walkthroughs for each mission and secondary quest lead you through Takkar's entire journey across Oros.

The expansive land of Oros has much more to offer than quests. Every Bonfire and Outpost is broken down with explanations of how to capture each one. Full explorations of all twenty-two Lost Caves indicate where to find the collectibles as well as how to find your way through the maze.

Complete everything the game has to offer with stats and specifics on every skill, weapon, tool, food recipe, and much more. Plus, for

SURVIVING THE WILD

This section contains everything you need to know about the beautifully harsh land of Oros.

THE HUD

Your HUD, or Heads Up Display, gives you all the information you need to help you stay alive on Oros.

MINI-MAP

The mini-map is located in the lower left corner of the screen, just above your health bar. Initially the mini-map shows the location of your beast and any marked enemies. As the game progresses and you unlock more skills, the mini-map gains the ability to show you the locations of resources and herbs.

If you have a Wolf as your companion, the mini-map shows a larger radius, allowing you to spot resources and topographical

HEALTH

Your health bar is below your mini-map in the lower left of the screen. Each bar starts as green and goes black when you've taken enough damage to lose that bar. The amount of bars you have depends on the Skills you have learned. Some skills add health bars, allowing up to a total of six.

CURRENT WEAPON/AMMO

Your current amount of weapons or ammo for the selected weapon appears on the bottom right of the screen. This only shows briefly after you've chosen the weapon, or recently thrown or used the weapon.

WATCH YOUR AMMO

Keep an eye on the ammo count! Try not to throw your last spear or club!

ENEMY AWARENESS

Small white arrows appear on screen and begin to fill when an enemy becomes aware of your presence. When the arrows are filled all the way, the icon flashes and the enemy begins attacking.

When the arrow isn't full, you can conceal yourself to make it rapidly fade away, allowing you to continue sneaking around the area undetected.

CRAFTING ICONS

Crafting Icons appear above the area that displays your ammo count. A hammer with a tent 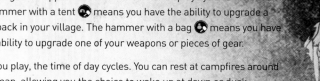 means you have the ability to upgrade a hut back in your village. The hammer with a bag means you have the ability to upgrade one of your weapons or pieces of gear.

As you play, the time of day cycles. You can rest at campfires around the map, allowing you the choice to wake up at dawn or dusk.

MOVEMENT

Oros isn't just a flat barren landscape, you need to master climbing, grappling, running, swimming, and sneaking through all the land. You can also use Fast Travel or the help of a nearby Mammoth to help you traverse the lands more quickly.

WALKING/SPRINTING

Move Takkar with the **Left Stick**. To move faster, press **L3** to sprint. Sprinting draws the attention of nearby predators and enemies. Some animals, such as the Woolly Rhino or Mammoth, may perceive a sprinting Takkar as an enemy and attack. Sprinting also scares nearby animals, making hunting much harder.

CLIMBING

Takkar can climb small ledges by simply pulling himself up. Most smaller ledges can be climbed by pressing **X/A**, causing Takkar to jump into the air and pull himself onto the object.

Other ledges that may seem a bit out of reach are marked with vines and are highlighted yellow when using Hunter Vision. Move as close as you can to the ledge, look up and follow the prompt, and Takkar pulls himself to the top of the ledge.

GRAPPLING

After unlocking the grappling claw, you are allowed to pull yourself up large cliff faces at certain points. These points are marked by a grappling claw icon at the actual grappling point. A cave painting of an eagle with its wings spread open is usually at the base of grappling points, signaling you to look up and locate the grappling point. When hanging from a grappling point, you can grapple to any other grappling point within range.

Once you are looking at the grappling point and within range, press and hold **Square/X** to throw your grappling claw up to the grappling point. Use **L2/LT** to go down, **R2/RT** to go up, **X/A** to jump, and **Circle/B** to detach yourself from the rope.

SWIMMING

When you enter water that is deep enough, Takkar immediately switches from walking to swimming. While swimming you

can use the Left Analog Stick to move around. To go underwater, change your camera angle with the Right Analog Stick to face under the water.

Enemies cannot spot you when you are under water so you can use this to help with a stealth approach on a group of enemies or animals.

Swimming is one of the best ways to escape enemies; quickly enter deep water and submerge yourself. Swim a short distance and reemerge. Even if they detect you, you can quickly sprint or use your bow to kill them from a distance.

STEALTH

Remaining concealed is important for surviving. Stay crouched to lower your audio and visual imprint in the environment. Crouching is essential for hunting. Bushes and boulders make up the majority of cover points in Oros.

When undetected, you can make short work of enemies by performing takedowns with **R3** when within distance. Submerging yourself in bodies of water also helps you stay undetected when moving.

HEALING AND FOOD

When you are damaged, press and hold **Triangle/Y** to heal yourself. The effectiveness of your healing depends on the type of food you are using and the different skills you have learned.

To view your available food recipes and set your quick heal options, press **D-Pad Left**. Constantly gather meat and plants to keep the necessary ingredients on hand for food crafting.

Keep helping Sayla to unlock new recipes, which both heal you and add temporary boosts to your abilities. For a full list of food check out the Food Recipes chapter.

RESOURCES AND CRAFTING

Resources are scattered around Oros and vary depending on the region you are in. To collect a resource, get in close then press and hold **Square/X** to collect it.

Different skills in the gatherer skill tree can increase your yields when collecting resources around Oros.

For a list of all the resources and crafting requirements, consult the Resources and Gear chapters.

REWARD STASH

As you progress in the game and liberate Outposts from enemy control, rewards go to you Rewards Stash. You can access your Reward Stash at any Outpost or Bonfire, as well as your Village.

WITHDRAWALS ONLY
You can only withdraw resources from the Reward Stash; you can't deposit excess resources for later use.

You receive rewards to your Stash every morning in game. The amount and type of rewards improves by upgrading the different huts in your village.

Reward Stashes can also be found at campfires, so stock up! Resources in the Stash do not count as being in your inventory, so you need to withdraw them for crafting or village upgrades.

THE MAP

The map menu allows you to apply a wide variety of filters to narrow down what you'd like to accomplish in Oros. You also have the ability to set custom Waypoints and Fast Travel from the map.

To zoom in on a point of the map use **R2/RT**, to zoom out press **L2/LT**.

Pressing **R3** centers the map cursor on the current position of the player.

FAST TRAVEL

Once conquered, Bonfires and Outposts allow Takkar to Fast Travel directly to their location via the map. Open the map and hover over the Fast Travel icon, then press **X/A** to travel to that area.

SETTING A WAYPOINT

To set a waypoint, hover over any objective or open map area and press **X/A**. To remove a waypoint press **X/A** again. The waypoint appears on your mini-map and HUD as a small square with a number showing the distance remaining to the waypoint.

FILTERS

There are seven different filters on the map, each allowing you to target specific objectives:

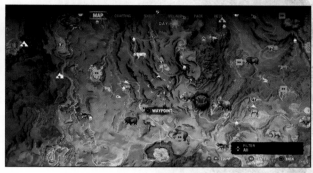

▶ **ALL:** This setting does not filter out any objectives, displaying them all at the same time.

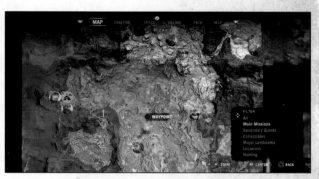

▶ **MAIN MISSIONS:** The Main Mission filter allows you to target the missions that progress the main story of the game.

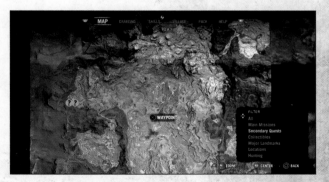

▶ **SECONDARY QUESTS:** These missions are not integral to the progression of the game's story. This filter is great for finding quick opportunities to level up and gain villagers.

▶ **COLLECTIBLES:** If you're looking for some easy XP, this filter shows you all the collectibles that you have discovered, but not yet acquired, during your journey through Oros.

▶ **LOCATIONS:** The Locations filter shows Campfires, Caves, and major Points of Interest. Plotting your route through the locations marked by a ? awards you easy XP as you travel.

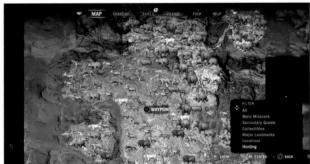

▶ **MAJOR LANDMARKS:** The Major Landmarks filter shows the location of all Outposts and Bonfires as well as your home base. This makes it easy to see which Fast Travel locations you have unlocked and which ones you still need to complete.

▶ **HUNTING:** The Hunting filter shows the standard locations that each animal is found in. This is great for hunting down a specific type of animal when you need their skin for crafting.

HUNTING KNOWLEDGE

Hovering over each animal shows their Hunting Difficulty, Loot, and any special trait the animal has.

COMBAT

Takkar has various weapons at his disposal, allowing him to kill enemies in a variety of ways. Every single weapon has the ability to be used as a ranged weapon.

FIRE

With the help of Animal Fat or a nearby fire, any weapon can also be used to carry a flame. To light a weapon on fire, hold **L1/LB** and choose the weapon with the **Left Stick**, and then press **Square/X** to ignite the weapon. This action removes a piece of Animal Fat from your inventory.

A lit weapon is extremely useful for scaring off predators, setting diversion fires, and staying warm in the cold north. When lit, however, your weapon loses durability until it eventually breaks. Try not to bring a mostly burnt weapon into battle as it will likely break after a few strikes.

DOUSING YOUR FLAME

Entering water or walking underneath a waterfall will put out your fire.

TAKEDOWNS

Takedowns are the best method for close quarters combat; they require no ammo and instantly kill any enemy. If an enemy is unaware of your presence, stay crouched and sneak up behind them to perform a takedown with **R3**. When upgraded in the Skill Tree, Takedowns allow you to take out chains of enemies, including the Elite Chieftains.

SELECTING YOUR WEAPON

Select your Weapon by holding **L1/LB**. This opens the weapon wheel, allowing you to choose which weapon and throwable item you want to have equipped for combat.

To toggle between different item types like clubs or bows, highlight the item with the **Left Stick** and then use **D-Pad Left/ Right** to switch between available options. You can quickly swap to your previously used weapon by pressing **Triangle/Y**.

WEAPONS

As you progress you unlock different weapons to help you survive in Oros. These weapons can each be upgraded to increase their durability and damage outputs. For full details and stats on each weapon, visit the Gear section.

Each melee weapon has three attack types, ranged, standard, and a heavy attack:

▶ **RANGED:** To throw your weapon, press **L2/LT** to lift it above your head for aiming, then press **R2/RT** to throw your weapon. The spear is by far the best thrown weapon in the game, gaining a damage bonus when thrown.

▶ **STANDARD:** The standard attack is a quick swipe or jab performed by quickly pressing **R2/RT**. This is your best attack when facing multiple enemies.

▶ **HEAVY:** Heavy attacks are performed by holding **R2/RT**. These attacks are meant to stagger and stun your enemy. This allows you to stop an enemy while they load up an attack, making it a great option when taking on Elite enemies.

All weapons grant bonus damage when attacking the heads of enemies. The only exception to this is the Elite Chieftain. The Elite Chieftain wears a thick mask, making attacks to vulnerable parts of the body much more effective.

WELCOME

SURVIVING
THE WILD

LAND OF OROS

TAKKAR'S JOURNEY

MAJOR LANDMARKS

LOCATIONS

VILLAGE
CONSTRUCTION

ENEMY TRIBES

WILDLIFE

GEAR

SKILLS

FOOD RECIPES

RESOURCES

COLLECTIBLES

TROPHIES/
ACHIEVEMENTS

THE ART OF OROS

CLUB

The Club is cheap and great for fighting multiple weak enemies. Since the club has a low cost, its best used when trying to carry fire from one place to another or to stay warm in cold areas.

TWO-HANDED CLUB

The Two-Handed Club is the big brother to the standard club. This club is slower but compensates by dealing a greater amount of damage. It is good for fighting Elite Enemies.

BOW

The Bow is a balanced and versatile long range weapon with great accuracy. When upgraded it gains a decent rate of fire bonus, allowing you to quickly put arrows into a charging target.

Make sure you have a good supply of spears. You can never go wrong with big sticks.

— *Vincent Pontbriand, Senior Producer*

LONG BOW

The Long Bow is slow to draw, but provides increased damage and aim zoom for unmatched long range precision.

DOUBLE BOW

The Double Bow offers fast performance and fires two arrows at once.

SPEAR

The Spear is a strong weapon, allowing you to easily get one hit melee kills when you land accurate shots to an enemy's head. The real benefit of the spear is found when you throw it. A thrown spear deals more damage than a melee strike. Using spears to eliminate an enemy from a distance can make the difference between life and death when facing certain foes.

WASTE NOT, WANT NOT
Once an enemy is dead be sure to go collect your spears protruding from their body.

THROWABLES

Throwables are located at the bottom of your weapon wheel. You can quickly use them by holding **R1/RB** to aim, then releasing **R1/RB** to throw the weapon. Different throwables can be unlocked in the Skills Menu. For a full breakdown on all throwables, check out the Gear chapter.

STONE SHARD

Stone Shards are thrown to damage enemies; headshots are lethal. Stone Shards can be upgraded to shatter Elite enemy's masks. Stone Shards can even be used during Takedowns if you have the appropriate Skills.

POISON SHARD

Throw Poison Shards at human enemies to drive them berserk, making them attack others.

FIRE BOMB

Fire Bombs shatter on impact, igniting enemies and animals.

STING BOMB

Sting Bombs are bags filled with angry bees. Throw them at your enemies and run.

BERSERK BOMB

Throw Berserk Bombs at human enemies to drive them berserk, making them attack others.

ROCKS AND THE SLING

Before you learn about the Sling, pressing **D-Pad Down** lets Takkar throw a rock. This helps distract enemies and singles them out for attack.

Once you have learned the Sling, holding **D-Pad Down** causes Takkar to start swinging the loaded Sling above his head. Rocks thrown from the Sling go much further and can be lethal if you hit an enemy in the head.

BAIT

Throw Bait to attract nearby animals. Some beasts attracted by bait can be tamed.

TRAP

Place these concealed Traps to surprise enemies and keep predators at bay.

SURVIVING OROS

Oros is full of life, and a lot of it wants you dead. Animals want to kill you, enemy tribes want to kill you, and even the weather wants to kill you!

SNAKES...I HATE SNAKES

Snakes are everywhere. Luckily for you, they like to warn you before they attack with a loud hissing sound. If you ignore or don't hear the sound, you can still spot them with your Hunter Vision.

Using a rock thrown from your sling is the best option for killing snakes as it does not take any resources to replace the rock.

If a snake lands a bite on you, poison immediately starts to take hold, adding a green hue to your screen and draining your health. This effect can be stopped if you have the correct food on hand.

DAY AND NIGHT

Day and night are like two completely different versions of Oros.

During the day, predatory animals are rarely found outside of their natural hunting areas. The main threat during the day is hunting

parties of the two enemy tribes that inhabit Oros. Keep your eyes and ears open and you'll make it through the day just fine.

The high visibility makes this a good time to travel longer distances to areas you haven't been before, preventing you from falling off an unseen cliff.

The night is a dark and dangerous place. Visibility is low and more predators come out to hunt. Exploring at night can yield unique animals, plants, and collectible items.

To help you stay alive at night, light your weapons on fire. Fire scares off weaker predators and lights the way, allowing you to avoid any environmental dangers.

THE GREAT WHITE NORTH

The northern area of Oros is covered in snow. In this area you need to stay warm to survive. A meter appears on the left side of the screen showing you how close you are to freezing. If this meter drains all the way, you take damage until you either find warmth or die.

Upgrading your Cold Gear in the Crafting Menu helps you stay warm longer.

Ultimately, the best way to stay warm is to light one of your weapons on fire and carry it with you into the cold. If you know you are going to come up on a fire soon, let the meter drain a bit and save your weapons from the durability loss.

ANIMALS OF OROS

There are many different types of animals that inhabit the land of Oros. The in-game map will guide you to which animals inhabit specific areas. The types and amounts of animals in the landscape change depending on the time of day.

DAY

Most large predators do not roam during the day, making your encounters with them less common outside of their normal hunting area. Daytime is best for hunting smaller animals for food and skins.

NIGHT

Hunting at night can be very dangerous as packs of Wolves roam Oros looking for food. Luckily, most roaming predators are scared of fire so having a lit club helps scare them off. Having fire also makes you easily spotted by non-predatory animals, so keep that in mind when you are the hunter.

To light a weapon on fire, hold **L1/LB** to choose the weapon with **Left Stick** then press **Square/X** to ignite the weapon. This action removes a piece of Animal Fat from your inventory.

HUNTING

Use your Owl and Hunter Vision to spot unsuspecting prey from a distance, allowing you to sneak up and line up a shot with your bow. You're not here to mount trophies, so aim for the head! Headshots are very effective at taking down animals.

If you did not kill an animal on the first shot, your Hunter Vision shows you the blood and scent trail leading to the animal you hit. Depending on how much damage was dealt on the initial attack, the animal may bleed out by the time you reach it, allowing you to easily skin it.

Spears do the most damage against animals, but they require the most amount of resources, making them an ineffective tool for hunting larger quantities of animals.

Skinning animals rewards you with generic and specific animal skins, meat, and animal fat. Keep your eye out for rare animals, they provide a rare type of skin that you need for certain upgrades. For a full list of animals including the rare variations, check out the Wildlife chapter.

BEAST COMPANIONS

While traveling through Oros it's always best to have a beast at your side to help you fight any roaming enemies or predatory animals. Not every beast in Oros can be tamed, but those that can each provide a special benefit to you.

BEASTS MENU

Press **D-Pad Right** to open the Beasts menu and see all tamable animals. Animals that you have yet to tame are grayed out, while animals you do not have the skill to tame are grayed out and also have a small lock placed to the top right of their image.

From the Beasts menu you can select a beast to call. Selecting your current beast companion dismisses it, while selecting a different beast replaces it. Upgrading your Beast Master Skills allows you to tame more beasts.

BEAST COMMAND

When tamed, your beast obeys your every command. To command your beast to go to an area or attack a target, aim with **L2/LT** then use **R1/RB** to issue the command.

To call a beast back to your side, press and hold **D-Pad Right**. This causes Takkar to whistle and your beast immediately returns to you.

HERE, BOY!

It is extremely helpful to summon your beast after big changes in elevation. In some cases, your beast may just spawn on the higher ground.

BEAST SURVIVAL

Elite Chieftains are the beast nemeses of Oros. Most smaller beasts quickly lose a fight with any Elite Chieftain. Bigger predators such as Mammoths and Cave Bears also pose a great threat to your beast.

When your beast is wounded, approach it and hold **Square/X** to heal it with Meat. If your beast dies, revive it from the Beasts menu or tame another in the world.

NO PET HOARDING

Taming two of the same beast does not allow you to have two of that beast. You may only have one beast of each type.

BAIT AND TAMING BEASTS

Bait is a necessity when it comes to taming a wild animal. To craft bait, open your weapon wheel and then highlight Bait on the bottom left. Bait is made from two Meat, which can be harvested from any animal in Oros. Once you have bait crafted and selected in your weapon wheel, press **R1/RB** to throw the bait. If any nearby carnivore is attracted to the bait, a small exclamation point pops up above their head to confirm they are taking the bait.

Once it is at the bait, approach the distracted animal slowly, and then press and hold **Square/X** to tame the beast. The tamed beast is then added to your available beasts in the Beast menu.

THAT NEW PET SMELL

A tamed beast replaces any beast you have at your side. You can call your old beast back from the Beast menu.

THE OWL

After bringing Tensay to your Village, you are granted access to your most valuable skill, the ability to call in an Owl to scout the area around you.

Press **D-Pad Up** to call in your Owl, then use your **Left Stick** to move the Owl through the air and the **Right Stick** to change where the Owl is looking. Pressing **L3** causes the Owl to fly faster through the air, making it easy to avoid any enemies. The Owl cannot hover, so it constantly moves forward. Use large circles around areas to capture every angle possible.

Your Owl stays active until it either collides with an object, is shot down by an enemy, or flies out of range. Only enemies who have been alerted to Takkar attack the Owl, otherwise it is left untouched.

The Owl can be upgraded to be more than just an eye in the sky. An upgraded Owl can tag enemies, direct your Beast, and drop weapons like Fire and Sting Bombs.

Hunter Vision can be used by the Owl; simply press **R3** to activate it while flying.

New Owl abilities can be unlocked in the Skills menu by building the Shaman's hut in your village.

BEAST SPECIALTIES

Each beast has special abilities to help you.

BEAST CATEGORY	PHILOSOPHY	NAME	PASSIVE ABILITY 1	PASSIVE ABILITY 2
Canines	Explores, gathers, warns the player	Dhole	Auto loots (skin) a carcass for you after the beast makes a kill	
		Dhole - Rare	Auto loots (skin) a carcass for you after the beast makes a kill	
		Wolf	Growls to warn of nearby predators/ enemies	Extends the fog of war discovery radius within a certain range and increases mini-map radius by 350 feet
		White Wolf	Growls to warn of nearby predators/ enemies	Extends the fog of war discovery radius within a certain range and increases mini-map radius by 350 feet
		Rare Stripe Wolf	Growls to warn of nearby predators/ enemies	Extends the fog of war discovery radius within a certain range and increases mini-map radius by 350 feet
		Snowblood Wolf	Growls to warn of nearby predators/ enemies	Extends the fog of war discovery radius within a certain range and increases mini-map radius by 350 feet
Felines	Stealth attacks, tracking, tagging	Sabretooth Tiger	Fastest Predator	
		Bloodfang Sabretooth	Fastest Predator	
		Leopard	Auto tags animals around it in a small radius	
		Jaguar	Stealth attacks idle target without alerting nearby enemies	
		Rare Black Jaguar	Stealth attacks idle target without alerting nearby enemies	
		Cave Lion	Auto tags NPCs around it in a small radius	
		Black Lion	Auto tags NPCs around it in a small radius	
Bears	Assault attack, tank, fearless	Cave Bear	Has higher targeting priority than the player, forcing enemies to attack the Bear first	
		Great Scar Bear	Has higher targeting priority than the player, forcing enemies to attack the Bear first	
		Brown Bear	Has higher targeting priority than the player, forcing enemies to attack the Bear first	When idle, randomly performs a dig animation, which directly gives you loot
Honey badger	Deterrent, wildcard	Badger	Repels all animals	Auto-revives itself once after being killed

JOURNEY PROGRESSION

Once the first mission, Path to Oros, is complete, you start building your Wenja village and help out the villagers on numerous quests. You must collect resources to build and upgrade huts as well as craft new weapons and gear. Completing quests, discovering locations, and capturing bonfires and outposts all earn XP. This, in turn, is used to purchase skills, available as you add specialists to your village.

MAIN MISSIONS

Eight specialists found through your travels offer up a variety of missions. Every mission earns XP while occasionally unlocking new abilities, gear, food recipes, and resources. Some missions are required to move the story along. Refer to the Journey Progression chapter to find out how they are unlocked.

THE TAKEN WENJA

SECONDARY QUESTS

A number of secondary quests also become available as you progress through the game. Beast Master Hunts, Village Missions, Help Wenja quests, Tribal Clashes, Cave Quests, and Wenja Events all earn you extra XP for completion. Take advantage of these side quests to quickly learn new skills. Full walkthroughs for all Secondary Quests can be found in their respective chapters.

WENJA EVENTS

Wenja Events happen randomly as you travel the land of Oros. Successfully completing them awards the player with XP and more villagers.

RESCUE

A small group of enemies marches a Wenja ally back to their encampment. Quickly kill the enemies before they can attack their hostage.

USE YOUR BEAR

Call in a Bear to attack the enemies. This causes them to prioritize attacking the Bear over you or the hostage.

Once all enemies are dead, move in and untie the hostage to complete the mission.

DEFEND

A group of four Wenja require your assistance against an onslaught of enemies.

SERIOUSLY, USE YOUR BEAR

Having a Bear is very useful as it draws the attacks away from the Wenja, allowing you to keep them alive easily.

Help the Wenja survive each wave of enemies and any remaining Wenja join your village.

CARRIER

These events require you to kill and search the Carrier. The Carrier is marked by an objective marker and is generally escorted

by two to four other enemies of the same tribe. When you initiate contact with the group of enemies, the Carrier attempts to flee before taking cover a short distance away.

You do not need to kill all of the enemies in the small hunting group, just killing and looting the body of the Carrier completes the Wenja Event.

GOOD DOG!

Using the Dhole allows you to stay away from the hunting group, while the Dhole kills and loots the Carrier.

BEAST REPEL

A group of predators attacks Wenja. Use your spears and arrows to kill them quickly before they can get in and attack your tribe. Once you kill all the animal waves, the Wenja join your village.

SKIRMISH

A small Wenja hunting group has stumbled across a group of enemies. Help the Wenja quickly kill all of the enemy invaders. The combat tactics you've used elsewhere serve you well here.

LOCATIONS

During your travels, you discover new locations such as caves and campfires. Unknown locations earn you XP as well as a few perks. Navigate or fight your way through Lost Caves to find two types of collectibles, Daysha Hands and Cave Paintings. Doing so completes the cave and earns a decent amount of XP. Discovered campfires act as spawn points; die and you respawn at the closest one. Unknown locations earn you bonus points just for walking through a new area.

OUTPOSTS

Outposts are heavily fortified areas held by the enemies. Liberating them unlocks a Fast Travel Point, access to the Rewards Stash, and a safe place to rest.

BONFIRES

Bonfires are large beacons that mark your territory once claimed. Get rid of nearby enemies and light the bonfires to claim them for your tribe. Claimed bonfires unlock Fast Travel points, offer safe places to rest, and provide access to you Reward Stash.

COLLECTIBLES

Different Collectibles are scattered around Oros. When you are in close proximity to them, they appear on your mini-map and remain marked until you collect them. Your progress on each type of collectible can be viewed on your cave wall. Each collectible awards a small amount of XP, with the exception of the Spirit Totems which award the player with a 2% XP boost.

▶ **IZILA MASK:** Once worn by Suxli's sacrifices, these mark Izila Land.

▶ **DAYSHA HAND:** Glowing handprints show sites of spirit energy.

▶ **SPIRIT TOTEM:** Totems ask spirits for safe and successful hunts.

▶ **WENJA BRACELET:** Worn for life, they represent the tribe's eternal bond.

▶ **CAVE PAINTING:** Study the cave painting to find a rare resource nearby.

The full list of collectible locations and descriptions of each can be found in the Collectibles Chapter.

LAND OF OROS

The sprawling world of Oros takes time to fully explore with its caves, mountains, waterways, and plains. As you move out from your village into more hostile territories, travel times get longer. Bonfires, Outposts, and a few Campfires act as Fast Travel locations, just like your village. Use these to quickly move around the map.

MAP KEY

 Sayla the Gatherer

 Ull

 Cut Mamaf Cave

 Your Village

 Batari

 Great Prashrawa

 Tensay the Shaman

 Bloodfang Sabretooth Hunt

 Mamaf Graveyard

 Wogah the Crafter

 Bloodtusk Mammoth Hunt

 Mash Baya Rocks

 Jayma the Hunter

 Great Scar Bear Hunt

 Nasan Run Valley

 Karoosh the Warrior

 Snowblood Wolf Hunt

 Prashrawa's Birth

 Urki the Thinker

 Altar of Suxli

 Praying Stones

 Big Darwa Fort

 Blajiman Stones

 Udam Homeland

 Fire Screamer Fort

Light your club and follow the footprints further inside to find Cave Lions roaming the interior. Keep your torch at the ready to keep them at bay, getting in attacks whenever possible. Once the threat has been dealt with, use Hunter Vision to find the Wenja hunter hiding in a small cubbyhole. Talk to him to heal him as he warns of more Tigers nearby. If you do not yet have enough healing plants, he tells you to find some. There are several bags containing plants in the cavern.

A group of felines, including a tough Sabretooth Tiger, must be dealt with before you can extract the Wenja from the den. Set them on fire, pelt them with arrows, or beat them down with your club or spear. Pay particular attention to the Sabretooth. If you can tame him, he is a great addition to your Beasts menu, though you do need the Tame Apex Predators skill before doing so. Clear out the beasts and return to the hunter to complete the mission.

INTO UDAM LAND

OVERVIEW

Head over to Sayla's hut and talk to the gatherer. She informs you that the Yellow Leaf is needed to craft an Antidote, which is required to reach Udam's leader, Ull. This plant is found in the bitterly cold wastes of the north. If you haven't already crafted some, grab Winter Clothing before heading out.

STRATEGY

Move up the west side of the icy north until Into Udam Land begins. Hop across the rock outcrops, take out the Wolves below, and search for the rare yellow plant. Take the Yellow Leaf and you are captured and thrown into a cell located in a cave to the north. Escaping is made tougher as your gear has been taken from you.

PREREQUISITE	Complete Vision of Fire and Trapped
MAIN OBJECTIVE	Find the Rare North Yellow Leaf in Udam territory
DIFFICULTY	Hard
AWARDS	1000 XP
SPECIAL	Requires Winter Clothing. Unlocks Rare North Yellow Leaves and Antidote.
ENEMIES	Udam Slingers, Udam Warriors, Udam Scourges, Udam Elite Chieftain, Udam Archer, Udam Spearman, Udam Elite Archer, Udam Elite Warrior

Climb the ledge at the back of the cell and grab the grappling claw from the corpse. Attach the tool to the grappling point above, move up on the line, and jump off the back wall. Detach as you reach the door and drop down. Head toward the cave entrance ahead, perform a takedown on the enemy checking your gear, and then grab it.

Step out into the bitter cold and sprint to the right, briefly stopping at the fire to get warm. At the next cave, light a torch and proceed inside. Udam occupy much of the cave system, so scout each area before running in. There is only one Udam that must be taken down and searched; your main objective is exiting the caves. You can sneak past many of the Udam. Whether you kill them all or just the ones in your way, your goal is to escape.

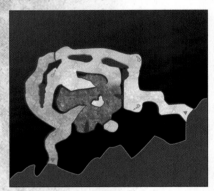

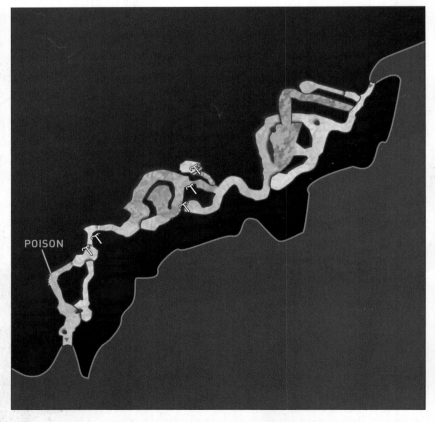

POISON

The first cavern has six Udam; two above, an easy takedown in a small room to the right, and three more in the middle. You can take out the upper two with two quick headshots. The far Scourge can be pulled away and taken care of with a takedown. The last two can be finished off or ignored as you follow the outside path up and out the far side.

Quickly sprint across another outside area to reach the next cave, which is a bit more complex. In the first room, the biggest threat is an Udam Elite Chieftain who watches over two Udam Warriors fighting at the far end. A lone Udam Warrior sitting by a fire is an easy takedown on the right. An Udam Warrior and Udam Archer sit by the central fire while others sleep. Finally an Udam Spearman patrolling a path around the central fire is also an easy takedown if done behind the rock. It is possible to get past this group while only taking down the lone Udam Warrior. Follow the narrow corridor to the right, drop behind the guy and perform a takedown. Descend off the right ledge and sneak around the outside of the room. Wait for the Udam Elite Chieftain to move to the central area and watch the two fighters. When the coast is clear move into the next area. If you are detected, stick around and take them down. You do not want to take the chance of alerting the next area too.

The leader is busy with two women on a rock above the middle of the next room. He is the one Udam that must be taken down. There are several guys around the outside of this area, including two Udam Elite Chieftains and a few Udam Scourges. It is tough getting to the leader without being detected, but take care of as many as you can quietly to limit the numbers who attack later. Start by taking out the two Udam Scourges straight ahead and to the left. Then, just circle around both directions, trying to get headshots on lone enemies or draw them out for takedowns. If all who remain are the leader and civilians, grapple to the upper ledge and take them out. If you are detected, seek out the leader and kill him while fending off the others.

It is time to flee the cave. Run into the next room and quickly eliminate the Udam Warrior and Udam Elite Archer on the narrow walkway. If anyone was left behind in the previous room, watch the mini-map to make sure they do not sneak up on you. Look for an Udam Elite Archer on the upper ledge ahead and quickly take him down. You are really close to the exit, but rot fumes block the lower route. Look for the grappling point above and use it to swing onto that upper ledge. Follow the path around the poison, drop down, and exit the cave. This completes the mission, sends you back to the village, and automatically hands over the Yellow Leaf to Sayla.

UDAM HOMELAND

With the Antidote, it is now possible to enter the Udam homeland and find Ull. The boss is extremely tough. Be sure you are well prepared before taking him on. Other areas are also available with a way past the rot fumes.

TENSAY THE SHAMAN

RECRUITMENT	Find Tensay and Complete Vision of Beasts
SKILLS	Beast Master Skill
SPECIAL	Ability to tame beasts, Owl, unlocks Udam's Big Darwa Fort and Izila's Fire Screamer Fort

Tensay is the psychotic, yet charming, Wenja shaman, intense and animalistic. He chews mind-altering plants, communicates with the spirits of nature, and holds audiences rapt with his colorful stories and animated personality. As the Wenja's only shaman, he is the keeper of the tribe's beliefs. When not lost in a hallucinatory spirit vision, he devotes his attention to healing the wounded, aiding births, and conducting funeral rites for fallen Wenja.

A year ago Tensay was captured and enslaved by the fire-wielding Izila tribe. They scorched his flesh with the fiery mark of a slave and forced him to erect their megalithic standing stones. After suffering months of back-breaking work, Tensay finally escaped and wrapped himself in a wolf skin to hide in the wilderness. Traumatized and half crazed, he set out to call upon a spirit strong enough to gather the scattered Wenja tribe and unite them against his former captors—the Izila.

Tensay the Shaman may seem a bit eccentric with the revolting concoctions he feeds to Takkar, but his missions offer up important aspects of the game. The ability to tame beasts and call for a scouting Owl are invaluable throughout your journey through Oros. Plus, his visions give you deep insight into the two bosses, unlocking both enemy tribe homelands along the way.

VISION OF BEASTS

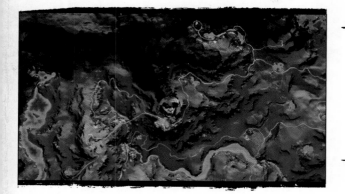

PREREQUISITE	Complete Deep Wounds
MAIN OBJECTIVE	Follow the Guide and Tame the Owl
DIFFICULTY	Easy
AWARDS	500 XP
SPECIAL	Call an Owl to scout an area
ENEMIES	None

OVERVIEW

Tensay hides out in a cave, northeast of the village—just beyond the Nakuti Bonfire. He has been waiting for Takkar to arrive and serves up a tasty-looking concoction. This sends the player into a hallucinatory trip.

STRATEGY

Be cautious when heading to Tensay's initial location as Udam Warriors and Udam Spearmen occupy the area. Move to the back of the cave, where Tensay takes over and Vision of Beasts begins. This simple mission introduces you to your extremely handy Owl. You just need to follow your guide. When on your feet or swimming, move down the path to the bright Owl. When in the air, fly right behind the bird, keeping an eye out for obstacles in your flight path. Eventually, you gain the opportunity to tame it.

BEAST MASTER

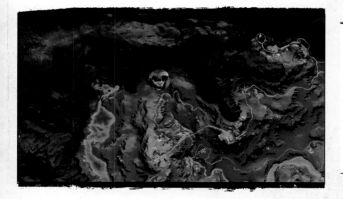

PREREQUISITE	Complete Vision of Beasts
MAIN OBJECTIVE	Find the wolf den and tame the White Wolf
DIFFICULTY	Easy
AWARDS	750 XP
SPECIAL	Ability to tame beasts, Tensay the Shaman in your village
ENEMIES	Udam Warriors, Udam Archers

OVERVIEW

Tensay claims you are the beast master and directs you to find the White Wolf and tame it. Completing this mission adds Tensay

to your village. Taming Skills are unlocked. Build Tensay's Hut and gain even more.

STRATEGY

Head northwest from the previous mission, approach the Tensay icon, and accept the mission. Call your Owl and fly directly south to find three Udam. They are tagged automatically as you fly over. Stealthily approach their location and quickly take them down.

Use Hunter Vision to pick up footprints that head south from the Udam camp to the Den of Walkwa. Crouch down and spot the White Wolf. Craft bait at the weapon wheel and toss it out toward the canine. Slowly approach and once you are close enough, tame it. This adds the White Wolf to your Beasts menu, so it can be called on at any time.

A couple of Udam are located just to the east; a great opportunity to test the beast out. Before dropping off the rocks, use Hunter Vision to spot the two enemies below. Send the White Wolf to the far target, while quietly taking down the nearest one. This completes Beast Master and adds Tensay the Shaman to your village.

XP FOR KILLS

Beast Kills do not get you as much XP as other kills such as Headshots and Takedowns. It is a quick and easy kill; just remember the payout is not as good.

BUILDING YOUR VILLAGE

It is time to start building your village. Give Sayla and Tensay huts and unlock skills, weapons, new items in your Reward Stash, and more. Once huts are built, talk to Sayla in the cave. She gives Takkar a new, powerful club as The Next Day begins.

VISION OF ICE

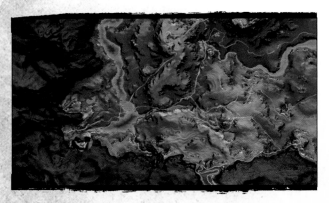

PREREQUISITE	Complete Attack of the Udam
MAIN OBJECTIVE	Find and destroy the stone woman statue
DIFFICULTY	Medium
AWARDS	750 XP
ENEMIES	Udam Warriors, Udam Spearmen, Udam Chieftains, Udam Archers

OVERVIEW

Tensay has concocted another of his hallucination-inducing cocktails. As Takkar takes a drink, Vision of Ice begins, allowing you to see through the eyes of Udam.

STRATEGY

Follow the icy path to the stone woman statue and attempt to interact with it. This transports you to another icy locale, equipped with a spiky club. Follow the path down the hill and pummel the Udam Warriors and Udam Spearmen who attack. You have unlimited clubs, so feel free to throw them at incoming fighters. Eventually you reach Udam Chieftains, equipped with a big, powerful club and better armor. They require a couple of club tosses to kill.

Just ahead, a big, stone woman statue stands in the way. Follow as it forges a path through the ice cave. Fight off the warriors that  appear, keeping an eye out for ground attacks from the statue itself—jumping to the side to avoid taking damage. Farther ahead, archers fire from side ledges; well-aimed clubs take care of them in one shot.

At the clearing, an onslaught of Udam Warriors and Udam Chieftains attack. Make quick tosses of your club to take them down. Udam Archers join in from above, requiring more precise throws. This goes on for a while. Avoid being surrounded as you finish them off. With the area clear, use a club to destroy the statue.

TAKKAR'S JOURNEY

HUNTING MAMMOTH

PATH TO OROS

JOURNEY PROGRESSION

MAIN MISSIONS

SAYLA THE GATHERER

TENSAY THE SHAMAN

ATTACK OF THE UDAM

WOGAH THE CRAFTER

JAYMA THE HUNTER

KAROOSH THE WARRIOR

URKI THE THINKER

CAPTURE UDAM BIG DARWA FORT

DAH OF THE UDAM

UDAM HOMELAND

CAPTURE IZILA FIRE SCREAMER FORT

ROSHANI OF THE IZILA

IZILA HOMELAND

SECONDARY QUESTS

BEAST MASTER HUNTS

VILLAGE MISSIONS

HELP WENJA: BEAST KILL

HELP WENJA: TRIBAL CLASHES

CAVES

✋ TAKING THE FIGHT TO THE UDAM

The small Udam camp has been destroyed, sending a message to the enemy tribe and now you have seen their icy home. It is time to prepare for the elimination of their clan. The fight for Oros begins as Big Darwa Fort becomes available to the north. It is not an easy fight though, so spend some time completing other missions, earning XP, and getting stronger before taking the Udam on.

THE TAKEN WENJA

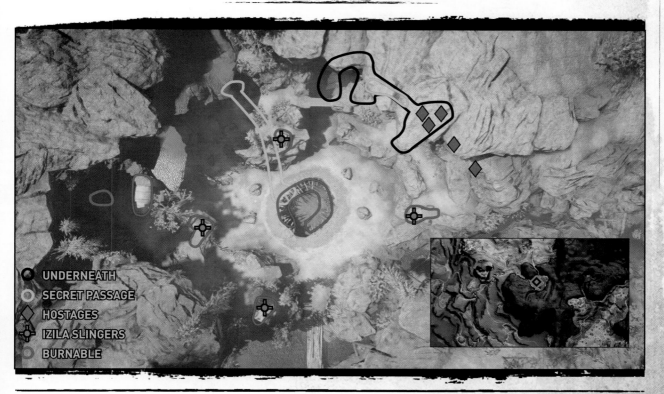

○ UNDERNEATH

○ SECRET PASSAGE

◇ HOSTAGES

✛ IZILA SLINGERS

○ BURNABLE

PREREQUISITE	Complete The Bone Cave
MAIN OBJECTIVE	Track the Wenja taken by the Izila tribe and free them
DIFFICULTY	Medium
AWARDS	1,000 XP
ENEMIES	Izila Slingers, Izila Archers, Izila Spearmen, Izila Warriors

OVERVIEW

The Izila tribe have taken Wenja and locked them up to the far east. There is still time to free them from their cages before they are used as tools by the sun walkers.

STRATEGY

Head east to the quest marker and accept the mission. Use Hunter Vision to follow the blood trail southeast toward the water. Follow the stream east through Mash Baya Rocks, investigating clues along the way. As you reach a bridge above, a scene plays out between the Izila and a couple of their hostages. Continue swimming, diving into a tunnel when you reach the waterfall. This leads into the Izila camp where they hold the hostages. Izila Slingers man watchtowers around the outside, while Izila Spearmen and Izila Warriors patrol the area.

Water tunnels wrap around the east side, leading all the way to the south end. Grappling points on the southeast and east allow for easy access to a couple of the Izila Slingers. Continuing in the water to the south, find a secret passage that leads north into the central pit. If you are detected inside, enemies pour into the hole, so be ready for a fight or flee back into the water. Stealth is an option for a while, but with the four watchtowers, it doesn't take long before you are detected.

Five Wenja hostages are being held on the west side. On the south side, look for the secret passage that leads right to them. Bust open their cages and untie them to set them free; with enemies present, they help in the fight. Once you have taken care of the Izila, ignite your weapons and set the place ablaze. The four platforms, cages, and wood spikes above the pit can be set on fire. The meter on the top of the HUD fills as it burns. More Izila fighters enter the area across the north bridge, so be on the lookout. Once the meter fills all the way, exit the camp After the scene, you must find a way out of the pit. Search for the underwater tunnel and swim to safety outside of the camp. After you escape the area, the mission completes and you return to the village.

✋ FACING BATARI

Wenja hostages have been freed from Batari's clutches, but there are more being forced to do her bidding. The sun daughter must be found and defeated in order to bring peace to Oros. Fire Screamer Fort appears on the map. This stronghold must be captured before you can reach Batari. Be sure you are ready before taking on this very challenging mission.

VISION OF FIRE

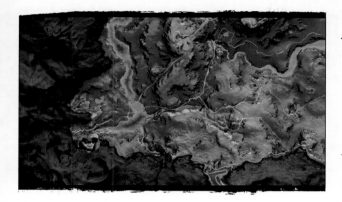

PREREQUISITE	Complete The Taken Wenja
MAIN OBJECTIVE	Discover what feeds Izila's fire
DIFFICULTY	Medium
AWARDS	1000 XP
ENEMIES	Izila Spearmen, Izila Archers, Izila Warriors

OVERVIEW

Your next visit to Tensay the Shaman offers up another drink and another vision. This time Takkar sees through the eyes of the Izila in a quest to find out what feeds their fire.

STRATEGY

Start out by interacting with the Krati ahead. This sends you to an Izila camp, equipped with The Fire of Krati bow. Move up the red path to reach the standing stones, killing the Izila along the way. Destroy the four stones, while fighting off the Izila Archers and Izila Spearmen.

In the next area, the moon threatens to block the sun during a lunar eclipse. Your goal is to shatter the moon with The Fire of Krati. Move up the path and kill any Izila that you see. Every time a triple-arrow shot is earned, launch them at the moon. Pay attention to damage indicators to find where the enemies are located. This also leads you up the fiery path. Be careful running into the final section as it is easy to get surrounded. Each successful hit with the triple-arrow further breaks up the moon until finally it explodes, completing the vision.

>  Tensay is always on edge. One second he could be joyful and charming and the second after he can be dangerously scary and violent.
>
> — *Jean-Sébastien Decant, Narrative Director*

 THE FIRE OF KRATI

This mission equips you with a special bow that fires a devastating meteor arrow. Kill five enemies to charge the Fire of Krati and gain a powerful triple-arrow shot as your next shot. After shooting the triple arrows you switch back to a meteor arrow.

>  Takkar is a reluctant hero. He comes to Oros to reunite with the Wenja, not to lead them. But Sayla and Tensay see the makings of a true leader in Takkar. Our story is about the resilience of humankind. No matter what is thrown in our path, we fight on and we form bonds. It's in our nature.
>
> — *Kevin Shortt, Lead Writer*

THE MASK OF KRATI

PREREQUISITE	Complete Into Udam Land
MAIN OBJECTIVE	Steal the mask of Krati from the Izila
DIFFICULTY	Hard
AWARDS	2000 XP
ENEMIES	Izila Elite Slinger, Izila Spearmen, Izila Elite Archer, Izila Warriors, Izila Archers, Izila Chieftain, Izila Elite Spearmen

OVERVIEW

Tensay the Shaman has a favor to ask of Takkar. Find the mask of Krati so that we can destroy their leader, Batari. The quest marker appears in far south Oros; approach it to begin the mission.

Find the narrow opening to the sacred cavern southeast of the Forest Tomb and follow the path until you drop into the water below. Swim through the tunnel toward the light to reach your destination. Call your Owl and take a minute to survey the area. An Izila Elite Slinger stands next to the mask of Krati with Izila Spearmen, Izila Archers, and Izila Warriors patrolling all around the area. Ivy to the right and a grappling point to the left offer access to the upper level, but watch out for the Izila. The more you can tag with the Owl, the less likely you are to be surprised.

Quietly move around the upper level and take out as many soldiers as you can with takedowns or headshots. The more you can eliminate from the cavern, the less you must face if and when the Izila Elite Slinger calls in reinforcements. As you get closer to the mask, the environment opens up, making it tougher to sneak around. A ledge on the north end gives great access to the Izila near the mask. Spend some time picking off the remaining foes while keeping an eye on the mini-map. Once the area is clear, run to the mask and snag it. It is now time to escape the tomb of Krati—hopefully unscathed.

You return to stable ground as many more Izila show up, many of which are Elites. There are several ways out of here; the following describes just one option.

Sneak over to the right ledge, wait for the Izila Elite Spearman to turn away, and quickly take him down. Remain crouched as you move across the bridge into the cave.

Turn left behind a short wall. An Izila Warrior above and Izila Archer below are easy targets for your bow. Hop over the ledge and climb the ladder on the left.

Peek around the next corner to spot an Izila Archer, quickly duck behind cover, and pull her toward you for a takedown.

Quickly take down the lone Izila Warrior ahead before he reaches the left turn, where three more Izila await. Quickly knock them out with your club or spear.

Remaining undetected is over, so sprint toward the quest markers to find the exit. It is possible to grapple across the front of the waterfall, but the safer route is around the left side.

 **IZILA HOMELAND**

This unlocks the Izila homeland, but you need the strength of a Mammoth to breach the gates. Purchase the Mammoth Rider skill before attempting this.

ATTACK OF THE UDAM

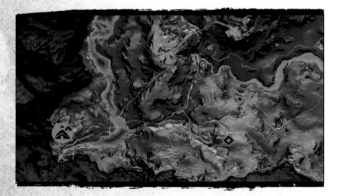

PREREQUISITE	Build Sayla and Tensay's huts and talk to Sayla
MAIN OBJECTIVE	Defend the Village from Udam. Kill Enemies and Destroy three Bone Trees at Udam Camp.
DIFFICULTY	Medium
AWARDS	500 XP
ENEMIES	Udam Warriors, Udam Archers, Udam Scourges, Udam Slingers

OVERVIEW

As your clan begins to make a new home for themselves in Oros, the Udam tribe takes notice and organizes an attack to once again destroy the Wenja village. Join with your fellow tribespeople and defend against the onslaught. Takkar is introduced to their evil leader, Ull, but he exits the area before you can go after him.

DEFEND THE VILLAGE STRATEGY

If it's not already at your side, call your White Wolf to assist in the fight. You can soften the Udam with arrows from afar, but the new club from Sayla and thrown spears do more damage. Warnings appear on screen when certain locations are under attack. First they go after the front gate and then the cavern gate. Use your canine's speed to your advantage and sic it on the distant Archers, while you go after the Warriors.

Watch out for Udam Scourges who toss poison bombs. These projectiles can eat away at your health, so make them a priority as you defend the village. Continue to watch the mini-map and go wherever help is needed. Eventually the attack is thwarted. Regroup with Sayla; it is time to take the fight to the Udam.

EFFECTS OF POISON

Bee stings, snake bites, rot fumes found later in the game, and poisonous bombs can all poison you. Once you are poisoned, your health slowly drains. At the moment you do not have an Antidote, so you must wait it out. Keep an eye on your health and be sure to heal when it gets low.

ELIMINATE UDAM CAMP STRATEGY

A small Udam camp, located nearby to the east, offers a chance to exact revenge on your enemy. Cautiously move up the hill toward the location and use your Owl to survey the area. Be careful if you have the Wolf companion as it may spoil a stealth attempt. Udam Archers and Udam Warriors occupy the retreat. They can be pulled outside the camp by tossing rocks, allowing you to perform takedowns on them without alerting the others. Or you can take the area over with brute force. Watch your back as reinforcements may have been called. Once the enemy has been eliminated, set the three bone trees, marked as objectives on your mini-map, on fire with burning arrows. Kill any remaining Udam Warriors to complete the mission.

BE CAREFUL AROUND FIRE

You always need to be cautious when setting targets on fire as it can easily spread through nearby brush, huts, and any other dry debris. Move clear of an area you wish to burn down to avoid taking damage from the flames. If you are set on fire, hold the Interact button to put it out or risk losing more health. It is even easier to set your companion ablaze, so be ready to heal it when playing with fire.

MORE WENJA FOR THE VILLAGE

More lost Wenja appear on the map to the east. Bring them back to the village and build them huts to unlock even more abilities.

WOGAH THE CRAFTER

RECRUITMENT	Complete Trapped and Blood of Oros
SKILLS	Crafting Skills
SPECIAL	Gives Grappling Claw and unlocks several great items for crafting

Wogah is a feral, dangerous, one-armed Wenja crafter—at once brilliant and completely deranged. One year ago the Udam tribe attacked his people. They massacred Wogah's village, captured him, and cut off his arm to feed on his flesh. Wogah staunched the blood flow and fashioned an ingenious device to break free from his cage. Ever since, he has lived the solitary existence of a hermit, chattering to himself and crafting traps to kill the violent Udam.

Wogah believes he is now the last surviving Wenja of the Udam attack. When he discovers the existence of other Wenja, his world is turned upside down as he rededicates his life to helping the tribespeople he feared he'd lost.

Wogah the Crafter lives alone in a nearby cave, thinking the rest of his fellow Wenja have been massacred. Because of this, it takes a while for him to warm up to Takkar. Once he does though, he offers a great selection of Crafting Skills and invaluable gear.

TRAPPED

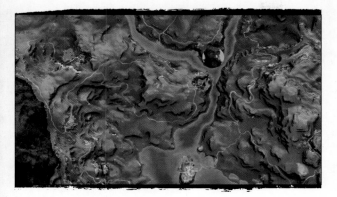

PREREQUISITE	Complete Attack of the Udam
MAIN OBJECTIVE	Escape the Cave
DIFFICULTY	Easy
AWARDS	500 XP
SPECIAL	Grappling Claw
ENEMIES	Jaguars

OVERVIEW

Once the Udam attack has been thwarted, new specialists appear on the map. Find and bring them back to the village to gain new skills and upgrades. Wogah the Crafter is found in a cave near the Shelter of the Lost. Climb the vines just to the east of this location and follow the wood path back west to find the cave. Enter to begin the Trapped mission.

STRATEGY

Wogah thinks he has caught another Udam and does not believe you are Wenja. You must find a way out of the cave to convince him otherwise.

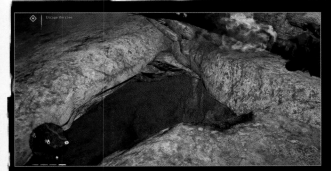

Light your torch and set the debris on fire to reveal a hole. Drop down to the lower level.

Head northwest to find a Leopard, tending to another Leopard carcass, and (if you have the skill) tame it with a piece of bait. Walk over to the body and pick up the grappling claw stuck in its side. This is an extremely useful tool as it allows for climbing and swinging to new heights.

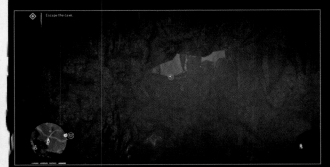

Return to the first cavern and spot a grappling point to the right. Use the claw to reach the ledge above and move to the end of the corridor.

Turn left and use the grappling claw to swing across the gap. Another grapple point allows you to descend into a big cavern below.

Four Jaguars attack as soon as you get within range, so be ready to keep them away with your torch. Climb out of the pit to the west and use the grappling claw on a point high up the right wall.

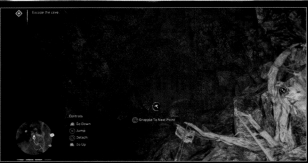

Continue up the wall ahead by ascending toward the first grapple point and switching to the next one when possible. You find an exit just ahead.

BLOOD OF OROS

BLOOD OF OROS

PREREQUISITE	Complete Trapped
MAIN OBJECTIVE	Find four Blood of Oros Rocks
DIFFICULTY	Medium
AWARDS	750 XP
SPECIAL	Wogah the Crafter in your village, unlocks Blood of Oros resource
ENEMIES	Udam Warriors, Udam Spearmen, Udam Archers

OVERVIEW

Return to Wogah so that he can get a look at the Wenja that he trapped. He introduces you to a great resource for weapons called Blood of Oros, but finding it has proven a tough endeavor. Find the precious material and Wogah will help the Wenja.

STRATEGY

Start the search at the objective marker to the northeast, where an Udam Warrior and Udam Spearman must be taken care of first. Just south of the campfire, burn off the branches from the dolmens and then interact with them to peer through the openings. Most have no result, but look through the one that faces southwest to find the Blood of Oros shining in the distance.

Climb to the sparkling location and investigate. More Udam fighters guard the site, where the four precious rocks are hidden. The overhead image shows the locations of the Blood Oros. Work your way around the outside of the area and eliminate the enemies.

✋ BEWARE OF THE CROCODILES

Be cautious as you enter the water around Oros, where Crocodiles often lie in wait. These predators do serious damage before you can escape their clutches. Use Hunter Vision to spot them hanging out near the water's edge. Put an arrow in a croc's head and collect the easy skin.

Now you are able to collect four of the rocks without worrying about the Udam. Search in the water and along the various ledges to the west and south to find them. Use Hunter Vision to make them stand out. Wogah joins your village once the you've obtained the fourth rock.

THE PEAK OF OROS

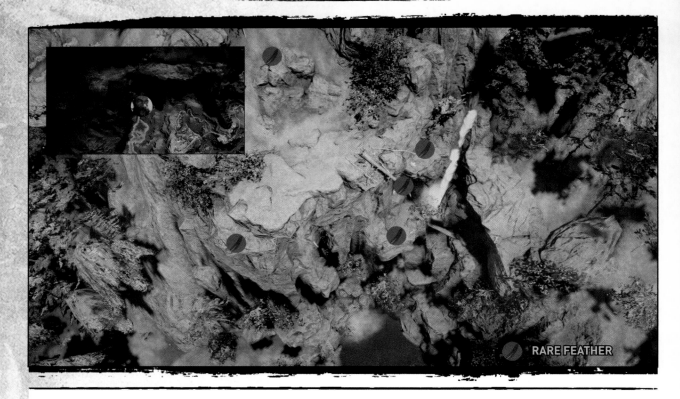

RARE FEATHER

PREREQUISITE	Complete Blood of Oros and build Wogah's hut
MAIN OBJECTIVE	Climb the cliff and collect Rare Feathers from the Eagle nests
DIFFICULTY	Hard
AWARDS	1000 XP
SPECIAL	Unlocks Rare Feathers
ENEMIES	Eagles

OVERVIEW

After building Wogah's hut, talk to him just outside and he offers to create new tools for you. But first, he wants you to collect Rare Feathers from Eagle nests to the north. Your new grappling claw allows you to reach the heights necessary to find these elusive resources.

STRATEGY

As you reach the water next to Eagle Cry Peak, the mission begins. Five Eagle nests are scattered up the cliff ahead. The mission helps get you familiar with the grappling claw as you climb and swing your way to the top.

Move around the left side of the lake and climb up the vines to the first ledge. Use the grappling claw on the first point ahead and swing across the gap.

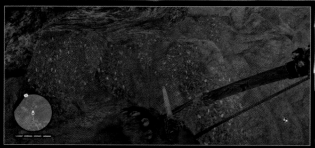

Climb and grapple up to the next ledge. Crouch and crawl under the low clearing ahead before ascending more vines.

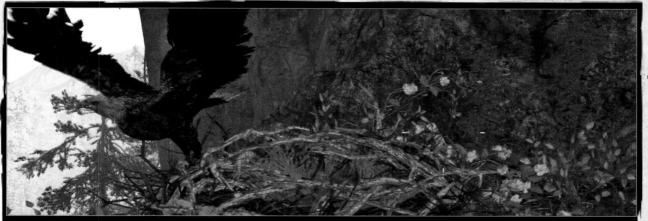

Turn around and grapple up to find the first nest. Grab the Rare Feathers that sit inside, turn around, and carefully cross the log that fills the next gap.

✋ BE AWARE OF ANGRY EAGLES

As you ransack the Eagle nests, you should expect the owners to not be happy. Listen for an Eagle to screech, signifying they are ready to swoop in on their prey. Quickly check the mini-map to see from where it approaches. Ready your club and time your swing so that you knock it out of the air just as it reaches you. If you are close to the edge, you could throw yourself off the side, so be careful. Staying on the move or holding a burning club out can also help avoid their attacks. More Eagles soar above as more nests are disturbed.

To the left is a weak wall that leads to a hidden room with two sacks inside. Watch out for the snakes. Back outside, use the grappling point high up the north face. Turn left and make a running leap to the next ledge where more Rare Feathers sit in a nest.

Three grappling points jut out from the cliff side ahead in succession. Use the grappling claw on the first, swing toward the second, attach to the second when the prompt appears, and repeat on the third. You can reach a fourth point on an upper ledge as you swing forward. The third group of Rare Feathers awaits inside another nest.

Ahead, vines lead up to the highest point. Watch out as the Eagle attacks become more frequent. Forward on the left is another Eagle nest, but you don't need it. Hop onto the fallen tree to the right and carefully walk out to the final nest to snatch the final group of Rare Feathers.

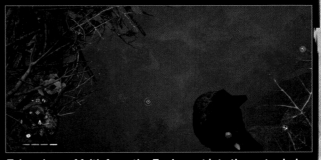

Take a leap of faith from the Eagle nest into the water below to complete the mission.

THE LOST TOTEM

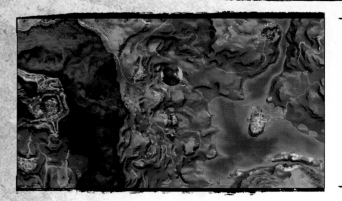

PREREQUISITE	Complete The Peak of Oros
MAIN OBJECTIVE	Recover scraps of the old Wenja totem from the Udam
DIFFICULTY	Hard
AWARDS	1000 XP
ENEMIES	Udam Elite Archers, Udam Elite Scourge, Udam Spearmen, Udam Scourges, Udam Warriors, Udam Slingers

OVERVIEW

Find Wogah just outside his hut. He talks about the Udam attack on the old Wenja home, which broke their totem in the process. He wants you to kill Udam and take back the totem scraps, so he can build a new one.

STRATEGY

As you near the Wogah marker, the mission begins. Your first objective is to tag the totem looters. Quietly approach their location on the Daywa Snake Path and aim at each Udam to identify them; a double circle icon appears above those who hold the totem scraps. They also highlight in red with Hunter Vision enabled. Stay in the shadows as you identify the three looters.

Once they have been exposed, set out to take them down. It doesn't matter how you do it—with stealth or all out warfare— you just need to kill and search the three looters. Once you are detected though, they tend to run, so be aware that a chase may be involved. Start by taking down the Udam Elite Archer as he stands guard on the rock above. Look for the three quest markers to quickly identify the scrap locations. Watch for poison bombs, Wolves, and attacking Udam as you collect the three pieces of the totem. The runners lead you into Lone Spear Camp, which is occupied by the Udam, so be alert for more enemies. Once you obtain the third scrap, the mission is complete. Talk to Wogah at the village to see the new totem.

My favorite character? Wogah the crafter. Because even if we are in the Mesolithic era, even if he is surrounded by other strong and brutish people, he was able to invent something to help him and his tribe survive. How cool is the grappling claw?!

— *Fabien Govini, Lead Design Director*

JAYMA THE HUNTER

RECRUITMENT	Complete On the Hunt
SKILLS	Hunting Skills
SPECIAL	Unlocks Beast Master Hunts, Long Bow, Double Bow, Sling

Jayma is a fierce, heavily-scarred Wenja hunter. She has spent her life in the wilds hunting the fiercest beasts. She's survived longer than most hunters who are often maimed or eaten by the beasts of Oros. She has a few faithful Wenja hunters who walk with her, eager to learn from this old master. She's in her twilight years and eager to pass on her experience to a worthy hunter. She has yet to find that hunter.

Jayma is a veteran huntress with numerous scars to show for it. From the first time you meet her, she taunts you—challenging you to hunt the fiercest beasts of Oros. She passes on her expertise with hunting skills that improve your Hunter Vision as well as unlocking the best long-range weapons in the game. She also introduces the four Beast Master hunts.

ON THE HUNT

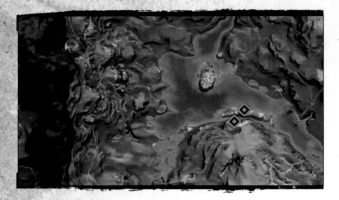

PREREQUISITE	Complete Attack of the Udam
MAIN OBJECTIVE	Track the Brown Bear
DIFFICULTY	Medium
AWARDS	500 XP
SPECIAL	Adds Jayma the Hunter to village
ENEMIES	None

OVERVIEW

Jayma is an expert hunter who is currently with her hunting party southeast of the village. She is brash and thinks that Takkar needs help improving his skills. Grab the Tame Apex Predators skill if possible before starting this mission.

STRATEGY

Approach the objective marker to meet the arrogant hunter. It is time to show her you are no slouch. Enable Hunter Vision to find Bear prints leading to the east. Follow them down the hill; stopping to investigate the damage the Bear has done along the way. Pay attention to the way the prints face as there are gaps in the trail. Continue in that direction to pick it back up.

 Jayma the wise hunter wears her wounds with pride. You can't rattle Jayma. She's seen the worst that Oros can deliver and she's ready to pass on her wisdom to you.

— *Kevin Shortt, Lead Writer*

Track the Bear south and then east to the big lake. The trail continues over a strip of land across the water, along the coast to the left and on over to the narrow island located to the northeast. Here you find your target. If you have the ability to tame Apex Predators, then toss bait out and add it to your companions; a powerful option for tougher foes. It also uncovers and gives you nearby resources when idle. Otherwise, take the Bear down with some spear throws. Cross the water to the south to show off your new pet to the hunters—if that is the way you handled it.

THE TALL ELK

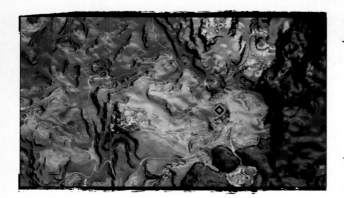

PREREQUISITE	Build Jayma's hut
MAIN OBJECTIVE	Hunt the Tall Elk
DIFFICULTY	Medium
AWARDS	750 XP
SPECIAL	Only available at night
ENEMIES	Tall Elk, Udam Spearmen

OVERVIEW

After building Jayma's hut, enter and talk to the huntress. She challenges you to take on the Tall Elk at nighttime. The Elk is most likely your toughest hunt yet, so prepare. Once you are ready, head out to the far west at night to find the mission start.

STRATEGY

After accepting the mission, turn to the south and follow the path of the fireflies up the hill. Eventually you reach an overlook at Halchi Hunt Run. Wait for the Tall Elk to show up below and get things started with an arrow or spear to the head. These animals are tough, taking quite a bit of damage before going down, so be prepared. Immediately sic your beast on it as it flees the area. You must take it down before the Udam do, so quickly chase after it.

Watch out when you catch up to the beast, as it charges at you. Step to the side to avoid taking damage. When needed, be quick with a heal and get back in the fight. Kill the Udam Hunters whenever the opportunity arises, but your focus is the Elk. Keep your pet after your target as you continue to hit it with your most powerful weapons. Once it goes down, approach and skin it to complete the mission.

🐾 THE GREAT BEAST MASTER HUNTS

Talk to Jayma at her hut after completing The Tall Elk. She challenges you to go after four elusive great beasts, unlocking the four Beast Master Hunts: Bloodfang Sabretooth, Bloodtusk Mammoth, Great Scar Bear, and Snowblood Wolf. Look for the quest markers on the map.

THE GREAT BEAST

PREREQUISITE	Complete The Tall Elk
MAIN OBJECTIVE	Join Jayma's hunters to take down a mighty Mammoth
DIFFICULTY	Hard
AWARDS	1,000 XP
ENEMIES	Mammoth

OVERVIEW

Visit Jayma in front of her hut to learn of a hunt that is already underway. Head out to Jayma's quest marker to the southeast, find the tree stump used for target practice, and accept the mission. Find the hunting path to the west at Nasan Run Valley and talk to the lead hunter to get things started. Call your strongest beast, but make it stay with the hunters for now. Since the Bear is strong and draws the enemies' attention, it is a good choice. Also, set a strong heal as the default before moving out.

STRATEGY

Find the Mammoth not too far away to the east, near the small body of water. Stay a safe distance away and get its attention with an arrow. If it moves in, quickly turn around and run back toward the hunters. Don't get too far away though, or the Mammoth loses interest. If you notice it heading back or see the message to lure the Mammoth, get its attention again. When you reach Nasan Run Valley with the target, the hunting party launches their attack.

Use up your spears on the Mammoth while keeping your companion busy attacking. Climb onto the south or east platform and attack from there, though it may be necessary to get back into the action if you run out of projectiles or your beast is knocked out. Try to keep the center rocks in between you and the target. If you find yourself in line with her charge attack, jump out of the way to limit the damage. Finally, she collapses.

KAROOSH THE WARRIOR

RECRUITMENT	Complete Brother in Need
SKILLS	Fighting Skills
SPECIAL	Unlocks Winter Clothing

Karoosh is a powerful, gregarious Wenja fighter. He suffers over the death of his only child. He had dreams of his young boy fighting alongside him for many years. Instead, his boy was killed by Mog, an Udam Warrior. Karoosh lost his own eye trying to defend his boy. Now he vows revenge. He is hunting for Mog and slicing through all Udam that come in his path.

For Karoosh, his revenge journey is a joyous adventure. It's in honor of his dead child. This quest for Mog is the closest Karoosh will ever get to fighting alongside his child and he is determined to live the adventure to its fullest. And he will not rest until Mog is dead.

Karoosh is a vital addition to your village if you plan to take on the Udam stronghold to the north. He offers powerful takedowns along with better clubs and spears. Most important though, his winter clothing allows you to survive longer in the bitter cold temperatures.

BROTHER IN NEED

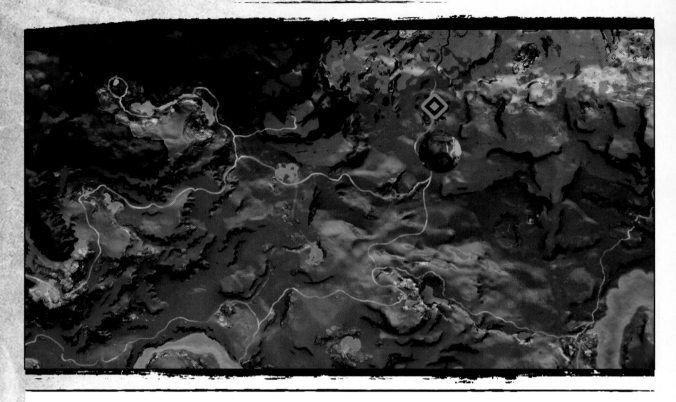

PREREQUISITE	Complete Attack of the Udam
MAIN OBJECTIVE	Protect a Wenja Warrior from the Udam
DIFFICULTY	Medium
AWARDS	500 XP
SPECIAL	Adds Karoosh the Warrior to village
ENEMIES	Udam Warriors, Udam Slinger, Udam Spearmen, Udam Archers

OVERVIEW

Find a Wenja hiding behind a tree, directly north of the Roaring Falls Bonfire. He needs you to help out a Wenja Warrior to the north who is under attack from the Udam.

STRATEGY

Call your strongest companion and run north toward Mamaf Foot Pond. As you approach the Warrior's location, Karoosh's health bar appears at the top of the screen. If this drains completely, you fail the mission, so work quickly. Move onto the rock outcrop to get a view of the situation; the Wenja attempts to fight off a group of Udam Warriors. Immediately sic your pet on one and pelt the others with arrows and spears. Once the Udam have been taken care of, meet the mighty Karoosh.

He wants your help burning the bodies to send a message to his mortal enemy, Mog. Spot three bodies and move them to the campfire. More Warriors attack as you do so, but it is possible for Karoosh and your beast to take care of them during the time it takes you to perform this task—just keep an eye on your friend's health. Watch out for an Udam Slinger on the rocks above. Take care of him with a well-placed arrow. Spearmen and Archers join the Warriors in the attack. Keep your pet busy and quickly move between the enemies. Defeat them all to complete the mission and bring Karoosh back to your village.

STOMP UDAM

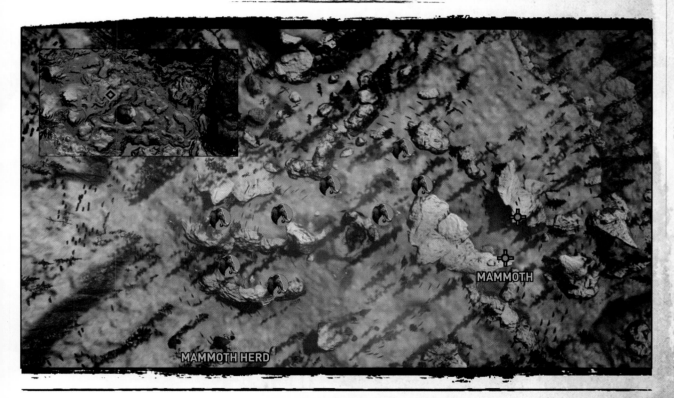

MAMMOTH

MAMMOTH HERD

PREREQUISITE	Build Karoosh's hut and purchase Mammoth Rider skill
MAIN OBJECTIVE	Save a Mammoth, mount the beast, and trample the Udam Hunters
DIFFICULTY	Hard
AWARDS	1,000 XP
SPECIAL	Mammoth Rider skill is required to unlock this mission
ENEMIES	Udam Slingers, Udam Warriors, Udam Elite Scourges, Udam Elite Archers, Udam Elite Spearmen

OVERVIEW

Build Karoosh's hut once the resources are available and talk to him inside. He warns of Udam who hunt the Mammoth in the far north and use the bones for their bone trees. Turn the animal against the Udam by mounting it and trampling the Hunters.

STRATEGY

After accepting the mission at the marker, head northwest to find a captured Mammoth surrounded by Udam. Move up the right rock and perform a takedown on the first Slinger, followed by an arrow to the head of the second. Sprint over to the Mammoth and mount it. Take off to the north and charge through the bone tree. There are three ways to attack with the beast.

MAMMOTH ACTIONS	
CHARGE ATTACK	Sprint Button
MAMMOTH ATTACK	Takedown Button
TAKKAR ATTACK	Hold Aim and press Quick Attack

Take the Mammoth west and demolish any bone structure you see. The shaded areas on the mini-map represent where they are found. Udam continually attack throughout the quest. Kill them as you move between the bone trees. Once the yellow bar at the top of the HUD fills, ride the Mammoth to its herd to the west and dismount.

EYE FOR AN EYE

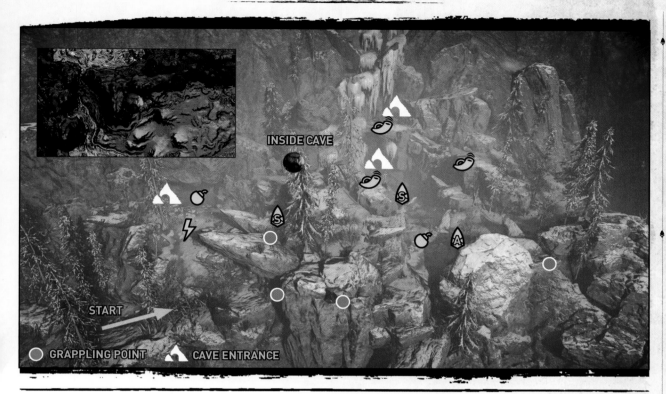

INSIDE CAVE

START

GRAPPLING POINT   CAVE ENTRANCE

PREREQUISITE	Complete Stomp Udam
MAIN OBJECTIVE	Catch up to Karoosh and join his fight against his Udam nemesis
DIFFICULTY	Hard
AWARDS	750 XP
ENEMIES	Udam Elite Warrior, Udam Elite Scourges, Udam Elite Spearmen, Udam Elite Slingers, Udam Elite Archers, Udam Elite Chieftain

> **The Mammoth is the beast most emblematic of the Stone Age. They are also gigantic and the shape of their tusks is unique.**
>
> — *Jean-Christophe Guyot, Creative Director*

OVERVIEW

Head over to Karoosh's hut and talk to the villager to find out the warrior has gone after Mog himself. Find his quest marker in far north Oros, deep inside Udam territory. He rests inside a cave on the east side of the mountain just south of Cave of the Drowned. If you already have three Green Leaves in your pack, this mission is easier to complete. If you don't yet have them, you are given an additional objective to gather them in the nearby area.

STRATEGY

As you approach the Cave of Frozen Knives, dismiss your beast and send out the Owl to survey the location. Udam litter the area, but it is possible to distract the enemies and sneak inside unscathed. We are going to take the stealth kill approach, though, and eliminate all foes. Note that the left cave entrance does not reach Karoosh.

Hide in the brush ahead and use rocks to pull the Elite Warrior over and take him down. Grapple to the rock ledge above and quietly perform a takedown on the Elite Spearman.

Move toward the cave entrance, wait for the Elite Scourge to turn his back, and eliminate him. With the left side taken care of, use the three grappling points around the east side to reach the northern area.

Drop down to the path and observe the Elite Archer and Scourge. Takedowns from the brush eliminate that threat without drawing attention from the Elite Slingers. Carefully move out to the path below them and kill the Elite Spearman who patrols the route.

Now only the three Elite Slingers remain as they stand guard on the rock ledges above. Quietly get behind each one, kill them with takedowns, and pull them away from the edge to avoid detection. Now you are free to enter one of the right cave openings and reach Karoosh.

Now that you have found Karoosh, hand him the three Green Leaves to get him back on his feet. Many more Udam approach your location, so you must fight your way out. The debris that blocked the path to the right is now clear so it is a straight shot out. Call in your beast if it's not already by your side. Stay close to Karoosh as you fight off the enemies, making sure his health bar is not reduced all the way. He does heal when not in combat. Watch your back, as Udam enter from the other side. Use bombs at the cave entrance to quickly reduce their forces. Once you get a short way down the hill, the mission is complete.

URKI THE THINKER

RECRUITMENT	Complete Urki's three missions
SKILLS	None
SPECIAL	-

Urki is the ancient ancestor of Far Cry's Hurk. He is a simple Wenja who always tries to make his life easier. He's continually working on new ideas. Unfortunately, his caveman brain is much slower than your average primitive man and his good ideas fall flat from terrible execution. He won't be long for this Mesolithic world.

Urki is just as crazy as his far flung descendant. He is not a specialist but he still joins the village, offering three missions and comic relief along the way. Takkar unknowingly helps out with Urki's off-the-wall ideas, which often lead to self-harm.

FLY LIKE BIRD

PREREQUISITE	Complete The Taken Wenja
MAIN OBJECTIVE	Help Urki learn to fly
DIFFICULTY	Easy
AWARDS	500 XP
ENEMIES	Bitefish, Izila Hunters, Jaguar

OVERVIEW

Find Urki the Thinker at Mayta Wenja Camp. Move close to the hut door to accept his first mission. He needs help making feathers so that he can fly like a bird. The nearby lake attracts all four animals that you need: Raven, Snow Bird, Bitefish, and Tortoises.

STRATEGY

Hunt and skin the four animals for Urki. Once you've obtained them, join him on the wood platform high up on the side of the cliff and hand over the ingredients. Return to the objective marker below to complete the mission.

▶ For Bitefish, use Hunter Vision to spot the predatory fish in the water. Wait for one to get close to the shore and take it out with a spear. You can also fight one off after it bites you in the lake. Jump in and skin it, but watch out for other Bitefish.

▶ Ravens land on rocks along the northwest side of the lake. Take one out with an arrow and skin it to obtain the Raven feather.

▶ Snow Birds are found walking around the grassy area of the center island. Just like with the Raven, take one out with an arrow and skin it.

▶ Tortoises are easy to find on the far shore, but they do need to be coaxed out of their shell. Knock one out with your club.

STRONG LIKE ROCK

● URKI ROCK

PREREQUISITE	Complete Fly Like Bird and return to the village
MAIN OBJECTIVE	Help Urki to protect himself from the Udam
DIFFICULTY	Hard
AWARDS	750 XP
ENEMIES	Izila Elite Warriors, Izila Elite Archers, Izila Elite Slingers, Izila Elite Chieftain, Izila Civilians

OVERVIEW

Return to Urki's hut to learn about his next scheme. He wants you to collect a particularly hard rock from a nearby Izila camp so that he can protect himself with "rock skin." Head over to the cliff above Drowning Huts and scout the area with your owl, being sure to tag all of the Izila, including the civilians.

STRATEGY

Follow the winding trail or use the grappling claw to reach the huts. There are four "Urki rocks" that can be collected, but you only need to grab three. Izila patrol the area around the structures well, requiring you to use distractions to take them down stealthily. Note that some Izila are less active at nighttime, when it is easier to get the stones without stirring up any trouble.

Give them a wide berth as you move around the left side and collect the rock next to the hay. Swim out to the end of the left dock, wait for the civilian to head back to camp, and nab the second. Swim to the left and make sure the coast is clear as you move toward the far stone. Return them to Urki and do what he asks to complete the quest.

URKI'S NEW STINK

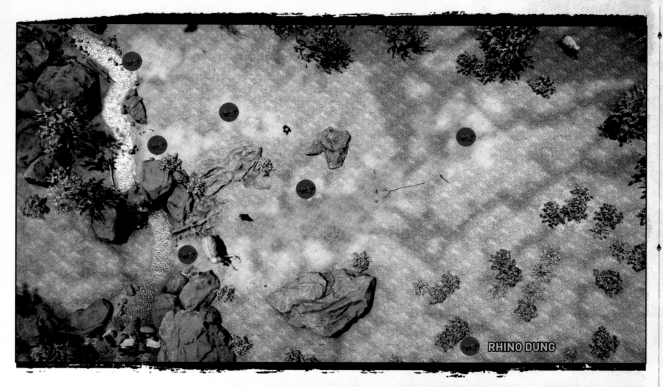

RHINO DUNG

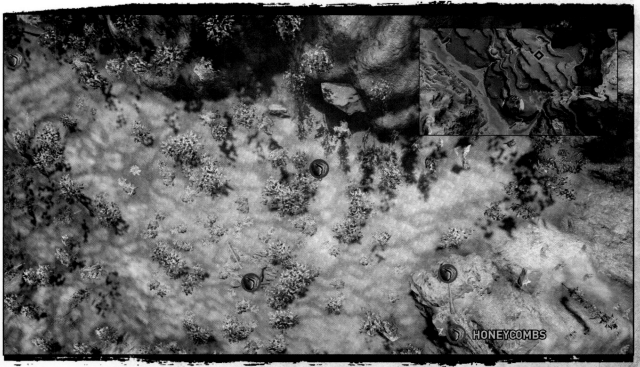

HONEYCOMBS

PREREQUISITE	Complete Strong Like Rock, buy Tame Apex Predators skill, and return to the village
MAIN OBJECTIVE	Help Urki defend himself against Bears by collecting stink ingredients
DIFFICULTY	Hard
AWARDS	1,000 XP
ENEMIES	Brown Bear, Woolly Rhino, Izila Hunters

OVERVIEW

For Urki's final request, he wants you to gather ingredients necessary to create a bear-repelling smell. You must find Rhino Dung and Honeycombs for the scent, and then tame a Brown Bear to test it. A clearing to the northeast offers up all of the above.

STRATEGY

Look for piles of rhino dung at the quest marker and search five of them to complete the first task. Rhinos are fairly passive, but they will attack if you give them a reason.

Just to the east, four beehives hang from the trees, but you only need three. Watch out for Izila Hunters who attack if you are detected. Reach up and grab the Honeycombs; Hunter Vision helps when they are hard to spot. Throughout this quest, keep an eye out for a Brown Bear. Throw down bait and tame the beast so that he can escort you back to Urki's hut. Talk to Urki and complete the mission by having your new companion attack.

URKI AT WENJA VILLAGE

After you complete his three missions, and bid farewell to Dah or Jayma, Urki finds a home near Tensay's hut in your village. Stop by and welcome him.

CAPTURE UDAM BIG DARWA FORT

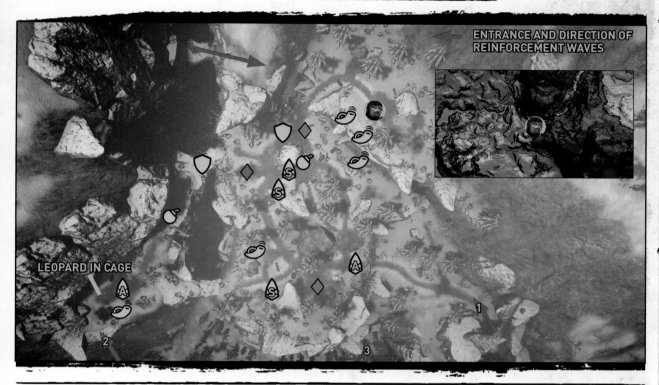

ENTRANCE AND DIRECTION OF REINFORCEMENT WAVES

LEOPARD IN CAGE

PREREQUISITE	Complete Vision of Ice and prepare for a tough battle
MAIN OBJECTIVE	Capture this heavily guarded Udam fort
DIFFICULTY	Very Hard
AWARDS	1800 XP
SPECIAL	Bonus XP for stealth, Fast Travel, Reward Stash
ENEMIES	Udam Elite Archers, Udam Elite Spearmen, Udam Elite Scourges, Udam Elite slingers, Udam Elite Chieftains, Udam civilians, Dah (Mini-boss), Wave Reinforcements: Udam Archers, Udam Elite Spearmen, Udam Elite Chieftains

SETUP

Once Vision of Ice is complete, the quest marker for Big Darwa Fort unlocks on the map. This mission is rated very hard and likely requires some preparation before taking on. Similar to capturing an outpost, the fort is littered with Udam fighters and alarms, with your first mini-boss, Dah, waiting at the finish. When you are ready, head to the location in the northeast. This fort must be captured before you can proceed toward the Udam leader, Ull, who is holed up in a cave on the other side of their homeland. The Heavy Takedown skill allows you to take down the large Chieftain enemies, making this fight a little simpler.

STRATEGY

There are three ways into the fort. Grapple points at two and three lead to the northwest corner and far west side of the camp respectively. From the far south, the camp can be entered up the main path. From there, you can go straight into the main gate or east toward Dah's position. Three alarms and two Udam Elite slingers mean that more than likely you must deal with reinforcements, who enter from the south and east when called. It is best to take out everyone north and west of Dah. Then, if more enemies are called, there are fewer to deal with at that point.

The northwest entrance is a great location to plan your attack. A caged Leopard offers a decent stealth companion if you don't have one already available. Start out by taking down the Udam Elite Archer, pulling him behind the cage, and destroying the first alarm. Use your Owl to scout out the post and then quietly eliminate the Udam Elite Scourge and Udam Elite Chieftain to the east. The enemies on the south side of the bridges change positions at nighttime.

The middle area can get fairly busy, so try drawing enemies out from groups with rocks. Carry bodies into the brush to avoid detection. The enemy civilians can be spared, but remember that they too can call reinforcements, so stay out of view. Once the area is clear, free the Wenja in the cage by busting it open and untying her.

RUN!

If things get hairy and reinforcements are called, flee outside the camp or onto the rocks in the northwest corner to heal and call a beast. Clear out any nearby pursuers and then make your way back into the camp.

Avoid Dah until you have defeated the rest of the Udam. When only he remains, sic your beast on him and launch arrows and spears at him. Stay clear of his powerful club and rot fumes. When your pet goes down, make a loop around the camp to draw Dah away and revive it. By avoiding the mini-boss, keeping your beast attacking, and pelting Dah with weapons, you eventually take him down. Instead of killing him though, Takkar invites him to join the Wenja village and teach the others how to make rot bane.

KILL THE UDAM LEADER

This is the first step toward the Udam leader, Ull, but to progress further you must complete Into Udam Land and get the Antidote food recipe from Sayla. This allows you to move through the rot fumes inside the northern passage and reach their homeland.

DAH OF THE UDAM

RECRUITMENT **Capture Udam's Big Darwa Fort**

For obvious reasons, Dah is unwelcome in the Wenja village. He represents the slaughter of many fellow tribespeople as well as the destruction of their old home, but Takkar sees the benefit that he can bring. Dah teaches you to craft Berserk Bombs and offers a few excellent skills. Sparing his life goes a long way in your travels.

WENJA WELCOME

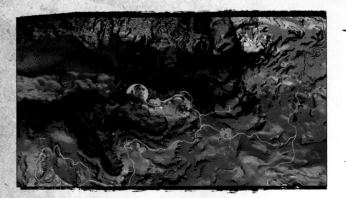

PREREQUISITE	Capture Udam's Big Darwa Fort
MAIN OBJECTIVE	Help Dah survive the anger of the Wenja welcoming party
DIFFICULTY	Medium
AWARDS	1000 XP
SPECIAL	Dah joins village
ENEMIES	Bitefish

OVERVIEW

Return to Dah's cage to find that the Wenja have taken him into the forest to watch him die. Quickly head to the Dah quest marker to save him.

STRATEGY

Head to the location, northeast of the village, and follow the stream past a waterfall to begin the mission. Run toward the water and slide down the vines to reach a rock platform, where Dah has been strapped down. The water rises and drowns the Udam if you don't repair the four water leaks in time. The white meter at the top of the HUD represents the water level. Once it fills, Dah drowns. You must approach each hole and interact with it to plug it. To make things worse, a bitefish attacks while you work. Mash on the indicated button to knock it off.

One leak is located on the wall ahead, two are down to the left, and the fourth is just below. The four locations are marked on the mini-map and appear on your HUD when you're heading in that direction. Small arrows point to any that are off screen. It doesn't matter in which order you take care of them, but the water level must get close to the one on the side wall

or it cannot be reached. After you have taken care of the leaks, climb onto the ledge and talk to Dah.

After the mission, talk to Dah at his cage and if the resources are available, build his hut. This unlocks his skills and a new mission.

BONE DUST

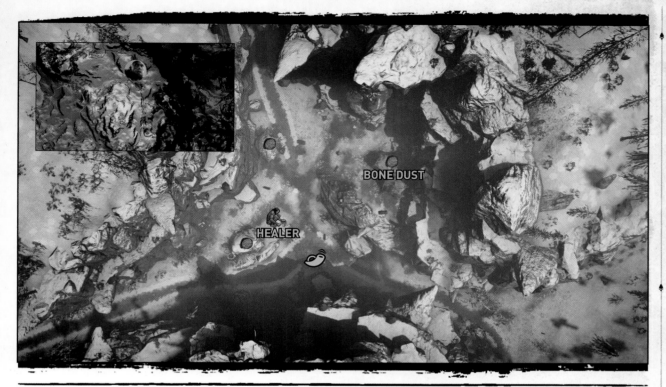

PREREQUISITE	Complete Vision of Ice and Build Dah's hut
MAIN OBJECTIVE	Find bone dust to help treat Dah's skull fire fevers
DIFFICULTY	Hard
AWARDS	1300 XP
ENEMIES	Udam Warriors, Udam Scourge, Udam Slinger

OVERVIEW

After building Dah's hut, step inside and talk to him. He wants you to grab bone dust from an Udam camp. This is the fix he needs for his fever.

STRATEGY

Head up to the north wastes and locate the quest marker, just south of the Big Darwa Fort. Approach Stone Mother Camp to begin the mission. The Udam are located in the valley below. Call your Owl to survey the area, being sure to tag the Udam healer near the southwest road. Now you just need to watch where she goes to find the bone dust, which is inside one of three huts around the camp.

You can stealthily sneak into the hut and swipe the dust or kill the Udam and grab it with ease. Starting from a high ledge, take out the Udam Slinger who overlooks the camp. Be sure to keep an eye on your cold meter. Fires can be found throughout the camp. An alarm sits on the south end, so destroy it with a fire arrow. Sic your beast and Owl on enemies below and finish them off with your bow. Descend to the ground and collect the bone

dust. If you did not find out the correct location, simply search every pot in the three huts. Escape outside the zone to complete the mission. Talk to Dah to hand over the bone dust.

SISTERS OF FIRE

SISTER

PREREQUISITE	Complete Bone Dust and Upgrade Dah's hut to level 2 (or move at least 150 meters from village)
MAIN OBJECTIVE	Kill the three deadly Izila sisters
DIFFICULTY	Very Hard
AWARDS	1500 XP
ENEMIES	Izila Elite Slingers, Izila Elite Scourges, Izila Spearmen, Izila Civilians, Izila Sisters

OVERVIEW

Talk to Dah outside his hut to learn about sun walker sisters that he has hunted for some time. He is unable to finish the job now and wishes for Takkar to kill them for him. Head to the far south, to find the Izila camp where the three sisters can be found.

STRATEGY

As you approach Stone Shadow Camp, the Sisters of Fire mission begins. Move up the hill and use your Owl to scout the camp. Staying put on the left side, sister number one is an Izila Elite Archer. To the right, the other two sisters, Izila Elite Chieftains, roam around the camp. Izila Elite Slingers stand guard atop the rock bluffs and wood watchtower. Climb over the flat rock to enter the south side and dispose of the guard on the rocks above. Then, quickly take out the sister and Izila Elite Scourge straight ahead.

Move around the backside of the camp and take down the second Izila Elite Slinger on the wood tower. He will jump down and wander a bit, if you don't find him there. Work your way over to the alarm and destroy it to remove the chance of reinforcements. From there your options are fairly wide open. Remember how tough an Izila Elite Chieftain Sister is before going after her. Don't expect to take her down with one arrow to the head. Be sure to search the three bodies to grab trophies for Dah.

UDAM HOMELAND

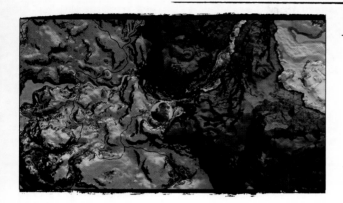

PREREQUISITE	Complete Into Udam Land and talk to Sayla
MAIN OBJECTIVE	Enter Udam Homeland, find Ull, and kill him
DIFFICULTY	Very Hard
SPECIAL	An Antidote is required to get through the deadly poison fumes

OVERVIEW

Fast Travel to Big Darwa Fort and find the tunnel in the back. This final Udam mission is split into three parts: Crossing the Udam Canyons and Raider Camp, capturing Mamsa Saja Bonfire, and entering Ull's cave with the ultimate goal of killing the leader.

GETTING IN

Rot fumes block your way to Udam Homeland, but by taking an Antidote, you can make it through the tunnel with time to spare. Cross the rock bridge to reach the poison caves. From there, proceed through the canyons to reach the first Udam camp.

CROSS UDAM CANYONS

OBJECTIVE	Cross through the Udam canyons
ENEMIES	Udam Elite Hunter, Udam Spearmen, Udam Warriors, Udam Elite Spearmen, Udam Archers, Udam Slingers, Udam Elite Archer

Udam Canyons is a long, narrow gorge that can be crossed either along the valley floor below, or on the rock ledges above. There is less resistance above, plus this gives you a better vantage point. It is not necessary to kill all of the Udam, but it is an option with more XP earned. Three groups of Udam must be dealt with, a camp and two watch posts. Easily deal with the three guys at the camp by getting behind the campfire, just be aware of the one on patrol.

Just ahead, quickly use the grappling point on the right to reach higher ground. Avoid being detected by the guard in the tower and grapple up another level to reach a lone Udam. Quietly drop him and then eliminate the watcher, either with your bow or let your Owl take care of him.

Follow the right ledge toward the second watch post, taking down the Archer along the way. Pull out the long bow and kill the Slinger in the watchtower. Kill the few remaining Udam or sneak past to exit the canyons.

RAIDER CAMP

OBJECTIVE	Cross through raider camp to reach The Hunting Valley
ENEMIES	Udam Archers, Udam Warriors, Udam Slinger, Udam Spearman, Udam Elite Chieftain

Cross the bridge to reach an Udam raider camp. Several Udam occupy the camp, but it can be traversed with minimal confrontation. Take cover in a bush and release your Owl to scout the area. Most enemies are found in the middle of the camp, including the Chieftain. Climb the vine and quietly take out the first Udam. Sneak along the left edge through the camp to avoid detection, tossing rocks to distract and move patrols away. The occasional loner gives you the opportunity for an easy takedown; just be sure to deposit the body behind cover or in the brush. Continue toward your destination until you reach The Hunting Valley.

There are plenty of resources to gather and wildlife to hunt in this open area. Take this opportunity to restock your supplies. A number of strong, tamable predators are present in case you haven't already added them to your roster, including Cave Bears and Sabretooth Tigers.

 What location draws me the most? The glacier. This is one of the biggest threats of this time, and home of the Udam tribe. It's also the farthest zone and one of the most beautiful with a very iconic backdrop.

— *Fabien Govini, Level Design Director*

CAPTURE MAMSA SAJA BONFIRE

⬤ GRAPPLING POINT

OBJECTIVE	Reach the Udam bonfire and claim it for Wenja
AWARDS	1200 XP, Population
SPECIAL	Fast Travel, Spawn Point, Reward Stash
ENEMIES	Udam Elite Hunters, Udam Elite Spearmen

A central bonfire offers the usual amenities close to Ull's cave—allowing you to easily travel Oros, access your Reward Stash, rest, and respawn nearby. Climb onto the vantage point on the west side and release your Owl to recon the camp, including patrols around the perimeter. Without an alarm or Elite Slingers, there is no threat of reinforcements. Clear out the outside guys first and then move in on those around the center, pulling them away if necessary.

ENTER ULL'S CAVE

OBJECTIVE	Find Ull's cave and enter
ENEMIES	Udam Elite Archers, Udam Elite Warriors, Udam Elite Spearman, Udam Elite Hunter, Udam Slingers, Udam Elite Chieftains

Your next objective is to reach Ull's cave, but an Udam camp sits just outside the entrance. Find a nice vantage point just north of the camp and tag the enemies with your Owl. There are a lot of them, so be sure to get them all. Two Chieftains are your biggest threat as they guard the main entrance. A second, secret entrance sits

just to the east. If combat is more your style, have your Owl thin them out with bombs before picking them off. Otherwise, cautiously move up the east side, killing lone Udam with takedowns and moving others out of the way. Enter Ull's cave at the left, smaller entrance. If you can perform heavy takedowns, you can enter the main entrance by waiting for them to separate and killing them.

FIND ULL

OBJECTIVE	Search the cave for Ull
ENEMIES	Udam Warriors, Udam Elite Chieftain, Udam Elite Warrior, Udam Hunters, Udam Slinger, Udam Archer, Udam Scourge

This cave system is big with one long path to the back, where you find Ull, but there are many side paths along the way. Keep moving toward the quest marker and you shouldn't get lost. Udam are only really a threat in the middle section and at the end where they protect their leader. Besides a lone Warrior, civilians are all you find in the first part of the cave and are easily avoided by sticking to the side, unless you brought a Bear companion, who causes a panic.

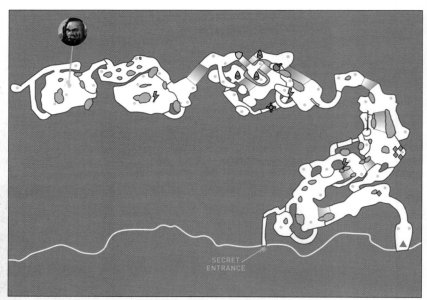

SECRET ENTRANCE

After the narrow, right bend, several Udam guard and patrol the next cavern. At first you only see a lone Warrior with his back turned. Kill and drag him into the previous room. Climb into the left tunnel and use the higher vantage point to survey the layout. Quickly take out the watchers above and wait for things to die down if the enemy was alerted.

Now work your way around the right side. Kill the Scourge on the small ledge, and then take care of the Hunters who wander the corridors below. Finish off the remaining Udam, including the Chieftain near the exit. In the next room, a solitary Warrior stands under an icicle. Shoot the ice to drop it on his head before following

the path into the room before the boss. Collect the weapons scattered around and prepare for a big fight, including calling in your strongest beast.

KILL ULL

OBJECTIVE	Kill Ull
ENEMIES	Udam Archers, Udam Elite Hunters, Udam Elite Spearmen, Udam Elite Warriors, Udam Spearmen, Udam Warriors, Ull

Ull stands in the middle of the final room surrounded by three soldiers. Throughout the fight, reinforcements enter from the sides. A tunnel runs underneath one side, offering a place to flee, while a ledge gives height advantage on the other. Look for puddles of water on the ground, indicating icicles that hang above. These ice shards can be hit with an arrow or spear, causing them to drop. This kills weaker enemies while stunning and hurting Ull. This is the best attack against the boss, taking off a good chunk of his health. It is fairly tough to pull off though, since you must time the attack and the ice shards are limited.

Ull is a fast, powerful Chieftain. He has armor that can be broken off by attacking it directly. With the protection removed, he takes more damage at that location. He wields a big club, has a devastating charge attack, and launches poison bombs. Keep an antidote buff active whenever Ull is around to nullify the rot bane's effect.

Once you are ready to take him on, enter the arena. Look right and shoot the icicle above Ull, stunning the boss. Quickly hop down behind him and press the Takedown button to stab him. Immediately back away as he swings and throw a couple of spears into him. Turn around and flee to another location to rest up and heal if needed.

Use the lower tunnel to get away from trouble. Be careful though, it is easy to get trapped with a large number of enemies. The ledge on the other side of the arena gives a good view of the room, but watch your back as reinforcements pour in from the small alcove. Kill the weaker enemies whenever you get a chance to limit their numbers. It can get overwhelming if left unchecked.

A strong beast does great damage to the boss, but it does not last long. Ull takes the animal down quickly. Draw Ull away and circle back around to your companion to get it back in the fight. As long as your beast is up, it should be attacking.

Continue to keep pressure on Ull, looking for opportunities to drop ice on him. Watch your health and keep your beast in the fight. Piles of spears and arrows lie near supply sacks. Seek them out when needed. Stay on the move and get in attacks when possible. When he falls, Udam Sanctum is complete.

SPEAK WITH DAH

After killing Ull, return to Dah and talk to him one more time.

> Ull's lair is both a spiritual safe haven for the Udam and a hell vision for anyone else.
> — *Jean-Sébastien Decant, Narrative Director*

CAPTURE IZILA FIRE SCREAMER FORT

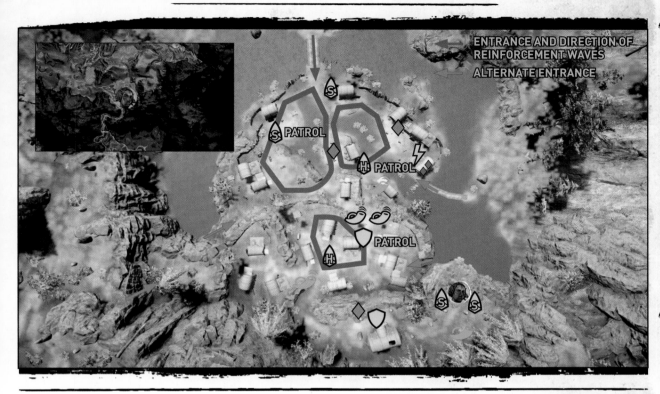

ENTRANCE AND DIRECTION OF
REINFORCEMENT WAVES
ALTERNATE ENTRANCE

PATROL

PATROL

PATROL

PREREQUISITE	Complete The Taken Wenjas
MAIN OBJECTIVE	Capture this heavily guarded Izila fort and confront the commander.
DIFFICULTY	Very Hard
AWARDS	1800 XP
SPECIAL	Bonus XP for stealth, Fast Travel, Reward Stash
ENEMIES	Izila Elite Slingers, Izila Elite Spearmen, Izila Warrior, Izila Elite Hunters, Izila Elite Chieftains, Izila civilians, Roshani (Mini-boss), Wave Reinforcements: Izila Elite Spearmen, Izila Elite Warriors, Izila Elite Hunters, Izila Elite Chieftain

SETUP

Once the Wenja are rescued from the Izila in The Taken Wenja mission, Fire Screamer Fort becomes available, which must be captured to gain access to the Izila Homeland and their leader, Batari. Head to their stronghold in the marshlands and spend some time surveying with your Owl, tagging every enemy force. Two Elite Spearmen guard your main target, Roshani, atop a plateau at the far end of the fort, while two Elite Slingers watch over the camp from watchtowers. Several more Elite soldiers patrol the grounds. At night, five of the hostiles sleep inside the hut.

STRATEGY

An alternate entrance on each side of the camp can be reached from the water, giving you quick access to the back half of the stronghold. If you wish to go after the mini-boss right away, access the western cliff and find the ivy at the south end that takes you down to a lower shelf. This gives you access behind the huts with a direct shot to Roshani and his immediate guards. Watch out for the Chieftain who patrols the path. If possible, take him down without alerting the others. From there, you and your beast can make quick work of the two Elite Spearmen and Roshani before reinforcements can reach you.

The more cautious approach is to methodically eliminate the Izila fighters, leaving Roshani for last. With three alarms and two Elite Slingers, it is very possible that reinforcements join the fight, so be ready. Work the two side water entrances to quietly take down the northern Izila. Next, pull each Elite Slinger from their post, staying clear of the big Chieftain who patrols to the south. If your Owl is able to attack Chieftains, have him do so when it is available. Always note the positions of Roshani's two guards as they can call in reinforcements if you are spotted. Clear out the bottom of the camp before following the south path up to your target, where a lone Chieftain awaits. From the bushes, get his attention with a rock and perform a takedown as he gets near.

👊 ROSHANI IS A TOUGH CHIEFTAIN

Roshani shares a lot of similarities to the Izila chieftain. He is a big melee fighter who carries a big fire-lit club. Watch for his ground slam attack as it launches mini fire projectiles at you. His swing attack is also devastating if it makes contact, but there is time to jump back out of reach.

If you decide to go it alone, work on the spearmen from a distance. Roshani lumbers your way once he detects your attacks, but you should have time to finish off the two guards before facing him. Use a club heavy attack to stun the mini-boss and then back away while throwing spears at him. Turn and run when things get hairy. Then, you can set up with more ranged attacks.

👊 FREE THE HOSTAGES

There are two Wenja being held in a cell on the east side. Add a couple of members to your village by sneaking into the camp along the wood walkway on the east side. Pull the Elite Warrior from his post and take him down. Watch the Izila as you bust open the cell door and untie the Wenja. This causes a ruckus as they flee through the front gate. You can wait for things to calm down or you can take advantage of the chaos and get in a couple of easy kills.

Call in a strong beast such as the Cave Bear or Sabretooth as you move in on the mini-boss. Send your companion after one Elite Spearman while you pick off the other with a bow or thrown spear. Now it is just Roshani against the two of you. With your beast tearing him to shreds, launch spears at him or move in with the club. It does not take too long for him to start pleading for his life. After a short talk, Takkar escorts the Izila commander back to the village, where you receive the Fire Bomb.

ROSHANI OF THE IZILA

RECRUITMENT	Capture the Izila's Fire Screamer Fort
SKILLS	Izila Skills
SPECIAL	Fire Bomb

Roshani is a proud but paranoid Izila Commander. He leads an impressive Izila fortress that has never suffered any threats from rival tribes. Like many Izila, Roshani has prideful faith in the Izila's place in the world. He's led a sedentary life and has limited combat experience. He earned his commander rank through charm and manipulation. He can talk his way out of troubles or into new opportunities.

Roshani has made enemies among the Izila over the years. He's known as a man who puts himself before all else, including his own people. It's a reputation that could catch up with him one day soon—and he knows it.

Upon capture, Roshani offers a powerful Fire Bomb to your arsenal. His Izila Skills are a great addition to your skill set, sharing the fire mastery that the Izila are known for.

TAKKAR'S JOURNEY

HUNTING MAMMOTH

PATH TO OROS

JOURNEY
PROGRESSION

MAIN MISSIONS

SAYLA THE
GATHERER

TENSAY THE
SHAMAN

ATTACK OF THE
UDAM

WOGAH THE
CRAFTER

JAYMA THE
HUNTER

KAROOSH THE
WARRIOR

URKI THE THINKER

CAPTURE UDAM
BIG DARWA FORT

DAH OF THE UDAM

UDAM HOMELAND

CAPTURE IZILA FIRE
SCREAMER FORT

ROSHANI OF
THE IZILA

IZILA HOMELAND

SECONDARY
QUESTS

BEAST MASTER
HUNTS

VILLAGE MISSIONS

HELP WENJA:
BEAST KILL

HELP WENJA:
TRIBAL CLASHES

CAVES

PREREQUISITE	Capture the Izila's Fire Screamer Fort
MAIN OBJECTIVE	Steal seeds for your village during an Izila race
DIFFICULTY	Medium
AWARDS	1250 XP
SPECIAL	Roshani joins village
ENEMIES	Izila Warriors, Izila Archers, Izila Spearmen

OVERVIEW

With Roshani safely in your village, talk to him to learn about seeds the Izila possess. Take his secrets, but leave the trader behind. Examine the pillar at the Roshani quest marker to accept the mission.

STRATEGY

Three bags of seeds can be found nearby as part of an Izila race, where Hunters prove their strength by getting to them the quickest; you just need to be quicker than they are. Izila Warriors, Archers, and Spearmen participate in the contest, but there is no need to fight anyone here.

In fact, it is a waste of valuable time. Sprint to each bag and flee the area. The first bag is just southwest of the closest standing stone. Hunter Vision highlights the bags in red, making them easier to spot. Head northwest and find the second resting next to a big boulder, just past a red plant.

Sprint east, navigating your way down from the cliffs as you race for the small island. The final bag rests at the end of the downed

tree. If an Izila gets to a bag before you, immediately give chase and take him down. Don't forget to collect the dropped item. After all three bags have been collected, a yellow zone appears on the map. Sprint to the closest edge of this zone to get far enough away from the enemy tribe and complete the mission.

BLOOD SACRIFICE

PRIESTESS
ENTRANCE

PREREQUISITE	Complete Vision of Fire and Build Roshani's hut
MAIN OBJECTIVE	Save a Wenja Hunter from an Izila sacrifice
DIFFICULTY	Hard
AWARDS	1500 XP
ENEMIES	Izila Spearmen, Izila Warriors, Izila Civilians, Izila Priestess

OVERVIEW

Build Roshani's hut and talk to him inside. He is worried that the Izila saw him at the village when they took a Wenja man and will come after him next. Roshani's danger doesn't worry Takkar, it is the Wenja, who has been taken to be sacrificed, that concerns him. There is still time to save him, so head for the quest marker at Blajiman Stones to find the victim.

STRATEGY

Only a Spearman, a Warrior, and three Civilians occupy the area at the moment, but shortly, three Spearmen and two Warriors escort in the Priestess from the southwest. She is your main target and must be killed before she reaches the Wenja. An alarm sits on each side of the temple, so if you are detected, reinforcements are called. There is not much need to send out your Owl, except that it can take out the priestess in a single swoop. Then you and a beast companion can clean up those who remain.

After a short time, another Priestess moves up the path and sprints for the Wenja. Quickly take her down and kill the rest of the Izila. Free the Wenja to complete the mission.

THE BLAZE

BURNABLE AREA
WENJA HOSTAGE

PREREQUISITE	Complete Blood Sacrifice
MAIN OBJECTIVE	Burn the Izila camp
DIFFICULTY	Hard
AWARDS	1000 XP, Population
ENEMIES	Izila Warriors, Izila Slingers, Izila Elite Warriors, Izila Elite Spearmen, Izila Elite Chieftain

OVERVIEW

Roshani wants you to frighten the Izila by burning their camp. Heed his advice and watch for Wenja captives who are often hidden around their villages.

STRATEGY

Travel to Sun Walker Ring and begin burning the place down. Find huts, hay in the fields, or basically anything flammable, and set it ablaze. A yellow meter shows your progress; fill it up to complete the mission. Izila attack from all around once they see their place on fire. Keep an eye out for Slingers who attack from ledges and atop the huts. Sic a strong beast on the Chieftain to limit damage.

Four Wenja captives are hidden around the camp. Free them before setting fires around them.

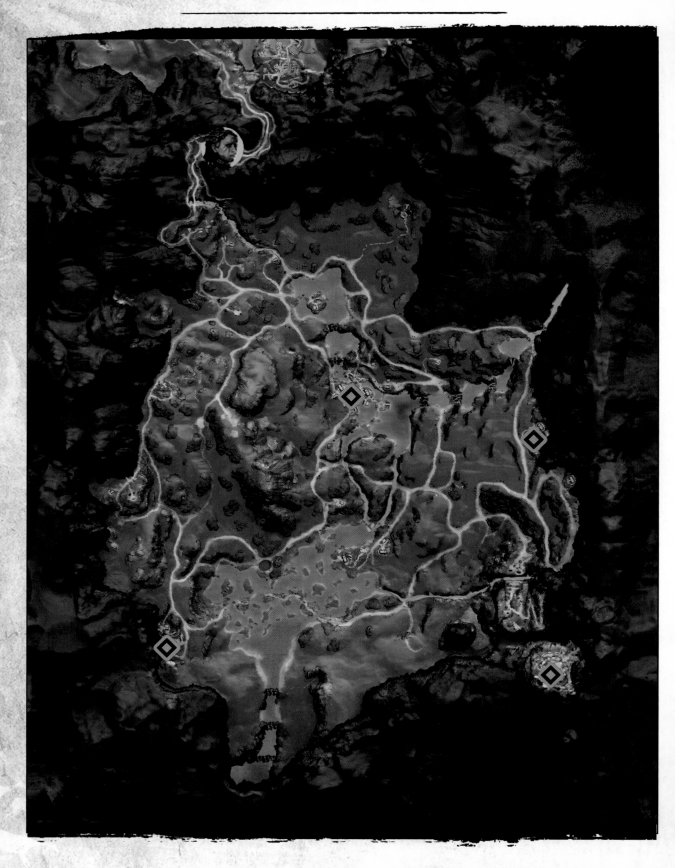

PREREQUISITE	Complete Mask of Krati and buy Mammoth Rider skill
MAIN OBJECTIVE	Enter Izila Homeland, find Batari, and kill her
DIFFICULTY	Very Hard
SPECIAL	Purchase the Mammoth Rider skill before attempting.

OVERVIEW

Fast Travel to Fire Screamer Fort and find a Mammoth. The entrance to Izila Homeland is just southwest from the camp. This final Izila mission is split into four objectives. Free the Wenja captives from the three locations—the training grounds, Izila Village, and Altar of Suxli—and then kill Batari.

GETTING IN

Ride the Mammoth south to the main gate and charge into it. Keep the charge attack going as you ram through the Izila fighters, only stopping when you do not see any more. Find the locked up Wenja on the left side of the path, dismount, and free him to learn of more hostages. If the Mammoth hasn't wandered off, get back on and use it to ram through more Izila to the south.

RESUPPLY

There are plenty of resources to gather and wildlife to hunt in this open area. Take this opportunity to restock your supplies. A number of strong, tamable predators are present in case you haven't already added them to your roster, including Brown Bears and Sabretooth Tigers.

WHERE TO NEXT?

There are three camps where Wenja are being held. Free them from their prison cells and they assist you in reaching Batari. These can be done in any order; we will work our way from east to west, making the training grounds our first stop. Follow the eastern edge south to find the camp. You come across Sajas Hill Bonfire first, which can be captured to give yourself a Fast Travel point.

FREE WENJA FROM THE TRAINING GROUNDS

OBJECTIVE	Free the Wenja in the training grounds
ENEMIES	Izila Elite Slingers, Izila Elite Spearmen, Izila Elite Warriors, Izila Archers, Izila Hunters

There are two Wenja prisoners being held in small cages toward the middle of the camp. It is wise to leave them be until the enemy has been taken of. They risk being killed if freed too early. An alarm is located in front of the big hut on the south side and another is found next to the dividing fence. If going for the stealth approach, take these out early on from long range.

Pick off the northern Slinger right away. Then, pull the other Izila away for easy takedowns. If you do not care about stealth though, there is a Mammoth just south of the camp. Clear out the training grounds by trampling the foes; make the two alarms a priority. Once it is safe to do so, release the two Wenja and then travel northeast toward the central village.

FREE WENJA FROM THE IZILA VILLAGE

OBJECTIVE	Free the Wenja in Izila village
ENEMIES	Izila Elite Slingers, Izila Elite Spearmen, Izila Elite Warriors, Izila Elite Archers, Izila Archers, Izila Warriors

Walkways connect a series of islands to the mainland, with three watchtowers looking over the area. Each one overlooks a prison cell that holds a Wenja prisoner. Send your Owl up to tag the enemies and the two alarms. Slingers man two of the towers, while several non-Elite Izila patrol the grounds. The village is wide open, making long-range combat an option—just be ready for them to become alerted.

If taking a combat approach, kill the watchtower sentries quickly with your bow and then recruit some help from your animal friends. The Owl can help out by dropping bombs on the Izila. Bring in a strong beast to distract the enemy while you get in quick takedowns. The village is very flammable, so be careful releasing the Wenja when danger still exists; the Izila love their fire weapons. With the three Izila village prisoners free, move east to the third location.

FREE WENJA FROM THE ALTAR OF SUXLI

UNDERNEATH ROCK OVERHANG

OBJECTIVE	Free the Wenja at the altar of Suxli
ENEMIES	Izila Elite Hunters, Izila Elite Warriors, Izila Elite Slingers, Izila Archers, Izila Spearmen, Izila Warriors

The Altar of Suxli is the grisly location where Wenja are sacrificed to Suxli. Two prisoners are held here. The lower area has two huts, an alarm, and one captive. The upper includes the altar, a third hut, another alarm, and the second captive in a cell on the back wall. Scout the place from the safety of the bushes. A Slinger climbs onto the roof of the main hut, so watch out for him. He is an easy target for your Owl. Archers start out on the upper ledge, while more soldiers roam the ground below.

Since the site is against the cliff, your options are fairly limited. Lure enemies out from the middle with stone throws and take them down out of sight. Use your long bow to pick off the upper enemies from the west. Focus on destroying the alarms early. Once the Izila have been taken care of, free the two captives before heading south to meet up with the Wenja.

REACH BATARI

OBJECTIVE	Find a way inside Batari's temple
ENEMIES	Izila Archers, Izila Spearmen

Approach Batari's temple to find out the bridge has been pulled back, leaving you no access. Fortunately, the freed Wenja are there to help. Talk to them and then cut the obelisk support ropes. At this point, the Wenja push the big standing stones down so you can get across. At the same time though, the Izila on the other side of the ravine start shooting arrows at them.

Hold them off by stepping to the front and taking them out with your own weaponry. If too many Wenja die, you fail. Berserk Bombs are great for confusing your foes, but they are also valuable against Batari, so only use them if you can spare them. Setting fires by igniting your arrows can deny the Izila a certain spot, but the flames eventually go out. With the four beams pushed away, the obelisk falls into place. Hop onto the bridge as you don the Mask of Krati. Run up the path and into the tunnel before Batari's temple. Nobody attacks while you wear the mask, so save your ammo. You can find supplies before and inside the tunnel, so take time to restock. Call your strongest beast and open the gate at the end of the passageway to find your target.

KILL BATARI

Cave Lion

OBJECTIVE	Kill Batari
ENEMIES	Izila Archers, Izila Spearmen, Izila Elite Spearmen, Izila Elite Warriors, Izila Scourges, Izila Chieftains, Batari

Batari stands on her own inaccessible platform on one end of the arena with a great view of the center, which is the best place to attack from. Take cover behind small stone walls and rock platforms. Stay on the move when possible to avoid taking too much damage from her fire arrows. She calls in reinforcements periodically, entering around the perimeter—most often the southeast corner. Sacks are found throughout the temple, so take advantage when you are low on weapons. A Cave Lion is locked up in a cage on the left, but you are free to call in any of your beasts.

Batari has a powerful bow equipped with fire arrows, making the Fire Resistance skill and Fireproof foods invaluable in the fight. Periodically, she moves behind the rocks and summons a wave of Izila soldiers, increasing in difficulty as you progress. She is strong against fire, poison, and bee stings, so the bombs should be saved for the reinforcements.

As soon as you are in range, whip a few spears at her head to get things started. Keep in mind that while she fights from her stage, you are not getting your weapons back. The four fire bowls can be destroyed with fire arrows or thrown clubs, eliminating much of her cover and exposing her to attack. Continue to throw spears and shoot arrows at Batari, taking cover to avoid her fire damage.

When Batari summons reinforcements, she hides behind cover and returns only after so many are dead or a certain time has elapsed. Concentrate on reducing these numbers during this time, sending your beast after them immediately. There are three waves of reinforcements that progressively get harder. Watch out as there are Chieftains and Scourges that occupy each of the waves. If you can get the jump on a wave of reinforcements, lob bombs as they enter. The southeast corner is your best bet.

When Batari gets low on health, she moves down the left ramp. Set your beast on her or try for a Death from Above Takedown. It doesn't take much at this point to finish her off.

Use the platforms as cover when fleeing from the reinforcements. Send a strong beast, such as the Cave Bear, their way. It can handle them while you attack Batari, as long as you keep it healed up. Whenever possible, save your projectiles against the Warriors. Take them down with your club behind the rock walls.

THERE IS STILL MORE TO DO

With Ull and Batari out of the way, Oros is finally at peace, but that doesn't mean the game is over; there is still plenty to do. There are still Wenja that need help, caves to explore, and collectibles to gather. If you haven't earned the second ending, there is that too.

SECONDARY QUESTS

While these quests don't advance the main story, they are a great way to earn XP and other rewards while exploring Oros.

BEAST MASTER HUNTS

Beast Master Hunts are epic hunting quests that send you on a mission to kill or tame these one of a kind beasts in Oros.

Upgraded spears are the best tool for taking down these beasts. Having a strong beast companion, like a Cave Bear, helps you tremendously.

Stop by your Rewards Stash and stock up on Hardwood before you begin these quests. Hardwood is used to craft traps in the areas of the Beast Master Hunts.

BLOODFANG SABRETOOTH

DIFFICULTY	Hard
AWARDS	High XP
SPECIAL	Tame the Bloodfang Sabretooth

You can begin the hunt during the day, climbing to the top of the waterfall near your cave. Once at the top of the waterfall you are notified that a Beast Master Hunt is nearby.

Use your grappling claw to pull yourself even higher until you finally reach an entrance to a cave that you are tasked to explore.

Once inside the cave, stay along the walls to the right; you come to a small ledge overlooking a large drop. Prepare yourself to jump a few small gaps in the upcoming ledge.

 **UDAM OUTPOST**

An Udam Outpost is located near the start of this hunt. You can choose to deal with it now, or save it for later, but either way, watch out for it!

Continue through the cave using the grappling point you come across to safely lower yourself to the side of a little bit of water.

Once you are on the rocks beside the water, you need to jump or swim across to the small landing, and then begin to climb the long vines upward.

Before you can reach the top of the vines, a short cut scene activates and the Bloodfang Sabretooth pulls away his Wenja victim.

After the cut scene, follow the blood trail out of the cave. With your Hunter Vision active, footprints begin to appear alongside the blood trail, eventually leading you to the first clue in the hunt—the Wenja that you saw get taken away in the cut scene.

Continue following the trail down the mountain, eventually having to use a grappling point. Just after you have lowered yourself from the grappling point you find another clue in the center of the path, a broken Udam Mask.

Slide down the hill as you follow the tracks south, eventually sliding into a pit of bones and bodies. Inside this small pit is a third clue, a dead Udam, killed by the Sabretooth.

The tracks then lead you to a small camp, which may be guarded by a few Udam. Some of them may even surround the next clue. Eliminate the Udam if needed, and then examine the pile of blood and guts.

> **My favorite beast is obviously the Sabretooth Tiger. I'm a cat person.**
>
> — *Vincent Pontbriand, Senior Producer*

After examining the clue, you have two sets of tracks to follow, each leading to a different location to fight the Bloodfang Sabretooth.

Head toward the western objective; this takes you to some ruins. This area has more trap locations which deal a great amount of damage to the Sabretooth without your dwindling down your weapons supply.

As you follow the path to the west, you come across another clue, a tree trunk that the Sabretooth has used to sharpen its claws.

Continue along the path which eventually leads you to your next clue, a spear that has been thrown into a large tree trunk. The Wenja that were at this camp weren't ready for the threat of the Bloodfang Sabretooth.

There are no more clues now, work your way to the objective marker. If it is daytime, a Wenja hunter is there waiting for you.

Use the daylight to set up traps. They are marked by a stone with white markings, as well as by a small white trap icon on your mini-map. The icon changes to red when you have placed a trap in that location.

GREAT BEAST TRAPS

Use the Rewards Stash next to grab a full load of Hardwood for crafting Great Beast Traps.

If you speak with the Wenja hunter, an objective marker is placed on the bed nearby. Use the bed to sleep until nightfall.

Please note that if you arrive at night and speak with the injured hunter, the Sabretooth spawns right away and begins attacking you, significantly shortening the amount of time you have to set up traps. Time your arrival accordingly.

You have a small amount of time to prepare traps once you wake up if you haven't already placed them. When Bloodfang Spawns, the angry Sabretooth is marked with an objective marker.

If you have a beast with you, they begin to attack Bloodfang. Use that opportunity to get as many headshots on the Sabretooth as you can. Run toward your traps, forcing Bloodfang to trigger them. The traps briefly stun Bloodfang, which allows you to get some headshots with your spears, dealing massive amounts of damage. While you run to the other trap, have your Two Handed Club equipped. The club is capable of stunning Bloodfang if he gets too close.

Once his health hits 50% he begins to run for his cave. You can still damage Bloodfang while he runs. A fast beast companion, like a Cave Lion or Wolf, can catch up and deal small amounts of damage to Bloodfang as he retreats to his cave.

Choosing the south objective results in a very similar experience. Follow the path south to the objective marker, keeping an eye out

for the next clue. A Wenja trap has damaged the Tiger with a blood trail leading to the forest.

Follow the trail into a camp and talk to the Wenja hunter. Build as many Spike Traps as you can around the site to better the odds of hurting the Sabretooth.

Sabretooth riding is the best.

— Jean-Sébastien Decant, Narrative Director

Sleep until dawn and deal with the beast as described for the west objective. Three Wenja hunters help with the hunt. As its health reaches 50%, it flees to the den.

Use your Hunter Vision to follow the trail. Try to run as straight as possible; this allows you to close some distance on Bloodfang as he retreats.

The entrance to his den is along the ledge that runs at the base of the cliff behind the water. The den itself, after you arrive from the entrance tunnel, is roughly ring-shaped with some changes in level.

Using the same tactics as before, force Bloodfang to chase you through the traps, then throw spears at his head to deal critical amounts of damage.

There are two available traps in Bloodfang's den, locate them and quickly set them up.

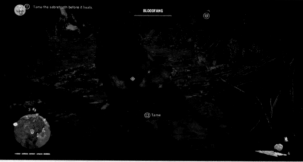

Once you have brought his health bar to nothing, the option to tame him appears. When you have tamed Bloodfang he joins you as your beast companion, allowing you to call for him whenever you'd like!

BLOODTUSK MAMMOTH

DIFFICULTY	Hard
AWARDS	High XP
SPECIAL	Bloodtusk Mammoth Skull

This area is in the snow, so having upgraded cold gear helps your hunt! If you don't have upgraded cold gear, be sure to stock up on Animal Fat as you want to be holding a lit weapon when you are not combating the Mammoth. You can also stay warm using fire pits and by visiting the edges of the Hot Springs pools.

Once you're in the area for the hunt, speak to the hunter crouched down by the fire. He tells you of the Bloodtusk Mammoth that is wreaking havoc on the Wenja.

After speaking with the Wenja hunter, head north and grapple down the cliffs. This will lead you to your first clue, a piece of meat and skin from the Mammoth on some wooden spikes.

Continue north either following the footprints with your Hunter Vision, or using the grapple points to quickly descend to the next clue. Hunter Vision can also highlight Resources and Traps. You find a dead Wenja that was crushed by the foot of the Bloodtusk Mammoth.

After examining the dead Wenja, three different places to fight the Mammoth are marked on your map. You can choose any of them to start with as the Mammoth always spawns at whichever you choose first. As you fight the Mammoth it retreats when damaged and takes you to each of the areas.

TRAP IT!
Traps are extremely effective against Mammoths. If you've brought enough wood, you can kill the Mammoth with traps alone.

To the west you have the Hot Springs. The clue leading into the hot springs area is another dead Wenja on top of a few logs.

There are plenty of traps in the hot springs that can deal heavy damage to the Mammoth. The geysers deal a great amount of damage if you can situate the Mammoth on top of one while it erupts. Snare traps located on the spring can help make this happen.

Focus on drawing the Mammoth into your traps, using your bow to kill off any Udam or smaller animals in the area, preventing them from accidentally triggering your traps.

After the Mammoth retreats, you can pick either of the remaining areas for the next part of the fight. You can also damage the Mammoth while chasing it from each battlefield.

To the north is the Glacier Valley. On your way there a group of trampled elk is your clue before entering the area

As you near the end of the cavern leading into the Glacier Valley, a large, blood-covered icicle protrudes from the ground. Examine it before entering the valley.

Use snare traps to hold the Mammoth in place before using your bow to shoot down the icicles that hang overhead to deal heavy amounts of damage. Icicles that can be shot down are highlighted when you use Hunter Vision. The high ground in this area is not safe as the Mammoth can easily take down bridges and grappling points by ramming into them.

96

The remaining area to the east is the Mammoth Graveyard. The graveyard has Udam warriors scattered throughout it. Kill the warriors before you set the traps and begin attacking the Mammoth. This prevents them from triggering your traps.

The Mammoth can easily be lead into the spike traps in this area as they are generally located between two objects, allowing you to funnel the Mammoth in for a direct hit on your trap.

Once you have downed the Mammoth, you must kill it and return its spirit to Oros. This kill is much like taming the other Great Beasts, you must get in close to the downed animal and press and hold the action button to kill the Mammoth.

If you wait too long before reaching the Mammoth and activating the kill, it gets back up with a small amount of health.

After killing the Mammoth be sure to collect the Bloodtusk Mammoth Skull from its corpse before leaving the area.

GREAT SCAR BEAR

DIFFICULTY	Hard
AWARDS	High XP
SPECIAL	Tame the Great Scar Bear

After entering the area to begin the search for the Great Scar Bear, you work your way through a cave system, swimming through a tunnel, then climbing up to an area containing a cave painting detailing the threat of the Great Scar Bear. Examine it.

Once you've inspected the painting, you end up facing the exit of the cave. Follow the path out of the cave and head north until you find some bloody footprints with your Hunter Vision. Follow the footprints to a small campsite and examine your next clue, the recently extinguished campfire.

Use the Reward Stash to stock up on Hardwood in your inventory and continue through the camp. As you follow the trail you come across three Izila Archers fighting off a single Brown Bear near your next clue. Use your bow to damage the Brown Bear and kill it before picking off the remaining Izila. Follow the tracks to your next clue, a beehive on the ground that was used by the Izila to attract the Bear.

CLEAR OUT THE AREA

Wolves can be an issue at night and in the early morning. Target their pack leader to disperse them quickly. Yaks are aggressive and will chase you. The area also contains Izila Warriors, who have no love for you. Clear them all out before taking on the Great Scar Bear.

Use your Hunter Vision to follow the Bear tracks north out of the camp, eventually coming across a spike trap that the Bear has tracked through. Examine the trap before continuing along the trail.

If you headed south when the trail splits at the bloody log, follow the second path as it leads to a bloodstained stone to the east.

Continue along the Bear's trail north to find bee clusters lying on the ground, used as a trap by the Izila hunters.

The tracks lead to a broken, blood-stained tree. A few Wenja villagers are nearby. Examine the blood on the tree and then use your Hunter Vision to follow the footprints leading north or south.

Follow the tracks as they head up the hill. They lead to a small pond below a waterfall with a few dead Izila Hunters near a downed tree at the edge of the water. Investigate the dead Izila Hunter at the edge of the water. Climb up the cliff from the base of the pond using the grappling claw, where you come into contact with the Bear fighting the Izila (or allies). Quickly grapple back down to the base of the cliff and turn to the left so that you are heading up toward the hill. Set the Great Best Trap there and wait for the Bear to come down the hill. After he hits the trap, quickly run (it helps to have a speed boost active) in the opposite direction so that you are on the other side of the pond. There is a line of traps that you can set. Two traps and one spear are enough to get him to start running away toward the cave. If you take him along this path, the Bear can hit more traps along the way, making the next phase easier.

Along the north path, a few Izila may scatter into the forest here as you approach a small camp containing the next clue. Once you've dealt with any Izila in the area, move into the camp and examine the broken tools on the ground.

An Izila Archer and Spearmen spawn just north of the fight. Kill them quickly before the Bear kills all of your allies. Note that you only have Wenja allies during this phase of the fight if you have liberated the outpost before reaching the Bear. If you haven't, you fight Izila and the Great Scar Bear here. Hop onto one of the nearby rocks and send your beast in to attack the Great Scar Bear. This keeps it distracted while you throw spears, making sure to aim for the Bear's head.

Once the Bear reaches 50% health it stands up and roars before running off into its cave. Continue attacking the Bear as it runs. It is never immune to damage, allowing you to hit it with arrows while it retreats.

As you enter the cave, set the first traps you come across, the Bear waits for you in the front cave area in this second stage of the battle.

The Great Scar Bear roars before he advances on you, sending bats flying out of the cave. When you hear the roar, fall back behind the snare traps inside the cave. These are located underneath unstable stalactites which you can bring down with spears or arrows. This causes them to fall onto the trapped Bear, inflicting huge amounts of damage. Be sure to order your own beast away from the snare before hitting the stalactites as they can also cause massage damage to your companion. When he has taken a bit more damage he retreats to his den in the back of the cave. Chase him into the den, quickly crafting more spears or arrows while you use your Hunter Vision to stay on his tail.

Once you are in the den, the Great Scar Bear has hardly any health. Send in your beast to distract him while you finish him off.

SNOWBLOOD WOLF

DIFFICULTY	Very Hard
AWARDS	High XP
SPECIAL	Tame the Snowblood Wolf leader.

The entrance to the Snowblood Dire Wolf Beast Master Hunt zone is in the far south. It is relatively easy to find. Follow the main river south and it takes you to the zone entrance. Keep following the river and you arrive at the quest giver.

Make sure to have your spear ready before accepting the quest from the dead Wenja body. Two Wolves immediately attack you once the cut scene ends. Kill the Wolves, stock up on Hardwood from the Rewards Stash nearby, and then head south toward the objective marker.

An Izila Hunting group is spread out in the forest near your first clue. Use your Hunter Vision to spot them, and the Wolves that are lurking in the forest. Once you've killed them, follow the blood trail to a dead Bear and examine it.

Follow the blood trail south, leading you down to a small pond. A group of three Izila Archers and three Wolves spawns just before you reach the water. Send in your beast to kill the Izila while you focus on killing the Wolves.

The next clue is a dead Izila Villager on shore next to a boat and a couple of nets.

Head directly south following the trail with your Hunter Vision, this short walk has no enemies, so use it to craft weapons and gather any materials you may need along the way. You reach a small camp with an overturned bowl which is full of fish, inspect it.

Run down the riverbed another short distance with no enemies until you come across a blood stained section with some broken spears. These broken spears are your next clue.

Follow the paw prints east to the standing stones. A group of four Izila, three Archers and one Spearman, attack you as you follow the trail. After killing them, you reach the hunting area for the first of the Snowblood Wolves.

Examine the dead Izila on the ground, then set all of the traps in the area and prepare yourself for the oncoming Wolf assault.

The Great Beast traps kill any regular Wolf in one hit and deal great amounts of damage to the Snowblood Wolf. This first Wolf dies much easier than the Alpha you fight in the third battle.

Once you free the caged Wenja, the assault begins. Head slightly north from the cage area as you free the Wenja. An objective marker spawns on the Snowblood Wolf to guide you to an opportune chance to take a good chunk of health off of the Wolf. As the Wolf appears, it howls from the top of a rock to summon the other Wolves, leaving it open to an easy headshot with your spear.

A fully upgraded spear takes the Wolf down to half health. Send your beast after it to finish it off and prepare yourself to take on five Wolves. Melee shots to the head with your spear can quickly kill the Wolves. If you kill them quickly, you never face more than one at a time, making this fight much easier. If you begin to get overrun, head through your traps, forcing the Wolves to set them off to continue their chase.

After killing the Wolf, head west toward the marsh. You can open your map and set a marker on the objective to help you head in the right direction. Use your Hunter Vision to locate the tracks leading you to a dead Izila Villager at the praying stones.

Arm the Great Beast Traps as you follow the path and then arm the ones next to the dead Izila before inspecting the body, as this spawns the second Snowblood Wolf.

Stand your ground and use your bow to pick off the Wolves as the advance on your location. If they begin to surround you, you can jump into the water and let your Beast take care of the Wolves. Wolves cannot follow you into the water, allowing you to put distance between yourself and them to heal and perform ranged attacks

After the second Snowblood Wolf is dead, head northeast for your final fight with the Alpha Snowblood Wolf. Set a marker on your map to help you stay on course. Following the prints with your Hunter Vision leads you to a small fishing camp. A bowl of fish spilled out onto the shore is another clue you can grab for bonus XP.

The tracks lead away from this fishing camp into another Izila camp partially engulfed in flames.

SNAKES!

Watch out for Snakes along the path, they are easily spotted with your Hunter Vision. The also provide an audio cue in the form of a hissing sound.

A dead Izila next to a stone in the ground is your next clue.

The paw prints take you to the Tomb of Teeth. Inside a Wolf guards your next clue, a dead Izila who attempted to hide from the Wolves.

Continue through the small tomb after examining the clue. When you emerge from the cave you are greeted by the Alpha Snowblood Wolf.

Use your bow to pick off the five regular Wolves that surround the Alpha from a distance. The Alpha and remaining Wolves retreat a short distance into the woods after you begin to fire your bow. There are Great Beast Traps in this area, but if you continue to keep your distance, focusing on killing the regular Wolves, these are not needed.

After you've killed off all of the standard Wolves, send your beast at the Alpha Snowblood Wolf and start throwing spears at it. When it reaches 50% health it begins to retreat. Use your beast to stall its advance and quickly finish it off with a few more Spears, avoiding a fight in the Snowblood Den.

Once you've critically wounded the Wolf, he is ready to tame. Approach him and claim the Alpha Snowblood Wolf as your companion.

VILLAGE MISSIONS

Once you build Karoosh's, Wogah's, and Jayma's huts, village missions become available. Quest markers show up on the mini-map and when you are in the village the quest giver is given the same question mark icon. Earn XP and unlock new quests as you complete the missions.

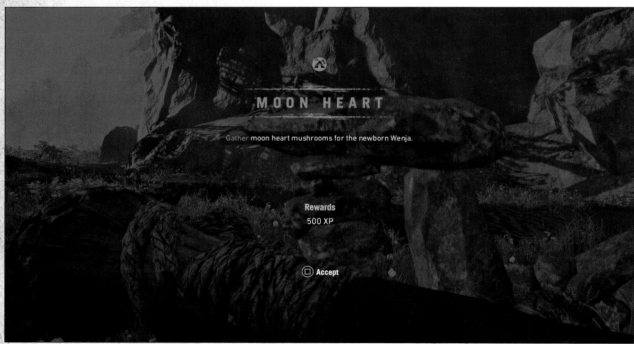

MOON HEART

Gather moon heart mushrooms for the newborn Wenja.

Rewards

500 XP

⬜ Accept

THE ROTTEN RIVER

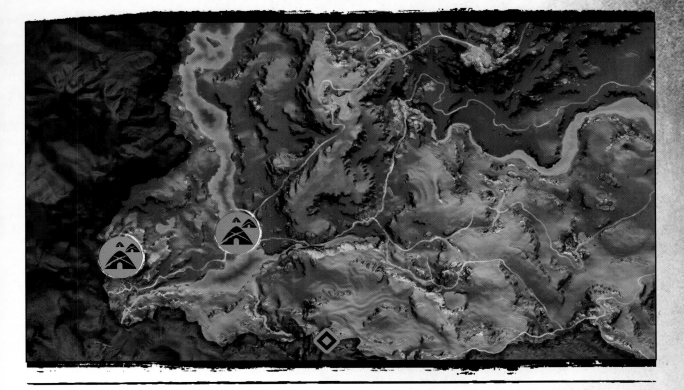

PREREQUISITE	Build Karoosh's, Wogah's, and Jayma's huts
MAIN OBJECTIVE	Find what spoiled the village water
DIFFICULTY	Easy
AWARDS	500 XP
PREDATORS	Dholes, Wolves

STRATEGY

After talking to the villager, head down to the river, find the dead fish inside the netting, and accept the mission. Investigate the water and then enable your Hunter Vision. Follow the trail of sickness to the south, across the path to the east, and along the shore further south. Investigate another net full of dead fish and continue to follow the trail up three waterfalls and into a cave to the east.

Inside the cave, bodies rot in the water. They need to be removed to prevent more sickness, but first you must deal with the hungry Wolves ahead. Once the area is clear, pick up the three bodies and drop them so that they are completely out of the water. Kill any remaining Wolves to complete the mission.

ROT FUMES

If you explore deeper inside the cave, you run into rot fumes that keep you from advancing any farther. Eventually you gain the ability to craft Antidotes, which allow you to move through the gas without taking damage.

SPIRIT TOTEM

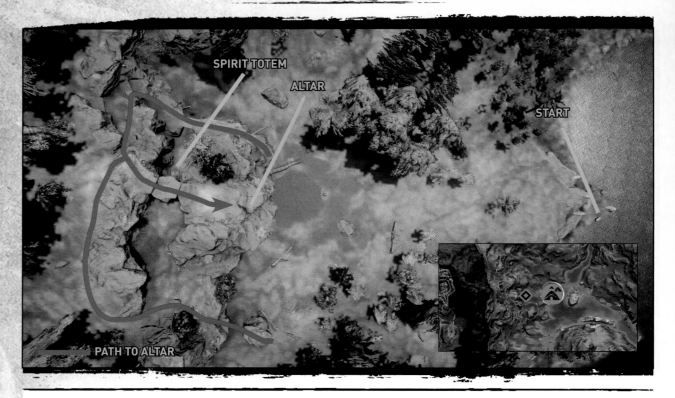

SPIRIT TOTEM

ALTAR

START

PATH TO ALTAR

PREREQUISITE	Build Karoosh's, Wogah's, and Jayma's huts
MAIN OBJECTIVE	Find the Spirit Totem and place it on the altar.
DIFFICULTY	Easy
AWARDS	500 XP
ENEMIES	Udam Warriors, Udam Slinger
PREDATORS	Brown Bear, Jaguars

STRATEGY

Talk to Manoo who hangs out west of Karoosh's hut. He wants you to help a fellow Wenja place a new spirit totem. A village mission marker appears on the map to the southeast. If available, use a nearby Fast Travel point to quicken the trip. Head west once the mission has been accepted. You must find the totem and place it on the altar, located on a cliff to the west.

Move west to find a high cliff, accessible around the north and south sides. Sitting just above is the altar where the totem must be placed. The spirit totem sits inside an opening accessible from the north, so move around the right side. Udam Warriors and Udam Slingers occupy the surrounding area, as does a Brown Bear, so move cautiously. Look inside the opening below the wood and spot the Wenja and the spirit totem. Grab the item and make your way up to the altar, taking care of the enemies and jaguars along the way. Place the totem to complete the mission.

MOON HEART

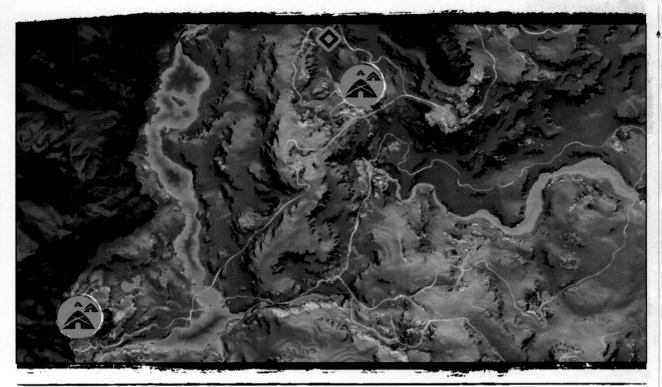

PREREQUISITE	Complete The Rotten River, Spirit Totem, and Vision of Ice
MAIN OBJECTIVE	Gather moon heart mushrooms from cave
DIFFICULTY	Medium
AWARDS	500 XP
PREDATORS	Wolves, Brown Bear

STRATEGY

A villager just outside your cave asks for help gathering moon heart mushrooms for a newborn. Head to the marked location just northeast of the Nakuti Bonfire and accept the mission. Enter the cave found to the north at Mansi Rest. There are eight spots in the cave where the mushroom is available, but only five need to be gathered. Two Wolves impede your progress, but are fairly easy to take care of with your lit club. A Brown Bear also makes an appearance and takes a little more work to take down. You are unable to tame it, but bait can be used as a distraction. Look for vines that lead to upper ledges and pick away at its health from there.

The fungus glows bright green in the dark and has a slight flicker when you are carrying a burning weapon. Explore the cave and grab five mushrooms. Head to the cave exit to find the villager and complete the mission.

SICK BEASTS

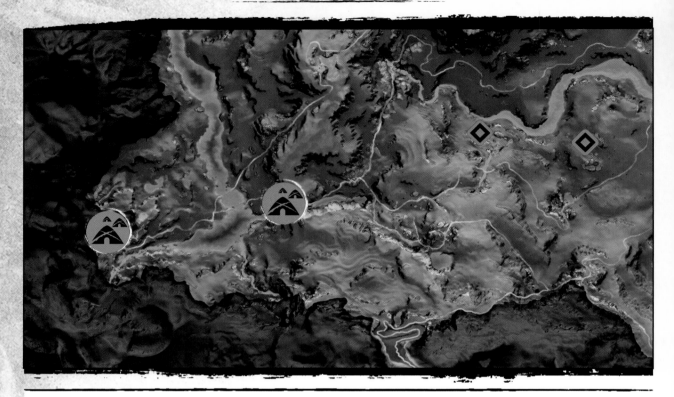

PREREQUISITE	Complete The Rotten River, Spirit Totem, and Vision of Ice
MAIN OBJECTIVE	Follow the sick beast's trail to discover what poisons the animals
DIFFICULTY	Medium
AWARDS	750 XP
ENEMIES	Udam Warriors, Udam Archers, Udam Spearman
PREDATORS	Boars, Jaguar, Rhinos

STRATEGY

Talk to Manoo in the middle of the village. He talks about a problem with sick beasts that is tainting the meat supply for the Wenja. A quest marker appears to the east. Head there to accept the mission and start the investigation. Signs of a sick Brown Bear give the first clue. Use Hunter Vision to track its trail along the stream to the east and then north to a small cave. Quietly dispose of the Udam who hang out at the entrance and proceed inside to find a sick Wenja who ate berries near the beehives. The cause has been found, now they must be burned. A Jaguar waits for you at the cave exit, so be careful.

Head east to find six bushes marked with objective markers. Set them all on fire to get rid of the sickness. A burning pot is here in case you want to conserve animal fat. Be careful as you set the bushes ablaze as the fire can quickly spread through the nearby grass. If you anger the nearby Rhinos, they do become hostile, so be ready with your spear.

BLOOD AND HONEY

(INSIDE CAVE)

WENJA EXIT PATH

PREREQUISITE	Complete Moon Heart and Sick Beasts
MAIN OBJECTIVE	Find the Wenja out gathering village supplies
DIFFICULTY	Medium
AWARDS	500 XP, Population
ENEMIES	Udam Elite Chieftain, Udam Spearmen, Udam Warriors, Udam Scourges, Udam Elite Warrior, Udam Elite Slinger

STRATEGY

Speak with Manoo again for the next village mission. A Wenja has not returned from fetching honey. Move out to the quest marker and accept the mission. Enable Hunter Vision and follow the blood trail to the west as it leads to an Udam camp. Several Udam occupy the area with an alarm situated between the two fires. Try to keep this operation stealthy—at least until the Udam Elite Slinger and alarm have been taken care of.

With the area clear of Udam, find the Wenja inside a small cave, northwest of the camp, and interact with him. At this point, you must escort him to safety. His health bar appears at the top of the HUD. If it depletes, he dies and you return to the previous checkpoint. Udam attack from all sides; use the mini-map to spot them early. Use a strong beast companion to increase the odds of the Wenja surviving. It may seem obvious, but be careful with fire, as the Wenja burn too.

MISSING HUNTERS

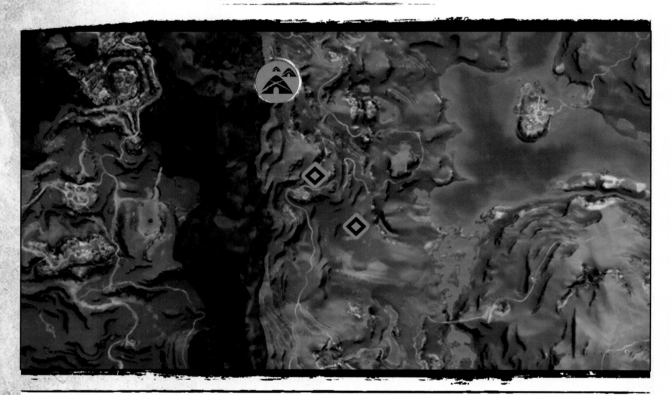

PREREQUISITE	Complete Blood and Honey
MAIN OBJECTIVE	Find the missing Wenja hunters
DIFFICULTY	Medium
AWARDS	500 XP
ENEMIES	Izila Elite Chieftain, Izila Warriors, Izila Archers
PREDATOR	Leopard, Wolves, Cave Lion

STRATEGY

The woman just outside Takkar's Cave is concerned about two Wenja hunters who haven't returned from an outing. Find their camp at the marker and accept the mission. Flip on Hunter Vision and track the blood trail to the southeast until you find a body. From there, the trail splits.

The left path shows evidence of an Izila attack. Continue down the hill to a rock overlooking five enemies surrounding a pond. Hiding inside a cranny below is a Wenja hunter. Eliminate the Izila threat, paying particular attention to the Izila Elite Chieftain, and then talk to the Wenja.

Return to the split and follow the other trail south up the side of the cliff to find the second hunter who cowers in fear. He wants you to deal with a nearby Leopard. Kill it and talk to the Wenja to complete the mission.

SONG OF THE SPIRITS

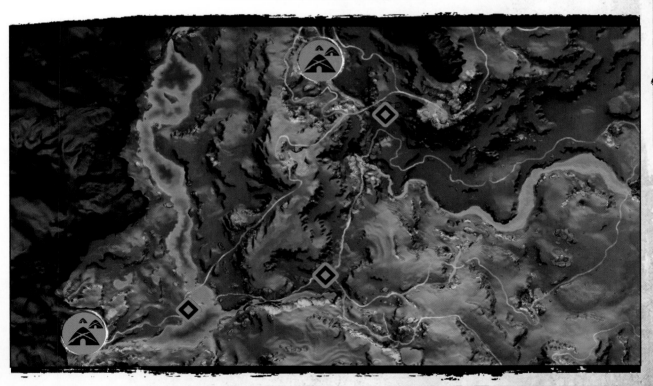

PREREQUISITE	Complete Blood and Honey
MAIN OBJECTIVE	Protect the Wenja procession from the dangers of Oros
DIFFICULTY	Medium
AWARDS	500 XP
SPECIAL	Mission is only available at night
ENEMIES	Udam Archers, Udam Spearmen, Udam Warriors
PREDATORS	Wolves, Cave Lions

STRATEGY

Manoo has another job for you; protect the Wenja voices from night beasts. If it is daytime, sleep until night and head out to the marker, northeast of the village. Call a beast for help and accept the mission. Run over to Prashrawa's Birth and interact with the woman to find four Wenja at the start of the celebratory progression. To complete the mission, at least two Wenja must survive. The four green diamonds at the top of the HUD note how many remain. Stay near the group with your trusty companion as they head southwest toward their first stop.

Keep an eye on the mini-map as predators attack. The longer you take defeating them, the more likely a Wenja dies. Continue the protection as they move to Stones of the Lost for another stop. Udam Archers, Udam Spearmen, and Udam Warriors attack from the east. Immediately sic your pet on one as you take another. Quickly take care of the enemies so no harm comes to the party. Watch out, as the Wenja bolt toward the nearby stream. Follow them west along the stream until they reach the finish at Wakwas River Stones.

BEYOND THE STONES

PREREQUISITE	Complete Missing Hunters, Song of the Spirits, and Vision of fire
MAIN OBJECTIVE	Find the Wenja hunter lost in Izila territory
DIFFICULTY	Hard
AWARDS	500 XP
ENEMIES	Izila Archers, Izila Warriors, Izila Elite Warriors, Izila Slinger

Talk to Manoo to learn of a Wenja hunter gone missing in Izila territory. Just southwest of Pardal's Perch, find the quest marker and accept. Using Hunter Vision, track the hunter to the southwest. Search the clues for bonus XP as you wind your way to the hunter. Eliminate the Izila in between you and the Wenja. Before talking to him, prepare for a big fight by calling your strongest beast and crafting weapons.

 **SHORTCUT**

The three clues take you quite a bit out of the way. If you don't mind forgoing the 300 XP, head up the left hill just after starting the mission. You can make a beeline for the hunter and save time.

The Wenja Hunter's health appears at the top of the HUD, which means one thing—you cannot let him die. Defend against waves of Izila as they attack from the south. Once ready, talk to him to get things started. Keep your beast busy as you aim your weapons at the incoming fighters. Glance at the mini-map often to avoid being surprised. Kill all of the Izila and talk to the hunter again to complete the mission.

SPIRIT GIFTS

PREREQUISITE	Complete Missing Hunters, Song of the Spirits, and Vision of Fire
MAIN OBJECTIVE	Recover the stolen gifts from the Udam camp
DIFFICULTY	Medium
AWARDS	500 XP
ENEMIES	Udam Archers, Udam Spearmen, Udam Slingers, Udam Civilians

STRATEGY

Talk to the woman outside Takkar's Cave to find out the Udam have been digging up Wenja graves and swiping the gifts left for the spirits. Head over to Stones of the Lost, grapple up to the rock high above the stream, and wait for the grave robbers. Crouch and step back to avoid being spotted. As soon as they leave, follow them to their camp to the southeast. Use Hunter Vision to follow their tracks.

Three lone Udam are easy takedowns as you follow the group's footprints, but eventually you reach the camp at Torn Flesh Retreat, where several enemies stand guard. Scout the place out from a high point or by calling in your Owl. You can get an easy kill with the bird on one of the lone watchmen, though if the body is found, the Udam become alerted. All of the Udam do not need to be eliminated, but it does make the recovery process much easier. You must find The Drum, Pot, and Necklace and return them to their rightful place.

Climb onto the northwest rock with the grappling claw to get good shots on the Udam Slingers to the right; watch for the left guy to move away and quickly take them both down. The outer Udam Archers and Udam Spearmen can be pulled away from the camp by tossing rocks just outside. Once the camp is clear of armed Udam, it is safe to collect the stolen offerings. Return the items to Stones of the Lost, placing them in the three marked locations.

BITER IN THE DEEP

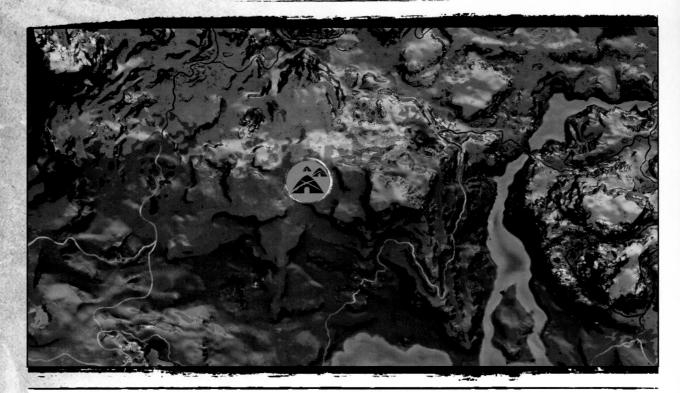

PREREQUISITE	Complete Spirit Gifts and Beyond the Stones
MAIN OBJECTIVE	Hunt the Rare Red Bitefish in its underwater lair
DIFFICULTY	Hard
AWARDS	1000 XP
PREDATORS	Brown Bears

STRATEGY

A villager wants you to kill and skin a rare Bitefish found in a deep cave far to the east. As you approach the location of the cavern, the mission begins. Look for rock outcroppings surrounding a deep hole at Dupaskaya Tooth Cave. A grappling point allows you to lower yourself inside. Move to a second grappling point as you move by, swing over to another on the ceiling, and finally grapple to a fourth to reach a ledge and solid ground.

Light a spear and follow the corridor into a big cavern, where two untamable Brown Bears wander the wet room. Kill one immediately upon contact or you may end up facing both at one time. With the predators defeated, climb the far ledge to find the remains of the Rare Red Bitefish. Skin it and leave the cave by moving between the grappling points in the same manner that you entered. Once out, the quest is complete.

LOST IN ICE

START

WENJA

DEAD BODY

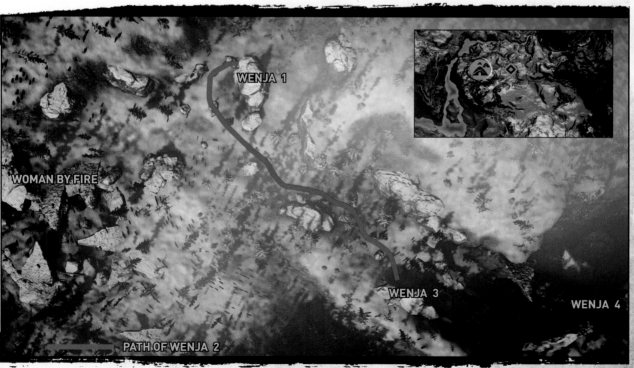

WENJA 1

WOMAN BY FIRE

WENJA 3

WENJA 4

PATH OF WENJA 2

PREREQUISITE	Complete Spirit Gifts and Beyond the Stones
MAIN OBJECTIVE	Help the Wenja lost in the cold
DIFFICULTY	Hard
AWARDS	500 XP
ENEMIES	Udam Warriors, Udam Spearmen, Udam Archers, Udam Scourge, Udam Elite Spearman, Udam Elite Chieftain
PREDATORS	Wolf, Cave Lion

STRATEGY

Visit Manoo to learn of Wenja who travelled to Udam territory in the ice hills and haven't been heard from since. Head to the new village mission marker west of Udam Homeland and accept the challenge. To find the Wenja, enable Hunter Vision and track them east, south, and east again until you find a woman warming up next to a fire. She tells you about Udam who have taken four Wenja south. All four, each represented by a quest marker, must be saved to complete the mission. Be sure to untie each one before proceeding.

Wenja 1 is surrounded by a group of Udam just to the south, as Wenja 2 is escorted away toward Wenja 3, who is also protected by several enemies. The fourth Wenja faces the most immediate danger—tied up on a rock ledge further west as a Cave Lion closes in. It is this final victim who acts as a timer for the mission; take too long and the feline gets dinner.

Quickly scout the south with your Owl, tagging as many Udam as possible and killing the left archer as he takes a break. Head south around the right side of the rocks and intercept Wenja 2 by taking down his escort.

Take down the Udam Archer as he climbs the rocks and then take his place up top. Look directly over the three remaining Udam, perform a Death from Above on one, and quickly eliminate the others. Free Wenja 1 and run west.

Send your Owl in to scout the valley, taking out the right Udam Spearman who stands guard over the others. Move up the left side and take down the left Udam Spearman. The remaining Udam surround Wenja 3 below. Drop off the ledge and quickly fight your way to the Wenja and untie him.

Ignore the Udam Elite Chieftain and sprint south to Wenja 4. Kill the Cave Lion and free the last Wenja, completing the village mission.

RINGS OF FIRE

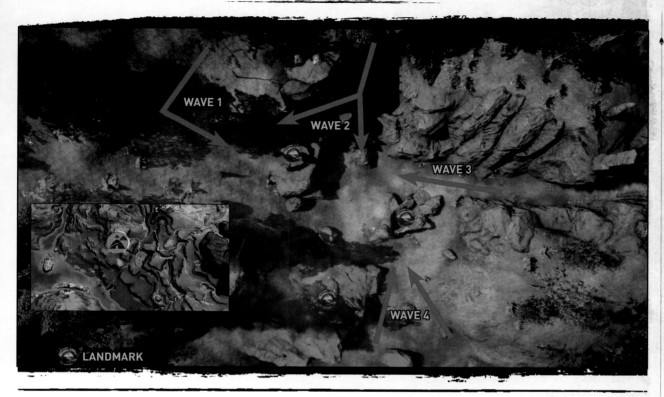

WAVE 1

WAVE 2

WAVE 3

WAVE 4

LANDMARK

PREREQUISITE	Complete Biter in the Deep and Lost in Ice
MAIN OBJECTIVE	Defend the Wenja landmarks from an Izila attack
DIFFICULTY	Very Hard
AWARDS	500 XP
ENEMIES	Izila Warriors, Izila Archers, Izila Spearmen, Izila Elite Chieftains

STRATEGY

Talking to Manoo starts the final village mission. Three Wenja rings are in danger of being burnt down by the sun walkers. Help defend the landmarks from the waves of Izila attackers. Before leaving, prepare for an Izila onslaught. Call your strongest beast; the Great Scar Bear is a great choice if it's available. The felines' speed is great against the smaller Izila, but the Izila Elite Chieftains are your biggest challenge, which requires strength. Set a fireproof food as your default; Ultimate Boost is your best bet. As you close in on Naymin of Spirits, quest markers note the locations of the three Wenja rings and the Izila begin their assault.

Four waves attack in all.

IZILA WAVES	
WAVE 1	Two Izila Warriors, two Izila Spearmen, Izila Elite Chieftain
WAVE 2	Izila Archers, Izila Spearmen, Izila Warrior, Izila Elite Chieftain
WAVE 3	Izila Spearmen, two Izila Elite Chieftains
WAVE 4	Izila Warriors, Izila Archer, Izila Spearman, three Izila Elite Chieftains

The number of remaining Wenja landmarks is noted in the upper-left corner of the HUD. Ideally all three stay upright throughout the quest, but as long as one survives, the mission is a success. Keep your beast busy as the Izila pour into the area. The weaker Izila attempt to divert your attention, but keep your focus on the fire wielding Izila Elite Chieftains. They are by far the biggest threat to the flammable rings. Stave off the firepower of the Izila without losing the three rings to complete the quest.

HELP WENJA: BEAST KILL

It's time to help your fellow Wenja by hunting down beasts causing various problems in their lives. Every mission starts by speaking to a Wenja tribesman. They tell you about an issue caused by wildlife and then a new marker shows up on your map. This next map marker actually starts the mission.

You can talk to each tribe member without starting the mission. So if you find yourself near one of the Objective starting locations, speak to the tribesman before moving on.

HELPFUL TIPS

Below are some helpful tips that will aid you in each Beast Kill mission, as well as facing beasts anywhere in Oros.

HUNT DURING THE DAY!

Hunting during the day helps you spot the animals and prevents other predatory beasts from spawning during your fight.

FOOD CHOICE

Making Scent Camouflage your quick heal food choice has a great impact on your ability to sneak up on predatory animals and get away when they decide to chase you. It does this by making it harder for the animal to detect you, and, on top of all of that it heals two health! Make sure you have a fair amount of Violet Leaves though, as it requires two Meat and one Violet Leaf to craft.

USE BAIT!

Using bait not only helps you tame an animal; it is a great way to call out and distract animals while you line them up for an easy shot.

BRING YOUR BEAST

Each Beast Companion awards you benefits; some of them are very helpful when hunting other animals

- ▶ **BEAR:** The Bear causes enemies, including other Beasts, to attack them first, allowing you to stay out of the fight while helping the Bear wreak havoc on your enemies.

- ▶ **BADGER:** All animals on Oros fear the Badger. Having a Badger at your side keeps even the most aggressive animals at bay, as long as you don't get overrun. The Badger even revives itself from death one time.

- ▶ **LEOPARD:** The Leopard is the only animal that can tag other animals. This ability to tag animals in a nearby radius prevents anything from sneaking up on you.

- ▶ **WOLF:** The Wolf reveals more terrain on your mini-map, helping you to see the different advantages the nearby terrain has to offer. It is also a decent fighter and growls to alert you to the presence of hostile beasts and tribes.

HELPFUL SKILLS

Take these skills with you into the Beast Hunting area and you dominate your prey.

- ▶ **SPRINT FOREVER:** You can run forever, giving you the ability to flee any bad situation.

- ▶ **TAME CANINES, WILDCATS, APEX PREDATORS, CUNNING BEASTS:** Having all of the taming skills unlocked allows you to tame creatures instead of killing them, which is much easier. You can also have much more powerful Beast companions, helping you in all aspects of the game.

- ▶ **TAG ANIMALS:** Both you and your Owl can tag animals. Once tagged, animals show up on your HUD or mini-map until they are eliminated.

- ▶ **ANIMAL WOUNDS:** Animal wounds increases the amount of damage your weapons inflict against animals.

- ▶ **MAMMOTH RIDER:** The Mammoth is the strongest weapon in the game. The ability to use a Mammoth against the Wolves and Bears in the Beast Kill missions is worth all of the skill points in the world. Plus, you get to ride a Mammoth so it's just flat out AWESOME!

KILLING THE BEASTS

DHOLES

ANIMAL COUNT	11
DIFFICULTY	Easy
AWARDS	800 XP + Animal Skins sent to your Reward Stash

After activating the mission, keep following the path and you find a Wenja hunter. Once you find the Hunter, use your Owl to locate all of the Dholes; this helps you plot your attack as you move forward. The first pair of Dholes is located at the end of the body of water. Headshots with your bow and arrows make short work of them. Looking in from the water, the next Dhole is located on the east side of the camp. Take it out from a distance as there are three more located at the opposite side of the camp.

THE RARE DHOLE

The Rare Dhole is located in the group of three Dholes on the west side of the camp so have some bait ready if you want to tame it.

If you don't have a shot on any of the Dholes, throw some bait to lure them out of their hiding spots. Head toward the back of the camp and start to approach the cave. Throw some bait to lure out at least one of the Dholes. This prevents you from fighting all three that reside in the cave at once.

Once you've killed them, finish off the two Dholes up on the hill to the southwest of the cave entrance and the mission is complete.

WILD BOARS

ANIMAL COUNT	7
DIFFICULTY	Medium
REWARDS	1000 XP + Animal Skins sent to your Reward Stash

Head north down the path after activating the mission. Stay crouched and have Hunter Vision on. You first come across four Boars. Line up a good headshot with your bow for the first Boar, then just try to hit the other three.

The headshot should instantly kill the first Boar and a trail of blood can help you track the remaining Boars. They are most likely to flee down toward the Boars on the beach. Do not go running after them; continue to stay crouched and follow their tracks until you have a shot on them.

Once you near the beach where the last three Boars remain, keep an eye out for a Bear. This Bear is alerted by all the violence happening on your side of the river and is likely to cross and begin attacking the Wenja hunter and the Boars in the area.

You can't attempt to save the Wenja Hunter, but it may be easier to just ignore the Bear and pick off the Boars before the Bear crosses the river to attack the Boars and Wenja Hunter.

Make sure to keep your distance so that the Bear focuses on the other Hunter and Boars before aggressing toward you. With all the Boars dead, you can flee, tame the Bear, or kill the Bear. The choice is yours as the mission is already complete.

JAGUARS

ANIMAL COUNT	6
DIFFICULTY	Medium
REWARD	1000 XP

After speaking with the Wenja and locating the mission start point, head west following a path that leads down into a small canyon. Once you bump into the Friendly Hunter, two Jaguars immediately attack.

HIT AND RUN
Jaguars are hit and run type animals so make every hit count! Your spear is your highest damaging ranged weapon and can make short work of a Jaguar.

Help the Hunter fend off the attack, and use your Hunter Vision to follow their trails. Wait for them to hide in a bush, then use your arrows to finish them off while they aren't moving.

One more Jaguar stands between you and the cavern's entrance. This Jaguar is located on a rock to the north behind a tree, just before the cavern and can easily be picked up with your Hunter Vision. Have some bait ready as you head into the cavern if you want your chance at taming the Rare Jaguar. Taming it is much easier than killing it if you have the appropriate skill set.

Once you have tamed or killed this Jaguar, you face three Jaguars at the same time at the end of the cavern.

Use your bow to injure them as they try to attack; this causes them to run away in pain. If you begin to get overrun, set some of the surrounding shrubs on fire. The Jaguars fear fire, so this causes them to scatter, allowing you to pick them off one by one. After clearing this trio of Jaguars the mission is over.

WOLVES

ANIMAL COUNT	9
DIFFICULTY	Hard
REWARD	1200 XP + Animal Skins sent to your Reward Stash

The safest, fastest and easiest way to complete this mission is simply riding a Mammoth in from the west and trampling all of the Wolves in the area. But assuming you do not have the Mammoth Rider skill here's how to do it on foot.

After accepting the mission, head east into the hunting area. Use your Owl to scout out the Wolves' locations. You quickly notice that they have the path surrounded. Stay to the north side of the path and use your Hunter Vision to locate the Wolves hiding in the brush. Take your time to aim for the head. You want to deal as much damage as possible so that they do not have time to "howl in" reinforcements.

There are six Wolves in the bushes before the Wooly Rhino. Make sure you kill them all before moving on past the Rhino. If they begin to surround you, light your arrow or club to scare them off.

Lighting the bushes on fire here may spook the Wooly Rhino, who is a much bigger problem to deal with than a few Wolves.

Give the Rhino plenty of distance as you move by, heading diagonally back down the south side of the hunting site. This will hopefully mean that you will face the Rare Wolf last, allowing you to tame it or kill it much easier.

Use your arrows to kill off the three remaining Wolves from the high rocks to the south. If they catch on to you, again use fire to scare them off and spread them out. Eliminate them one by one and then have your spears or bait ready to kill or tame the Rare Wolf.

CAVE LIONS

ANIMAL COUNT	5
DIFFICULTY	Hard
REWARD	1200 XP + Animal Skins sent to your Reward Stash

After accepting the mission, light one of your weapons on fire and head east, where you find a hunter at the beginning of the hunting area.

On the south side of the rock they are standing in front of, there are two Cave Lions. Pull out your spear and activate your Hunter Vision to locate them.

Get in close enough to land a Spear on one of them, if you have upgraded your spear and land a headshot, this could be the end for the Cave Lion. The other Cave Lion flees in a random direction; follow it and take it down with your spear.

HALT!
A thrown spear or fire stops a Cave Lion from charging you.

Now with almost half the Lions eliminated, head down to the north side of the small pond's edge and throw some bait. This attracts the Rare Black Lion, you can chose to tame or kill it. Either option takes it off your amount of Cave Lions left to kill. Across the water from you there is a lone Cave Lion. This Lion may be a bit tough to hit with a spear so use your bow to land a headshot and then Hunter Vision to follow its tracks and finish it off.

A small cave in the back of the pond houses the last two Cave Lions, throw some bait to draw them out.

BE GENEROUS
Don't be afraid to waste bait. If no animal takes it, you can quickly pick it back up and place it in your inventory.

Ideally one of the Cave Lions will come out; attack it with a spear. If it runs, do not cross the mouth of the cave, instead prepare another spear and take on the Cave Lion still residing in the Cave.

This will leave it pinned in the cave for a follow up attack. Once the Lion is dead, hunt down the last injured Cave Lion to collect your reward.

BADGERS

ANIMAL COUNT	9
DIFFICULTY	Hard
REWARD	1200 XP + Animal Skins sent to your Reward Stash

After accepting the mission, quickly run south into the hunting area. Badgers are attacking a friendly Wenja Hunter. Use your spears to make short work of them and try to save the hunter. If he survives, he makes excellent bait as you make your way south toward a cave in the camp.

THE BEAR IS MIGHTIER THAN THE BADGER
If you have a Bear now is a great time to use it. The Badgers attack the Bear, and the Bear makes short work of the Badgers, making this mission easy.

If the hunter did not survive your initial encounter with the Badgers, toss bait a few meters in front of you and wait to see if it pulls any Badgers out. You can use this opportunity to tame a Badger if you'd like. Even if you've already tamed a Badger, you can still tame another. This is much easier than trying to hit them while they speed around. Push forward using this method to prevent being overrun by Badgers.

HONEY BADGER DON'T CARE!
Honey Badgers just don't care; hence they aren't scared by fire.

Three of the Badgers are located in the small houses along the path forward: one in the hut to the east and two in the fenced area to the west.

After you kill them, a short incline leads to a bush that is hiding two Badgers just before the cave. Use a spear or bow to line a headshot up on one of them before they detect you, then hunt down the other. Do not chase it if it runs to the south as that leads you into three more Badgers.

Head toward the mouth of the cave slowly; a Badger hides in the brush just to the right of the cave entrance. Take him out with a headshot, then throw some bait to call out the remaining Badgers one by one. A couple of Badger Headshots later and you have saved the day for this Wenja Village.

 My favorite beast companion is the Honey Badger. When he dies…he doesn't really, because he don't give a damn.

— *Jean-Sébastien Decant, Narrative Director*

LEOPARDS

ANIMAL COUNT	8
DIFFICULTY	Hard
REWARD	1200 XP + Animal Skins sent to your Reward Stash

If you have a Bear tamed, bring it with you. The Leopards are weak, but very aggressive and stalk you before quickly jumping out for an attack. A Bear forces them to attack it before attacking you, making this mission incredibly easy.

Grab your spear and be ready to perform heavy attacks. The Leopards attack so quickly that taking time to aim and throw your spear my cause you to miss and deal no damage at all. The Leopards come running straight at you with no warning, leaping from their cover and closing the distance quickly.

The Leopards are so aggressive that you may not even make it through half of the hunting area before facing all of them. It is a good idea to have a lit club ready to scare them off if too many begin to attack. Once they scatter, activate Hunter Vision and hunt them down. If you strike a Leopard with your Spear head-on, it bleeds and runs away, allowing you to quickly hunt it down.

You can also throw bait around to distract a few Leopards, jumping in to tame one if you have the skills!

Once you've killed all eight of the Leopards, you complete the mission.

BEARS

ANIMAL COUNT	7
DIFFICULTY	Very Hard
REWARD	1400 XP + Animal Skins sent to your Reward Stash

The best way to accomplish this mission is by grabbing a Mammoth from the area to the east and riding it into the hunting Area. You'll be able to easily trample Brown Bears and Cave Bears without issue. You can even use Spears to weaken the Cave Bears from atop the Mammoth to make things easier.

If you haven't learned how to ride a Mammoth yet, you need to rely on your Hunter Vision to get you through this quest alive.

First use your Owl to locate the Bears, making sure to make note of the location of the Cave Bears and Brown Bears

separately. Head south once entering the hunting area. This pits you against your first Brown Bear. Use arrows while the Bear is at a distance, then shift to spears once it is in close range. Use this tactic on the next two Brown Bears to the north. With them down, you can focus on the Cave Bear that is north of the entrance of the hunting area.

Set a few traps on the ground if you have them available on the route you plan on using to retreat. These deal damage to the Bear if it chooses to chase you. Use your arrows, making sure to aim for the head, to deal the greatest amount of damage. You can use bait to stall it momentarily or even tame it if you haven't yet tamed a Cave Bear.

Stay crouched and use Hunter Vision while you head farther east into the camp where you encounter another Cave Bear. Employ the same tactics used to kill the last Cave Bear to make short work of this one. Continue pushing into the camp until you come across a cave containing two Brown Bears.

If you've kept your distance you can pull the first Bear out of the front of the cave, kill them, and then pull the second one out. If you accidentally pull both Bears out of the cave, use some bait to distract one while you kill the other.

With all of these Bears dead, the mission rewards are yours!

CAVE LIONS 2

ANIMAL COUNT	6
DIFFICULTY	Medium
REWARDS	1000 XP and Animal Skins sent to your Reward Stash

While taking out six Cave Lions may sound like a challenging task, this quest takes place in a large area allowing you to sneak up and fight one Cave Lion at a time.

Use your Hunter Vision and stay crouched as you move through the grass heading towards the waterfall. Your first three cave lions will be on the east side of the waterfall.

WILD BOARS

Wild Boars in the area may distract the Cave Lions, allowing you to easily take aim and land critical hits with your Spear.

A Black Cave Lion is in the west side of the hunting area. Use bait or wait for it to attack some of the local wildlife before you attempt to attack.

The Black Cave Lion is much stronger than its standard Cave Lion counterparts.

If you are having trouble locating any of the Cave Lions, call in your Owl and use it to scout out and mark their locations.

WOOLLY RHINO

ANIMAL COUNT	4
DIFFICULTY	Hard
REWARDS	1200 XP and Animal Skins sent to your Reward Stash

Woolly Rhinos can deal out a ton of damage, assuming you let them get close enough. Take advantage of their non-aggressive nature, by beginning your attack with a spear to the head from a distance. You'll want to kill them as quickly as possible, since they will attack in a group if they reach another Woolly Rhino.

Your Beast can distract and slow a Woolly Rhino's attempt to flee, but it will likely take a lethal amount of damage in the process so be ready to revive your Beast.

Keep your eyes out for the two Two Horned Woolly Rhinos that are in the hunting area. They have more health and deal more damage than the standard Woolly Rhino. Leave them for last, lessening the chances of them running off and recruiting another Woolly Rhino to fight you.

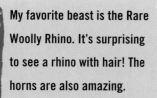

My favorite beast is the Rare Woolly Rhino. It's surprising to see a rhino with hair! The horns are also amazing.

— *Mickael Labat, Art Director*

HELP WENJA: TRIBAL CLASHES

The Wenja are always in need of a helping hand when it comes to taking their land back from their enemies, the Udam and the Izila. These quests are a great source of XP and also award a great amount of skill points, helping you unlock more skills at a rapid pace.

TRIBAL CLASH: KILL

Tribal Clash: Kill missions turn Takkar into a "stone" cold assassin. Unlike other missions where you kill wave after wave of enemies, here you have a very specific target.

At first these missions may seem a bit daunting, especially if you are looking to get your XP bonus. But with help from your beast and Owl, these quests become incredibly simple.

Having the Owl: Attack II skill allows the Owl to take down your target by itself. This simplifies your goal to just getting in, searching a body, and getting out.

Two other great skills to learn are the Heavy Takedown and Search Takedown. These allow you to take down and search your target's body in one go, cutting down the time that you are exposed. If an enemy spots a dead body or your beast, it does not break your stealth bonus.

DRAGGING THE BODY

When taking down an enemy, hold Left Stick in any direction to begin dragging their body while killing them. Use this to pull them out of sight or into a bush while you finish searching them.

The following walkthroughs are written with the goal of providing you the stealth XP bonus for each mission. This missions can also be easily accomplished with a "Smash and Grab" style where you run in, quickly tag team the targets with your beast, and then escape the area.

KILL: ONE

Udam Warriors have been hunting Wenja near their homes. Take out the Udam leader, then search the body.

DIFFICULTY	Easy
AWARDS	Weapon Resources
SPECIAL	1 Skill Point, Bonus XP for Stealth

Get to the northeast side of the map, climbing to the top of the waterfall. Call in your Owl and order your beast to start attacking the Elite Slinger in the Cave.

Once you've ordered your beast to attack, use your Owl to takedown the target. With the Slinger and target down, jump into the water below the waterfall, and pull yourself up to loot the body of the target.

Then, simply turn back toward the water and use the grappling point at the top near the waterfall to pull yourself out of the area and complete the mission without being noticed.

KILL: TWO

Strong outpost defenses protect powerful Udam leaders. Take out the leaders, and then search the bodies.

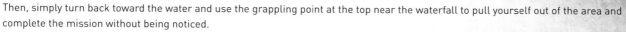

DIFFICULTY	Hard
AWARDS	Weapon Resources
SPECIAL	1 Skill Point, Bonus XP for Stealth

Head into the objective area from the west. Before advancing, call in your Owl to locate the enemies and Udam Leaders that are your targets. There are two targets in this one, you need to kill and search both bodies for completion.

Once you've scouted out the locations of all the enemies, use your Owl to takedown the first target located near the center of the camp, next to a small campfire.

Slowly move in from the east, circling around toward the high ground on the south side of the area. Call your beast in to attack the Spearman on the left while you use your bow to kill the Warrior on the right.

Send your beast to then attack the Elite Slinger on the high ground in the north side of the camp. Continue to move along the south side, killing a Scourge and placing yourself on the rocks above the Elite Chieftain and your target. Use some rocks to lure the Chieftain into range of a thrown spear, then quickly take him out while remaining hidden on the high ground.

With the Chieftain dead, slide down from the rocks and perform a takedown on the remaining target. The last thing you need to do is simply walk over and search the body of the other target that your Owl had killed at the beginning of the fight and your mission is complete.

129

KILL: THREE

An Udam Hunter with the strength of a Mammoth is threatening local Wenja. Take out the Hunter and his scout, then search the bodies.

DIFFICULTY	Very Hard
AWARDS	Weapon Resources
SPECIAL	1 Skill Point, Bonus XP for Stealth

Enter the area via the small cavern to the south. Have your spear ready and quickly take out the Elite Warrior that is guarding the entrance.

Call in your Owl to scout out the enemies, and take out one of the Elite Slingers. Wait for the Owl to cooldown, then use it again to eliminate the other Elite Slinger.

Slowly move into the camp, staying crouched, and sneak up behind the Chieftain who is facing the caged animal.

Once you are within range, perform a takedown on the Chieftain, then retreat into the bushes behind you, looking west toward your first target. Throw a rock away behind the target. This draws the attention of your second target. Once they are close to each other, call in your beast to attack one of the targets.

Quickly move in and perform a takedown on the other target while your beast has the remaining enemies distracted.

With both targets dead and searched, you can retreat the way you came, or move across the camp and kill the last Elite Spearman in the camp to complete the quest.

KILL: FOUR

Udam Hunters are catching and killing Wenja for food. Take out the Hunters and then search the bodies.

DIFFICULTY	Medium
AWARDS	Weapon Resources
SPECIAL	1 Skill Point, Bonus XP for Stealth

Use the grappling point on the cliff to the north of the objective to pull yourself into the objective area.

Once you climb to the top, send your Owl south to scout out the enemy locations. Use your Owl to kill the Elite Slinger, then move toward the camp.

From the high ground above the camp use your bow to kill the Archer, Spearman, and Scourge that surround your first target. Free the caged animal next to your target. The freed Wolf quickly kills them.

Use the vines to the east to slide down into the camp. Slowly move in with Hunter Vision active, working toward the cave opening. The Wolf that you've freed is still alive and enemy Udam appear from the cave to try and kill the Wolf.

They fail, leaving you with two bodies to search and a Wolf to kill. Once you've searched the bodies, the mission completes. Killing the Wolf is optional, but it will likely turn to attack you once all other enemies are eliminated.

KILL: FIVE

Izila have taken over a fishing location, starving the local Wenja. Take out the leader and then search the body.

DIFFICULTY	Medium
AWARDS	Weapon Resources
SPECIAL	1 Skill Point, Bonus XP for Stealth

Head south into the objective area, sticking to the high ground once you are close by. Use your Owl to call your beast in on one Elite Slinger, while you kill the other with your Owl.

From the high ground above the camp, use your bow to kill the Archer and Spearmen that surround the target and order your beast to attack the target itself.

Let your beast kill any of the remaining enemies, making sure to stay crouched and hidden to avoid losing your XP bonus.

For extra safety, you can call in your Owl to scan the area for any remaining enemies before hopping down from your position to search the body and complete the quest.

KILL: SIX

Wenja captives are being worked to death by cruel Izila leaders. Take out the leaders, then search the bodies.

DIFFICULTY	Medium
AWARDS	Weapon Resources
SPECIAL	1 Skill Point, Bonus XP for Stealth

After accepting the quest, head west into an area surrounded by tall stone pillars.

Call in your Owl to mark the enemies, then take down the Elite Slinger with your Owl. The Izila are kept fairly close together in this camp so use your beast to make entry and thin them out before attempting to enter yourself.

A single shot to the head from your bow can kill any enemy in this camp, including the targets, making it the weapon of choice while you wait in the bushes.

Once your beast has cleared out all the enemies, use your Owl to double check that there are no Izila left alive in the area and then search the bodies of the two targets to complete the quest.

Stay hidden in the bushes and continuously call in your beast on every enemy in sight. Be ready, as some of them may flee the area and run toward you.

KILL: SEVEN

Izila priests are killing Wenja for bloody sacrifice. Take out the Izila leaders, then search the bodies.

DIFFICULTY	Very Hard
AWARDS	Weapon Resources
SPECIAL	1 Skill Point, Bonus XP for Stealth

Once you have accepted the mission, head east toward the mission area. Call in your Owl, and notice there are no enemies visible in the area aside from one Elite Slinger. The Elite Slinger is located above the entrance to a small cave.

Enter the cave cautiously, and take the path to the right.

USE YOUR LEOPARD
Having a Leopard as your beast helps you greatly inside the cave. It marks targets around corners and through walls before you even make contact with them.

Use takedowns on each enemy you come across, including your first target, until you reach the Elite Chieftain.

Turn around and head back toward the entrance, this time taking the left path. This path brings you right up behind the second target; perform a takedown and then head back for the exit.

Once you are outside, you're in the clear, just keep walking until you exit the mission area.

KILL: EIGHT

Izila priests are performing strange rituals in a tomb. Take out their leaders, then search the bodies.

DIFFICULTY	Hard
AWARDS	Weapon Resources
SPECIAL	1 Skill Point, Bonus XP for Stealth

Head through the trees to the west, calling in your Owl as you come across an area with a lot of standing stones.

Use your Owl to Eliminate the first of three Elite Slingers in the camp, then send in your beast to kill the others, one by one.

Head to the small hill on the south side of the camp. Use your beast to pick off each enemy inside the camp, keeping an eye out for the Elite Chieftain that may try to climb the hill to get to you.

When your beast is injured, retreat farther away from your position on the hill and heal them. If you have no food, call in a different beast to take their place and continue the battle. Once you've killed all three Elite Slingers, the Elite Chieftain, the two targets, and the Slinger, there are no witnesses left to watch you search the bodies of the two targets, allowing for an easy victory.

KILL: NINE

Udam Hunters are killing Wenja in the area. Take out the Udam leader, then search his body.

DIFFICULTY	Medium
AWARDS	Weapon Resources
SPECIAL	1 Skill Point, Bonus XP for Stealth

This quest leads you into an Udam infested cave. As you enter the cave, go left. Continue along the left path until it takes you to an open area. All of the Udam are in this area: a Warrior, Elite Scourge, Elite Spearman, two Elite Slingers, and the two Udam Leaders that are your target.

The first enemy you come across is the Elite Warrior who is right at the bottom of the path you took in. Use your spear to quickly kill him. The Elite Slinger on the high ground in the center of the open area patrols to a side of his post facing you.

He is out of range for your beast, so use another spear or a few quick arrows to knock him down. Use a Sabretooth Tiger, preferably Bloodfang, to take out each enemy below, including the targets. Call your beast back to you for healing when necessary.

You may need to adjust positions to get a lock on the final target on the opposite side of the cave. Continue along the path and you find a small platform with a climbing spot.

Stay behind the stalagmites to prevent yourself from being spotted and losing your stealth bonus.

KILL: TEN

A Wenja hunting party was ambushed by the Izila. Take out the Izila leaders, then search the bodies.

DIFFICULTY	Hard
AWARDS	Weapon Resources
SPECIAL	1 Skill Point, Bonus XP for Stealth

After accepting the quest, head north up the river. Once in the objective area, call in your Owl to spot the Two Elite Slingers on the high ground and locate the two targets patrolling with the rest of the Izila below.

Use your Owl to take down one of the Elite Slingers while you remain back at the edge of the objective area.

A warrior patrols the ramp to the high ground. Kill him quickly or he turns around and spots you.

Once the warrior is dead, call your Sabretooth in to kill the target. Once he has killed the first target, immediately order him to kill the second one. You can also use your Owl to kill the targets. Remember to loot the body.

If you can't see the second target, you can call in your Owl if it has cooled down and order your beast from there. Once you have killed and looted both targets, retreat out of the area to complete the mission.

KILL: ELEVEN

The Izila attacked Wenja who were building a new camp. Take out the Izila leaders, then search the bodies.

DIFFICULTY	Hard
AWARDS	Weapon Resources
SPECIAL	1 Skill Point, Bonus XP for Stealth

After accepting the mission, grapple and climb your way up to the mission area, then call in your Owl to scope out the camp.

While you have control of your Owl, order your Sabretooth to kill the target in the front of the camp. Once it has killed the target, assuming your beast still has a good amount of health left, send it off to kill the other target.

Once both targets are dead, simply grapple back down to the area below where you first accepted the quest.

TRIBAL CLASH: DESTROY

DESTROY: ONE

LOCATION	Cut Mamaf Cave
DIFFICULTY	Hard
SPECIAL	1 Skill Point

Have your beast at your side as you approach this camp from the south. Call in your Owl to get a good look at the position of the lookouts, as well as the position of the Scarecrows as these are your main objective when you begin to destroy this base.

Start by picking off the Archers on the upper level with lit arrows, this causes them to catch fire, thus lighting any objects they touch ablaze. Send your beast in to attack the enemies near the campfire. Light your club and circle around the camp, lighting the large spike walls, smaller wooden walls, and Udam Scarecrows. As the meter fills, reinforcements begin to swarm in from the east and west side of the camp.

Since you've already destroyed most items on the outside of the camp, move inside and take out the meat transporters and the small shelters they have built. This quickly finishes off the destruction meter.

When the meter has filled all the way, your objective changes from burning the Udam camp to simply fleeing the area. This is a much easier task than attempting to take on the waves of reinforcements that are about to fill the camp.

DESTROY: TWO

LOCATION	Dead Tree Camp
DIFFICULTY	Medium
SPECIAL	1 Skill Point

Stock up on Animal Fat and get ready to wreak some havoc from the top of a Mammoth. Mammoths are located right next to the quest giver, hop on top of one and pull your bow out. Follow the path up into the camp and charge!

Your Mammoth destroys smaller wooden objects and the Udam enemies below. All you need to do is light some of your arrows on fire and shoot for the tents and the tall Udam Scarecrows (which can also be destroyed by melee or Mammoth).

136

The Scarecrows are facing out toward the cliff, near the entrance and exit to the camp. If you think you've got everything, but the meter is full, check the large rock near the campfire in the center of the camp. A handful of meat transports are leaning up against it.

Continue circling around the camp until you've stomped and burned the place to the ground.

DESTROY: THREE

LOCATION	Cave of Sun Walkers
DIFFICULTY	Medium
SPECIAL	1 Skill Point

Once inside the cave, immediately begin lighting the bundles of wood on fire; this helps raise the destruction meter quickly. Stay moving once you are inside the cave. Use your Two Handed Club to not only light everything inside on fire, but to quickly dispatch enemies that inhabit this cramped cave.

Moving slowly and staying crouched allows you to sneak up on groups of enemies. When this happens use your bow to make short work of them.

It's good to bring your beast into the cave with you, this prevents any enemies from sneaking up behind you while you move around the cave. Look for the megaliths and smaller huts inside the cave as you circle around; these help your destruction meter fill rapidly.

When your meter is full, an Elite Izila Spearman and Elite Warrior spawn, they are easily taken down by thrown spears. You can choose to just ignore them and flee the cave to complete the mission. Besides XP awarded for the kills, there is no bonus for killing all the enemies.

DESTROY: FOUR

LOCATION	Pur Tanhin Rocks
DIFFICULTY	Hard
SPECIAL	1 Skill Point

After accepting the mission, use the grappling point on the cliff to the west of the objective area, then use the vines to pull yourself up into the area for the mission.

Continue working your way up to the high ground in the north side of the camp, killing the Warrior near the fire if you wish to remain undetected.

Once up on the high ground, turn back down toward the camp and begin shooting lit arrows down into it. Call in your beast to distract the Izila while you aim for the big Megaliths (large stones supported by wood) and the wooden cat walks. The destruction meter quickly fills as more things catch fire.

Once you've killed off a few enemies, drop down into the camp and light your club on fire, using it to light the stacks of wood, cages, huts, and any remaining objects you can find. This prevents you from running out of arrows and Animal Fat.

Stay constantly moving to prevent yourself from being overrun by any enemies. Killing them is not the goal; you're just there to burn the place to the ground!

When you've filled the meter, use the grappling point that you initially used to enter as an escape, allowing you to bypass fighting the remaining enemies.

DESTROY: FIVE

LOCATION	Yagi Canyons
DIFFICULTY	Medium
SPECIAL	1 Skill Point

Enter the cave and immediately begin lighting the Udam Scarecrows and small bundles of wood on fire.

Take the path to the east, using your Hunter Vision to spot enemies before they spot you. Use your beast to kill enemies while you focus on lighting things on fire. The most common item in this cave is the meat transporting sleds.

The sleds are lined up on all the walls of the cave. Continue to locate them and burn them as you move in a circle around the large cave. Don't forget to destroy the bundles of wood. You need every little bit of wood in this cave to burn to fill your destruction meter.

If you've taken care to burn and destroy everything in your path as you circled around the cave, you should have your meter filled by the time you reach the exit.

An Elite Archer waits for you at the exit as you try to leave. Kill him or move past him and exit the area to complete the mission.

DESTROY: SIX

LOCATION	Chanting Cave
DIFFICULTY	Hard
SPECIAL	1 Skill Point

A few Izila guard the path into this cave. Kill them with your bow, then slowly work your way into the cave system.

The destructible objects are all located in an open area with a handful of Izila patrolling around. Use takedowns on close enemies and call your beast in on the enemies that are located at the opposite end of the cave.

Bundles of wood are your primary target here, with the majority of them being in the north end of the cave near a waterfall.

Make sure to destroy every piece of wood you can as you work through the Izila. If you've hit all the pieces of wood, you won't even need to burn the final stacks of wood in the north end.

When the bar fills, jump into the water near the waterfall in the north side of the cave. This counts as clearing the area and completes the quest.

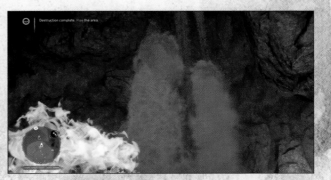

ESCORT

Escort the Wenja to their destination and defend them against any threats. Rescued Wenja join your village and increase the population.

These quests have you following a Group of Wenja as they fight through enemies and ambushes along the path home. Always have your beast with you. Sending your beast to start the attack on the ambushers prevents them from targeting your Wenja allies, especially if that beast is a Bear.

Stay in the front of the group, only slightly behind the leader so you don't accidentally advance past an ambush.

Use the short time between engagements to heal you or your beast, and craft more weapons if needed.

ESCORT: ONE

Heavy rains have flooded Wenja huts. Now your people need your help to reach higher ground.

DIFFICULTY	Easy
AWARDS	Population
SPECIAL	1 Skill Point

Cross the river and head south to find the Wenja in their flooded camp. Speak to one of them and follow them east out of the camp. After a short walk, two Udam Archers spawn and begin to attack immediately.

Quickly charge the Archers using your bow to fire arrows at them while you close the distance.

As the Wenja begin to turn south, two Archers spawn on the high ground to the east. Take them out with your bow, or charge up there and kill them with your spears. Three Udam Warriors attack at the end of the small hill that the Archers spawned on. Run up to them with your spear and quickly kill them before they can advance on your Wenja allies.

Follow the Wenja into an open area with a small pond to the south. A horn sounds and a group of four Warriors runs out and begins to attack from the east side. Meet them with your beast and your spear, quickly killing them before focusing on the two Archers that have spawned to the west.

The Archers will most likely still be trying to get into a position to fight the Wenja, retreating back into cover. Charge them with your spear or club in hand, quickly killing them and clearing the final path for the Wenja. Once the Wenja reach the small camp at the end of the path, the mission ends.

DON'T KILL YOUR FRIENDS
Two friendly Wenja villages will run toward you, do not mistake them for Udam Warriors.

ESCORT: TWO

Some Wenja need your help to reach a sacred place where they will honor the spirits.

DIFFICULTY	Medium
AWARDS	Population
SPECIAL	1 Skill Point

Head north to the Wenja who are waiting for your escort. Speak with them and follow the path north out of the camp leading you along the mountain side. As you come up on a large broken tree that hangs over the path, you find three Udam Warriors who are not expecting you, as there are observing their freshly killed Boar. Use your bow and the element of surprise to quickly kill them before they are even aware of your existence.

Continue on the north path, going under the broken tree. A patrol of Udam are heading south on the same path toward you. Three Archers and two Warriors make up the group. Hold you ground when you see them appear, and send a volley of arrows their way. As the Udam begin to advance, a Brown Bear joins the fight. Attack the Bear while keeping your distance, allowing the Bear to continue targeting Udam until it meets its demise. Kill off any remaining Udam or have your spear ready to finish the Bear if it survives the fight.

As you follow the path north, a group of three Udam Warriors comes running out of the trees to the east. Use your bow to thin them out, then switch to your spear if any of them make it close enough to strike.

Make sure you have plenty of arrows and spears made as you approach the holy site at the end of this journey. It is guarded by an Elite Chieftain, two Warriors, and two Archers.

Send your beast into battle and be aggressive. Use your bow while you close the distance to the site, then switch to your spear to quickly kill the Warriors and Spearmen. Throw your spears at the exposed midsection of the Chieftain before he can get close to your group of Wenja. Once the Wenja enter the area the mission completes even if you haven't killed off all the Udam in the area.

ESCORT: THREE

Some Wenja need your help to reunite with their companion lost in the snow.

DIFFICULTY	Hard
AWARDS	Population
SPECIAL	1 Skill Point

Speak to the Quest giver and head south to find a group of Wenja sitting around a campfire. Speak to any of them to begin your journey.

The Wenja lead you west down the cliffs. As the path ends you are greeted by two Wolves. Quickly kill the Wolves and the Wenja continue on.

A dead Elk is on the ground to the east. Two Udam Archers are working on the corpse. Send in your beast and use your bow to eliminate them.

Next you come across some pikes in the ground, defending a small Udam encampment. Four Warriors come running out of the camp. Use your bow to pick them off quickly, or have your spear out and ready to take them on with melee attacks.

If you have the Chain Takedown skill, you can move near the pike fence and then activate the takedown as they come out. This allows you to quickly kill all four Warriors without them having a chance to injure the Wenja.

Continue following the Wenja. Once you hit a rock bridge, you attract the attention of a Sabretooth Tiger.

Use your Hunter Vision to keep an eye on it. When the Sabretooth is at a distance, take your time to line up headshots with your bow. Three or four shots to the head should kill it. If it gets in close, use your spear, throwing it for maximum damage.

PROTECT THE WENJA
Remember, you can always heal yourself, but you can't heal any of the Wenja in your group.

Your next engagement is in a small Udam camp tucked into a cavern along the path to the east. Stay in front of the Wenja and use your bow and beast to quickly kill the Spearman and two Archers that are warming themselves by the fire.

Follow the path east out of the camp, this leads you to your last fight. Six Udam Warriors appear a distance from you and begin to charge. Do not immediately attack them. A Mammoth comes from the south and starts fighting the Warriors.

Use this time to deal as much damage to the Mammoth as possible, a few Warriors are much easier to fight than a healthy Mammoth. Even with the help of the Udam Warriors, the Mammoth quickly crushes them and heads your direction. Use your spears and aim for the Mammoth's head, making sure to constantly strafe to avoid its attacks. Once you have killed the Mammoth the Wenja walk a short distance to a small camp and the quest is complete.

ESCORT: FOUR

A Group of Wenja captives has escaped the Izila and want to return to their tribe.

DIFFICULTY	Hard
AWARDS	Population
SPECIAL	1 Skill Point

Accept the quest and head west down the hill, crossing the river to find the group of Wenja that needs your assistance.

After you speak with them, they lead you north along the path to their home. Your first engagement comes just as two paths on your mini-map merge to one. A group of Izila, two Warriors and two Archers, spawn directly in front of you.

Quickly use your bow to kill them. Headshots are not important here, hitting them anywhere prevents them from attacking which protects your Wenja allies. Send in your beast to draw their attention while you and the Wenja easily kill the Izila.

Wait for the group to advance and keep an eye on the cliffs to the east. A horn sounds and another group of Izila spawns on top of the cliffs. If you react quickly enough, you can kill the two Archers and the two Warriors before they can come down to your level to attack.

As the path begins to slope downward, Izila are waiting in ambush in the bushes ahead.

Use your Hunter Vision to quickly spot them, then call your beast in to stop the Warrior's advance while you quickly take out the two Archers.

STOCK UP

There's some wood scattered in the area of this fight, pick it up if you need to craft more arrows.

The path begins to slope south into an open grassy area. Six Izila (two Warriors, two Spearmen, and two Archers) spawn on the other side. Send your beast in to take on the Warriors, this also draws the attention of the Spearmen.

The Wenja attack the closest targets which are fighting your beast, so use your bow to take out the Archers that are in the back, hiding in the bushes, before you shift your focus to the Izila engaged with your beast.

At the end of this fight, two Wolves spawn. The Wolves walk into the area and then stop to howl. Use that time to place a couple of headshots with your bow and then follow the Wenja as they follow the path back to the north into your final battle.

A stone structure along the path has two Elite Warriors and two Archers waiting for your group of Wenja.

Be the aggressor and use your bow or spears to quickly take down the two Elite Warriors before they have a chance to react, then move around the stone pillars and kill the two Archers. Your Wenja tribesmen are still walking up the path. Once they enter the area behind the stone pillars the mission is complete.

ESCORT: FIVE

Some Wenja Hunters were attacked by Udam and now need your help to reach safety.

DIFFICULTY	Medium
AWARDS	Population
SPECIAL	1 Skill Point

You follow the stream south to your destination in this Escort mission. This makes it very easy to stay ahead of the group and clear potential threats before the enemy gets close.

DON'T GET TOO FAR AHEAD!

Some ambushes are triggered by the group and can't be fought ahead of time.

The Udam bring their first attack upon the group as the river begins to bend and head directly south. Kill a Warrior and two Archers on the west side before looking east and killing the two Archers that spawn in an attempt to flank to group. You can use your beast to help you take them down and speed things along.

A Dhole is engaged in a fight with a Brown Bear. Use your spears to quickly take down the distracted Brown Bear and then kill the Dhole.

After the Bear is dead, a Warrior and Archer spawn in the woods to the east. Rush them with your spear to catch them before they get within range of your Group.

Two Dholes run out toward your group as they chase a few Monkeys from the forest. Kill them, then head downstream to a small Udam camp which is the final destination for your group.

Four Dholes run across your path. Take as many out as possible with your bow as they attempt to attack you from behind momentarily.

While the Dholes finish their run, an Udam Archer and Warrior spawn on the riverbank. Kill them before worrying about the remaining Dholes as they aren't much of a threat to the Wenja. Have your Spears ready as you move forward.

Two Archers are on the riverbank, a Spearman and Warrior are next to a small campfire on the south side of the river. Kill them quickly and then head into the forest to the north of the small camp and locate the Elite Chieftain who is hiding in the brush. Kill him and you have secured the safety of the Wenja.

ESCORT: SIX

The angry Bloodtusk Mammoth trampled a Wenja camp. Now the survivors need your help to find shelter.

DIFFICULTY	Hard
AWARDS	Population
SPECIAL	1 Skill Point

The survivors are found down the hill, directly east of the quest giver, taking shelter under a rock overhang. Talk to the leader to begin the quest. Immediately head west and take care of the two Jaguars that approach. Send your beast after one while you take care of the other.

At the pits, the Wenja cautiously slow down, sensing trouble ahead. Move to the west side of the big rock as your group comes to a halt. Up the next hill, more Udam head your way, including a Chieftain. There is a chance that other Wenja are already entangled with them.

Being sure not to get too far ahead of your group, move further down the path and cut off the Udam Warriors and Archers. Kill them quickly to keep the Wenja out of trouble. Continue down the hill toward the tar pits as more Udam attack.

Send your beast ahead as you start picking off the lesser Udam Warriors. Once they have been thinned out, run up the hill ahead of the Wenja survivors and toss some spears into the Chieftain. Team up with your beast against the large Warrior until he drops. With the area clear, allow the group to reach their final destination at the nearby camp.

SEARCH AND RESCUE

Search and Rescue quests task you with saving a Lost Wenja by tracking their steps and searching for clues along the way. If you find and search each of the clues along the path to them, you are rewarded with a small amount of bonus XP. These clues are not needed to complete the quest. Rescued Wenja join your Village and increase the Population.

SEARCH AND RESCUE: ONE

A Wenja hunting party was ambushed and killed by the Udam. Search for the lone Wenja who returned to avenge his dead brothers.

DIFFICULTY	Very Hard
AWARDS	1375-1595 XP, Population

Follow the bloody footprints to the cliff edge, carefully using the fallen tree to cross the gap. Farther up the path a single Scourge guards the first clue, a dead Udam with Wenja arrows stuck in him.

Look up from the clue and use the two grappling points to climb to the top of the mountain. A warrior is visible on the rocks to the east; kill him with your bow and then examine the dead Udam.

Two Udam Spearmen run toward the location of the clue. Kill them as they try to climb down to you, then use the climbing spots to move forward.

Another Spearman is further down the cliff's edge. Use your bow to kill him from a distance, then carefully use the fallen tree to cross another gap in the mountain. Have your spear ready. You quickly come across an Udam Hunter, Spearman, and Chieftain.

Your spears allow you to quickly take out the Hunter and Spearman, leaving you to deal with the Chieftain by himself instead of facing all three at once. Once the Chieftain is dead, make sure you've crafted or picked up your spears as you face one more enemy before finding the missing Wenja.

The path leads you into a cave that is home to a Brown Bear. The Bear is busy sniffing the ground when you walk in, so throw a spear at its head and keep throwing spears until the Bear is dead. Once you've killed the Bear there are no other enemies, push farther into the cave and climb up to locate the lost Wenja. Speak to them to complete the quest.

SEARCH AND RESCUE: TWO

An Udam has been attacking Wenja and dragging them away. Search for his latest victim.

DIFFICULTY	Hard
AWARDS	1175 - 1363 XP, Population

Light a spear or club in the small camp where you accept the mission. Use your Hunter Vision to follow the footprints down the path.

A group of four Wolves guards your first clue, a broken pot, you can either try to kill them or use your already lit fire to scare them away and examine the clue.

After examining the clue, follow the blood trail west up the mountain. You reach a small campfire that you can use to warm up, or to reignite a weapon.

Follow the path farther and be ready for a surprise attack from a few Leopards. If you have your fire out, they quickly shy away once you point it in their direction. In the same area of this attack you come across a decapitated corpse. This corpse is your last clue before finding the missing Wenja; examine it to gain Bonus XP.

The path of blood leads into a cave; inside you find the heads of the two missing Wenja among a stack of skulls. Suddenly, Udam pour in from the mouth of the cave. Two Elite Warriors rush in; use your spears or two handed club to put them down quickly before the Elite Chieftain enters.

Try and kill the Chieftain before he works his way into the cave, this prevents you from getting into a close quarters fight, giving you the advantage.

The quest automatically completes once you have killed the Udam, avenging the deaths of the Wenja.

SEARCH AND RESCUE: THREE

Two Wenja are missing. Search for clues near the fishing spot.

DIFFICULTY	Medium
AWARDS	975-1131 XP, Population

After accepting the mission, activate Hunter Vision and follow the path down toward the southeast. Broken pots are scattered along the path. After a short walk, you find a broken pot surrounded by a pack of three Dholes.

Use your bow or spear to fight them off, then interact with the broken pot near the net on the ground. After interacting with the pot, equip your spear; you'll need it in a moment.

Continue following the path leading southeast along the river, using your Hunter Vision to follow the trail of blood. Just before the path splits into two directions, a Wenja comes running toward you with a Bear right on his trail. Use your spears and aim for the head of the Bear, quickly killing it and saving the Wenja.

Speak to this Wenja and then follow them to the last Wenja. The remaining Wenja is located on a small platform in the cave behind the waterfall.

Two Wolves are harassing the Wenja from below the platform. Use your bow or spears to quickly dispatch the two Wolves and then speak to the Wenja on the platform to complete your mission.

SEARCH AND RESCUE: FOUR

Two Wenja Hunters are lost deep in Izila territory. Search for them.

DIFFICULTY	Very Hard
AWARDS	1175 XP, Population

Once you've accepted the quest, head west, following the tracks across the water into a small cavern.

At the mouth of the cavern three Izila Hunters are scouting the area. Keep your distance, staying crouched in the bushes, and call your Owl to get their exact positions, killing one of them if you have the ability.

Although they wear masks, you can still kill them in one shot to the head with your bow.

With the group of Hunters dead, head down the path where you come across an Elite Warrior and a patrolling Archer. Kill him with your bow, then take out the Elite Warrior who is crouched down inspecting a body.

Move up and inspect the body next to the Warrior, you find that it is one of the missing Wenja Hunters.

Use your Hunter Vision to follow the trail of blood. You find another team of Izila investigating a body.

DON'T MISS OUT

It is possible to just sneak by this group and continue following the footsteps, but passing them by means you miss out on Bonus XP.

Use your Owl to spot the locations of the Scourge, Spearman, and Elite Spearman that are guarding the body. There are plenty of bushes nearby that allow you to use your bow or spears while remaining concealed.

Examine the body in the camp; it is a dead Izila that has Wenja arrows protruding from its body. Your last encounter with the Izila is a few steps away. Pull out your spear and follow the trail of blood. A small stone encampment holds the missing Wenja.

Use your spear to quickly kill the Elite Spearman and Elite Warrior that are holding them captive. Then simply walk up to the Wenja and complete the quest.

SEARCH AND RESCUE: FIVE

Two Wenja have escaped Izila captivity, but now one of them is missing. Search for her.

DIFFICULTY	Medium
AWARDS	975-1150 XP, Population

After accepting the quest, head east to find a Cave Lion guarding your first clue. You can either kill this Cave Lion or light one of your weapons on fire and move in to scare it off. Search the corpse next to some broken slave collars.

Climb the vines next to the waterfall, pulling yourself up onto the boulders above. Follow the blood that eventually leads you to cross the edge of the water. Don't worry about the water pulling you over the edge of the waterfall, Takkar is very strong!

Use your Owl to locate the Izila Scourge and Slinger across the river. Once you've spotted them, use your bow or Owl to take them out, and then cross the river.

Once you are at the other side you find another broken slave collar. Interact with it for bonus XP.

The blood trail leads into a cave, ending at a spot of water. Use your Hunter Vision to spot the fish and kill it with your bow or a spear before jumping into the water.

Follow the blood trail to a climbing point and then a large vine rope to the east. Once you've climbed the vines, an Izila Scourge is out near the water's edge in the direction you need to go. Take him out with your bow, then stay along the rocks and perform a takedown on the next Izila enemy who is crouched down by the fire.

Take the underwater passage into the next area, pulling yourself up and finding the missing Wenja. Speak to them to complete the quest.

SEARCH AND RESCUE: SIX

The Izila have brought a Wenja to a nearby mountain for sacrifice. Search for him and stop the sacrifice.

DIFFICULTY	Hard
AWARDS	1175 XP, Population

Follow the trail north up a few climbing spots. You come across a camp containing three Izila enemies: an Elite Spearman, a Spearman, and a Warrior. Maintain distance and use your bow to kill off each enemy from the bushes, avoiding a melee fight.

Inside of the small camp you find a small broken pot next to the campfire which can be examined for bonus XP.

Continue following the path up the mountain. Stay crouched; there are three more Izila Spearmen ahead. Two of the Spearmen are engaged in a friendly bout. While they are distracted, take down the one closest to you and then focus on the other two. Using a bow from a distance can make short work of them, but the easiest way is to perform a takedown and then use the Chain Takedown skill to quickly kill both of them without alerting any other enemies.

Sneak into the center of the camp and locate the broken slave collar near the altar. Examine the collar for bonus XP.

Sneak toward the Slinger at the far end of the camp and perform a takedown. This is your last stop before facing the Izila who are holding the Wenja.

Stay in the bushes as you head north up the path to the final location of the Wenja. He is being guarded by a Chieftain, two Slingers, and a Spearman. Use your bow to take out the Slingers and Spearman from the bushes.

The Chieftain remains far enough away to not notice his allies dying. Eliminate him any way you see fit. Once all of the Izila are eliminated, move in and talk to the tied up Wenja to complete your quest.

SEARCH AND RESCUE: SEVEN

The Udam tribe has captured Wenja for meat. Search for their camp to save the Wenja.

DIFFICULTY	Hard
AWARDS	1175 XP

After talking to the quest giver, head east down the hill to find the starting point. Accept the quest, enable Hunter Vision, and follow the blood trail southeast through the valley. Watch out for possible Udam as you move down the hill and across the water to find the first clue. A dead Wenja lies next to a Mammoth carcass.

Next, the trail heads north. Cautiously move into the clearing as Udam archers patrol the area. With help from your beast, kill them before going up the hill.

Follow the trail under the unstable snow and down the right path into a sheltered area. An Udam Spearman and Archer guard the path with their backs turned; use takedowns to kill them without detection. Examine another Wenja body that lies nearby.

Continue north through the water and up the other side. Kill the Udam at the top of the hill, including a dangerous Scourge. Just north at Hungry Hollow is an Udam camp. Stop before moving in and send your Owl ahead to scout the area.

Several Udam inhabit the camp, including a Chieftain who stands guard on the upper level. Send your beast after the Scourge first to take away his threat of poison and pick off as many enemies as you can from the area below. Move up the path to find the last Wenja body at the back of the camp. With no survivors, no one joins your village, but you do still earn a decent chunk of XP.

SEARCH AND RESCUE: EIGHT

A Strange poison is killing the Izila. Search for clues to find the source.

DIFFICULTY	Hard
AWARDS	1175 XP, Population

After accepting the mission, use your Hunter Vision to follow the bloody footprints to the south. Have your spear out and ready to kill a handful of Dholes that are scattered throughout the forest. Kill them as you come across them to keep from being overrun.

Your first clue is a shattered pot next to some tools along the path of footprints. Continue following the footprints that lead along the riverbank. A group of Izila, consisting of two Spearman and one Scourge, are in your way. They are scattered pretty far from each other, allowing you to take each one out without the others being alerted.

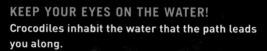

KEEP YOUR EYES ON THE WATER!
Crocodiles inhabit the water that the path leads you along.

Your next clue is just down the path, a dead Izila with a bite on his wrist.

Continue along the path as it begins to lead you a little further inland, away from the water. Once you are in an open area you are ambushed by two Spearmen and two Archers.

They do not advance, so use your bow to take them down. An Elite Chieftain spawns behind the enemies; use your beast to attack them once they appear.

Two warriors spawn to try and assist the Elite Chieftain. Kill them off and continue south toward the mountains.

Snakes line the path into the Cave of Whispers, which is your final destination in this quest. Use Hunter Vision to locate the snakes in the bushes and kill all three of them before moving into the cave. Examine the Izila in the cave to complete your quest.

SAVE CAPTIVE

These quests begin immediately after speaking with the Quest Giver. All surviving hostages are added to your Population, so stay undetected to prevent them from being killed.

Enemies killed by your Owl or beast do not cause the enemies to execute hostages. Hostages are only attacked once you yourself have been spotted.

Killing all of the hostiles immediately frees the Wenja, so you do not need to untie them after you have cleared the area and have been rewarded the Population. At least two Wenja captives must survive or the mission fails.

SAVE CAPTIVE: ONE

Some Udam want to eat fresh Wenja meat. Free the captives.

DIFFICULTY	Easy
AWARDS	Population
SPECIAL	1 Skill Point

Accept the mission and call in your Owl to scout out the location nearby. Use the Owl to kill the Warrior on the south side of the camp standing next to two hostages.

Continue east, staying on the high ground to the south of the camp. Once you are in position, pull out your bow and kill the first Spearman that is closest to the water on the north side of the camp. Next, kill the Archer who is crouched down searching a dead body. Take your next shot on the Warrior standing between the two hostages near the campfire.

Only one enemy remains. Quickly shoot the last Archer, who is facing away from the campfire and is still unaware his allies are dead.

SAVE CAPTIVE: TWO

A Few Udam are keeping Wenja Captives in a freezing cave. Free the Captives.

DIFFICULTY	Hard
AWARDS	Population
SPECIAL	1 Skill Point

Take a short run east to the objective area, sticking to the high ground on the north side of the area once you reach it. Call in your Owl and spot the hostages and Udam guards. Use your Owl or bow to take out the Spearman on the west side of the area while he is away from the camp.

From the rocks, kill the Slinger that is farther into the camp before moving forward to prevent being spotted.

Call your beast in on the Scourge standing next to two hostages at the far east side of the camp. While your beast attacks, drop down off the high ground and move onto the main path leading into the camp.

This new position gives you a shot on a Spearman and a Scourge located near the fire. They are now looking back toward the enemy your beast killed, allowing you to quickly take them out with a few well-placed arrows.

A Spearman will likely try to engage your beast after it has killed the Scourge. Use your bow to help your beast kill the Spearman.

One last Slinger is outside of the camp to the east. You can free all of the captives in the camp before hunting him down, if you wish. Once all of the Udam are dead, the mission is complete.

SAVE CAPTIVE: THREE

The Udam have discovered a new game—make Wenja captives fight beasts. Free the Captives

DIFFICULTY	Very Hard
AWARDS	Population
SPECIAL	1 Skill Point

This quest may seem quite hard at first, considering it takes place indoors. However, using your beast to kill each enemy quickly clears the place out and prevents any alarm from sounding. When your beast is injured, call it back and use meat to heal it. If you don't have meat, you can always call in another beast to take its place.

After accepting the mission, follow the path east where it leads you to a couple of climbing spots into a cave called the Shwadari Fight Den.

Stay crouched as you enter the den, activating your Hunter Vision to spot the Udam that surround the center. Do not leave the high ground at the cave entrance.

Use your bow to first take out the Warrior across the cave, and then pick off the Spearman and Scourge across the room. Look to the right and kill the Spearmen located just below you. For the closer enemies like the Chieftain, call in your beast to take them down. Using your beast on the nearby enemies prevents you from accidently exposing yourself to the other enemies.

If the mission doesn't clear, work clockwise around the cave, slowly releasing captives until you come across any enemies that may be holding their positions behind the rocks.

When the captives are freed they run out of the area, preventing them from being killed by the remaining enemy.

Once all enemies are down, the mission is complete.

SAVE CAPTIVE: FOUR

Some Wenja are trapped in a freezing cave. The Udam will eat them soon. Free the captives.

DIFFICULTY	Medium
AWARDS	Population
SPECIAL	1 Skill Point

After accepting the mission, sneak to the east side of the objective area; there will find some vines that lead up onto the high ground above.

You can also jump down from the high ground and land right behind a group of three captives, allowing you to free them before all of the Udam have been killed.

Call in your beast as a distraction on the enemies farthest away from you. Once they are distracted by your beast, use your bow to pick them off one by one until they are all dead.

SAVE CAPTIVE: FIVE

Izila are sacrificing Wenja near a roaring waterfall. Free the captives.

DIFFICULTY	Medium
AWARDS	Population
SPECIAL	1 Skill Point

Head north toward the objective area but stay to the west side of it until you come across a grappling point.

Use the grappling point to pull yourself onto a small ledge containing a bag of loot, grab the loot, and use the next grappling point. This point leads you to a path that takes you right behind the Izila and captive Wenja.

Use your Owl to take out the Slinger that is on the high ground, then follow the path and climb up. Stay crouched and use the bushes for cover.

Order your beast to attack the Scourge, this prevents them from throwing a fire bomb and accidentally killing the hostages. Pick off the Warriors that begin to advance on your beast and then focus on the Spearmen. Once you and your beast kill off the Izila, the captives join your population!

SAVE CAPTIVE: SIX

Wenja captives are being forced to mine stone for the Izila. Free the captives.

DIFFICULTY	Very Hard
AWARDS	Population
SPECIAL	1 Skill Point

These Wenja captives can be liberated very easily from a head on approach with the help of your beast. First take out the Archer on the highest ground. If enemies begin to spot you, retreat down the small hill until they can no longer see you.

The captives are held in a small cave that is blocked by a gate, so freeing them without killing off all of the Izila is very dangerous as you are likely to be spotted.

Once you've killed the top Archer, call in your beast to take on the Warrior and two Spearmen in the camp. The enemies on the second level begin to work their way down to the base level of the camp. While they are moving, they are not looking in your direction, making them extremely vulnerable to attack. Quickly take out the two Scourge and the Archer as they work their way down to combat your beast. If your beast dies call in another beast to continue the fight.

SAVE CAPTIVE: SEVEN

Izila are forcing Wenja to build their standing stones. Free the captives.

DIFFICULTY	Medium
AWARDS	Population
SPECIAL	1 Skill Point

Call in your Owl to locate the enemies. A Warrior is attacking one of the captives. Use your Owl to stop the attack, then send in your beast to attack the Spearman located next to the captive.

This draws the attention of the nearby Scourge. Stay in the bushes and use your bow to stop him before he throws a Fire Bomb.

Your beast should now be fighting a Warrior that has run over from the south side of the camp. Ignore that fight and pick off the Spearman near the hut on the west side of the tent.

While doing this, your beast has likely killed the Warrior and moved on to fighting the last Archer in the camp. Once the Archer is killed, the captives are added to your population.

SAVE CAPTIVE: EIGHT

Izila are toying with their Wenja Captives, releasing them only to hunt them down. Free the Captives.

DIFFICULTY	Hard
AWARDS	Population
SPECIAL	1 Skill Point

Slowly follow the path to the south; an Izila Spearman and Scourge patrol the edge of the objective area. Hide in the bushes and call in your Owl.

After scouting out the enemies, use your Owl to kill the Archer that is overlooking the captives being held around the campfire. Once you've killed the lookout, send your beast in on the patrolling Scourge. This pulls all of the enemies away from the captives.

Slowly move up and use your arrows to support your beast, killing the two Spearman and two Archers that come to fight him. If you have the Chain Takedown skill, you can save some arrows and move in close to finish all four of them quickly once they leave their positions.

This fight ends quickly, and the Wenja are free to join your population.

SAVE CAPTIVE: NINE

Izila warriors have trapped Wenja captives at a sacrificial altar. Free the captives.

DIFFICULTY	Hard
AWARDS	Population
SPECIAL	1 Skill Point

After accepting the quest, use the grappling points to pull yourself closer to the objective area. Once you've used the second grapple, stay to the north of the objective area, and head east until you hit the cliffs.

Use your Owl to locate the enemies inside the camp, and then have it perform a takedown on the Elite Scourge.

A path leads up to a small cave opening with a Wenja Captive inside. You can free this captive without attacking any enemies.

Once you've freed that captive, start killing the Warriors and Archers that scatter the camp.

Call in your beast to begin attacking the Izila and slowly sneak into the camp and untie the Captives. Depending on the effectiveness of your beast, you may be able to free all of the Captives before the Izila are wiped out.

SAVE CAPTIVE: TEN

Wenja gatherers have been captured by Udam raiders. Free the captives.

DIFFICULTY	Hard
AWARDS	Population
SPECIAL	1 Skill Point

Head out to the objective area. Once inside the objective area, call in your Owl to spot the enemies. The Udam are easily visible in this completely outdoors camp. Call your beast in to begin attacking the Elite Udam Warrior on the east side.

This attack draws all of the enemies in toward the center of the camp, allowing you to easily gain access to the high ground in the north. Assist your beast in combat with your bow and Owl takedowns.

Only one Elite enemy populates this camp, making it incredibly easy for a Bear to kill all Udam without retreating to heal. Once all Udam are dead, the captives are free.

SAVE CAPTIVE: ELEVEN

Izila are sacrificing Wenja captives to their sun goddess, Suxli. Free the captives.

DIFFICULTY	Hard
AWARDS	Population
SPECIAL	1 Skill Point

Follow the objective marker into a cave. Once inside, follow the path, choosing to go through the vine covered tunnel when the path forks.

After you've walked through the vines, a small fire lights the balcony that will be your spot for picking off all of the Izila in the cave. Start by taking out the three Archers on the high ground. Once you've killed them, call your beast in to start fighting the Spearmen and Warriors on the ground floor.

When your beast begins fighting, peek over the edge and help finish off the remaining Izila with your bow.

OUT OF ARROWS?

If you are out of arrows, most of these enemies are in close enough range to be killed by a rock thrown from your sling.

You can continue around the back side of the cave and begin to free the Captives even if you haven't killed all of the Izila. However, this is risky as they have to run through any living Izila to get out of the cave, leaving them vulnerable to attack.

CAVES

These caves require a bit of exploration as well as combat to get through each lair of the caves.

A Grappling Claw is required to complete all of these caves, this is acquired very early in the game from Wogah, so you may have to advance the story further with him if you have not yet unlocked it.

Make sure to stock up on Animal Fat; this allows you to light your weapons without having a static source of fire nearby. You can conserve the amount of fat you use by lighting an object nearby on fire, allowing you to light future weapons from that. Small campfires work best for conserving your flame.

Falling into water extinguishes your fire. Try throwing your lit weapon across the water into some objects so that you can light your weapon again without using fat.

CAVE OF BLOOD CLAWS

DIFFICULTY	Medium
REWARD	780 XP

Follow the short path into the cave, then take a long leap down into the water below.

Take a look around to locate the objective marker, if it doesn't show up use your Hunter Vision to locate the small bit of Cedar nearby and head that way.

Climb up the path you reach and stay crouched while you follow it. You come up on what looks like a small bonfire guarded by an Udam Warrior. Take him out with your bow, then jump across the broken bridge and light the bonfire.

Stay near the bonfire and use your bow to take out the Leopard that guards the area below, then hop down and follow the path to a climbing spot at its dead end.

MASK YOUR SCENT!

Having the Scent Camouflage food option is great for sneaking through this cave without having to deal with angry Leopards.

After climbing the second climbing spot you are in a room with three Leopards. Use your bow with flaming arrows to not only keep Leopards away from you due to their fear of fire, but to make tracking them much easier since they catch fire when hit.

OUT OF THE FRYING PAN...
When a Leopard is hit with fire, it may try to jump into the water to put itself out, causing it to drown.

Once you've killed the animals, run toward the waterfall, locating the grapping point that is just above it.

Follow the path through to the backside of another waterfall. Have your spear ready as another Leopard attacks you the moment you step through the waterfall and into the water.

Use your Hunter Vision to locate the climbing spots across the room, you will climb four different times to reach the top, then follow the wooden platform to a dead end marked by an Eagle Cave Painting.

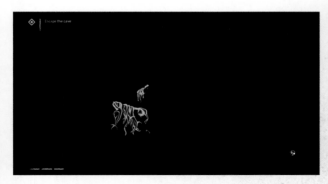

Look up to find two grappling points. After reaching the top, watch your step and follow the platform. Once you enter a larger cave area, light the platform on fire. This fire spreads all the way up to the small bonfire, scaring off the Leopard, and lighting the way out of this area.

You have to jump a few gaps to reach the next area so be sure to watch where you step as falling could be fatal.

Once you reach a large cliff, look left and stick to the wall. This path take you to the bottom of the cliffs. When in the water at the bottom, use your Hunter Vision to locate climbing spots. These two climbing spots lead up to a grappling point.

Pull yourself up to the top of the grappling point, then look up and pull yourself to the top of the next grappling point.

When you reach the top you need to jump a few gaps on the path leading toward the objective marker. Light the small bonfire near the top to help light the way.

Follow the path into a large day lit area containing an Udam warrior fighting a Leopard that blocks your path. Use the broken down tree that leads up into the light to find your way out.

CAVE OF THE DROWNED

DIFFICULTY	Medium
REWARD	780 XP

Once you've entered the cave, drop down into the water and head left, away from the waterfall. Once you see a point to climb, use it. You come across a small camp of Udam containing two Archers and a Warrior. Use your bow, and take the one farthest from the fire out first, then look left and take the other two out before they notice you.

After a brief moment outside looking over the water you swam through at the beginning, you come across a cave with a small fork. Both point at the same stretch of water.

BITEFISH

This water is inhabited by Bitefish. Use your bow to make short work of them and gather their resources if you need them.

From the left side of the fork you can use the above grappling point to swing to the platform on the right side. Be careful! If you touch the water while swinging you immediately lose your hold on the grapple.

You can also swim across the water, through the gap between the two platforms, before locating a climb spot hidden on the back side of the right platform. Either way you choose to go, it is best to kill the Bitefish before swinging or swimming to avoid taking any unnecessary damage.

Once you are on top of the right platform jump the small gap to the other platform and follow the path to another body of water. A Red Leaf, two North Yellow Leaves, and North Black Rock inhabit this platform; grab them before moving on!

Stay underwater and follow the stream until it dead ends behind a small Udam camp. Climb up into the camp. Five enemy Udam inhabit the camp: three Archers and two Spearmen. You can either use your position to take down each enemy with a bow, or use the bushes and cover to move through the camp onto the next area. If you alert them to your presence, quickly jump into the water and dive down to ditch them.

Head though the camp toward the next way point where you will hit a wall. When facing the wall, look left for a small rock ramp that you can climb up, this is marked with an Eagle Cave Painting.

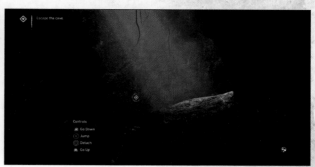

Once on there, look up, and slightly back toward the camp and you will find a grappling point.

Hold **(R2/RT)** to pull yourself up and prevent from touching the water. Now you will need to swing yourself back and forth **(LeftStick)** and throw yourself over the small wall that was blocking your progress.

Once in the water on the other side you will swim through a small tunnel. Quickly swim left to the small ramp! Three Bitefish and one Crocodile inhabit this water making it a very dangerous place to spend more than a few moments. Since you are already out of the water, you will not need to kill these creatures unless you want their resources. Follow the ramp up to the small bridge, do not cross it and stay along the wall.

This will eventually lead you into the water. Continue swimming through the water, staying under to avoid any Udam in the camp noticing you. Be sure to use Hunter Vision as a Crocodile is waiting near your exit.

If he is in the way you may need to retreat back to where you came and use a spear or bow to take him out.

If you've stayed along the wall this whole time, you go up a small ramp that leads to the left side of the waterfall, from there all you have to do is swim straight through a small body of water and you are free from the cave.

CAVE OF WEEPING ROOTS

DIFFICULTY	Medium
REWARD	780 XP

This cave contains the highest amount of Udam, however, it has many routes that lead you past them without conflict.

First enter the cave by sliding down the entrance. Once inside, follow the path down to a small drop off where you find an Udam Spearman looking over the Leopard he just killed.

SEEING RED
Things that can be destroyed by fire or melee show up as red when in Hunter Vision.

Take him out any way you see fit, then light your weapon with the nearby fire and use it on the roots of the plant that block your way.

Once through the passage you cleared, look right just before the sun hits the ground in the new area you enter. Use fire to again destroy that root, allowing you to bypass all of the enemies in this room.

Follow the small tunnel to its end and you find yourself at a cliff. Straight in front of you on the right wall there is a Grappling Point.

Use that Grappling Point to quickly swing across the gap onto the other ledge. Stay crouched and sneak up on the Spearman that is guarding the fire nearby. Perform a quick takedown and then move forward.

COLLECTING ROCK
A piece of Northern Black Rock is behind the destructible roots next to the small camp.

Another patch of tree roots blocks your advance. Use a lit arrow or spear to destroy it before attempting to use the Grappling Claw to swing across.

Once across, you fall down a small drop before being forced to crouch through a very small tunnel.

This area is full of enemies. Stick to the wall to your left and keep a low profile. A caged Boar is at the top of the ramp. Free it from a distance to distract your enemies, allowing you to pass the animal cage to reach a patch of rocks that can be broken down with your club. Quickly break them down and follow the path to a small drop, then drop down and continue along the path.

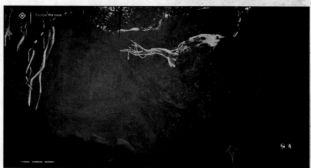

The path leads you into a larger room. Quickly perform a takedown on the first enemy you see along the walkways. This prevents you from being spotted in the next step.

Head a few steps back toward where you exited the tunnel and then locate the Grappling Point that lets you swing across to the area with the large dinosaur bones.

Jump onto the small wall leading into the water, from there, use your bow to take out the Crocodile and two Bitefish that inhabit the water. You can also use the stalactites hanging from the roof to help pick off any Udam in your way. With the water clear you can simply swim over to the climbing point and exit the caves.

If you do not have a shot on them, you have to take on the Udam that surround the area. This can easily be done from the bottom of the path. Take down the two Udam, an Elite Warrior and a Spearman, nearest the fire.

The rest of the enemies (Udam Scourge, Elite Archer, Archer, Elite Slinger, and Slinger) attack you one by one. As long as you use your bow effectively they should never be able to get close enough to begin attacking you.

Head to the climbing point across the way and kill the Crocodile and two Bitefish, if you haven't already. Climb the vines and follow the path to your direct left taking you out of the cave.

MAJOR LANDMARKS

OUTPOSTS

Outposts are hostile camps controlled by enemy tribes. Claim them all to make Oros safer for the Wenja. Claimed outposts can be used as Fast Travel points in the Map menu and also act as an access point for your Reward Stash.

Outposts are heavily fortified with enemies which would be impossible for Takkar to take on all at once. This means you need to plan your attack and plot your moves to prevent yourself from being overrun by enemies.

PLANNING THE ATTACK

There are many things to factor in when you want to take over an Outpost. While you can avoid stealth and attempt to take on each enemy in hand to hand combat, you get a large XP bonus for clearing out the outpost while remaining undetected, with a smaller bonus for completing the outpost without reinforcements being called.

STONE AGE UAV
Use the Owl to scout out the enemies' exact positions before making your move.

REINFORCEMENTS

If you are spotted during a raid on an outpost the enemies begin to call for reinforcements to join the fight. Clearing an Outpost without raising the alarm will net you an XP bonus.

STATIONARY ALARMS

Stationary Alarms can be found throughout the encampment, and are marked as a white horn on your mini-map once you've located them. These can be operated by any enemy in the camp.

To prevent them from being used, you can walk up to them and press **Square/X** to crush them without the use of your weapons. This action is performed without any additional movement from your character, so you can stay concealed in a bush.

You can also destroy the Alarm by hitting it with any weapon including a ranged weapon, like your bow or a thrown rock.

BURN IT DOWN!
If you don't have a clear shot on the Alarm, you can light a fire on an item attached to it (post, tent, bush, etc.) and the Alarm will be destroyed once the fire reaches it.

ELITE SLINGERS

Elite Slingers carry a Horn on them at all times. When they have discovered you, they reach for their horn. You can stop them from calling for reinforcements by attacking them. If you are at a distance, quickly throw your weapon or a rock to stun them, then quickly kill them. Elite Slingers wear masks so it takes two headshots with a Bow to take them out. A thrown spear to the chest is the best way to put down an Elite Slinger from a distance.

THE APPROACH

A stealth approach is not only the safest, but will net you the most possible XP if you can eliminate all enemies in the camp without being spotted.

BEING SPOTTED
To count as being spotted, the awareness meter must fill all the way. If an enemy raises their weapon to attack you, you have been spotted.

If you fail a stealth approach, you can remove yourself from combat and Fast Travel to another location, then return to try again without forfeiting your XP bonus.

In general, it's a safe bet to eliminate any type of Alarm before taking out other enemies, this takes a lot of pressure off you, while you eliminate all enemies in the base.

Always scout out possible hiding spots as well as a good exfiltration route on the off chance that you get surrounded and progressing forward is too hard. Some enemies patrol around the camp; use your Owl to observe their routes. Depending on the time of day, some enemies leave their patrol routes in favor of a spot near the fire, or a bed in their tents.

TIME OF DAY

While the amount of units in an Outpost does not change at any time of day, their positions, however, do change. If you'd prefer to wait for a specific time of day to begin your attack, find the closest camp site, light the fire, and sleep until the time you choose to attack.

DAY TIME

Attacking an outpost during the day allows you to plan your attack much easier due to the lack of predators and the visibility of the enemies. The enemies are also a spaced out farther from each other so singling them out for attack is a little easier. However, you are much easier to spot, enemies will be on patrol routes, and gaining access to the alarms to Destroy them is much harder.

NIGHT TIME

Night Time allows you to infiltrate the Outpost much easier, enemies are more likely to be asleep and around the campfires. With most of the enemies centralized in a few locations, it's much easier to disable the Alarms preventing an unwanted reinforcement call. Stealth approaches are much easier at night and, in general, a night time approach is the best option, but don't expect all of the enemies to be asleep.

A patrolling unit can creep up on you in the darkness without your noticing so always make sure you stay aware of your surroundings.

WHERE'S A LEASH WHEN YOU NEED ONE?

Keep an eye on your beast. Having them accidentally start an attack on an Outpost may cause a few sleeping enemies to wake up, effectively ruining your night time advantage.

Staying on the outskirts of town at night means you are likely to run into a pack of roaming Wolves or other dangerous night time predators. This can not only slow you down, but the fight may alert the enemies at the nearby Outpost.

WELCOME

SURVIVING
THE WILD

LAND OF OROS

TAKKAR'S JOURNEY

MAJOR LANDMARKS

OUTPOSTS

BONFIRES

LOCATIONS

VILLAGE
CONSTRUCTION

ENEMY TRIBES

WILDLIFE

GEAR

SKILLS

FOOD RECIPES

RESOURCES

COLLECTIBLES

TROPHIES/
ACHIEVEMENTS

THE ART OF OROS

Locating enemies at night time is hard due to the lack of light, make sure you use Hunter Vision and your Owl to plot your way into the base and locate all of the enemies.

Check out the specific walkthroughs for each outpost below to get full enemy counts and stealth walkthroughs.

OUTPOST LIST

Name	Difficulty	Awards	Special
Kapal Outpost	Easy	500 XP, Population, Village Resources	1000 XP for stealth, Fast Travel, Stash
Swaras Outpost	Easy	500 XP, Population, Village Resources	1000 XP for stealth, Fast Travel, Stash
Payska River Outpost	Medium	500 XP, Population, Village Resources	1250 XP for stealth, Fast Travel, Stash
Piki Meat Outpost	Medium	500 XP, Population, Village Resources	1250 XP for stealth, Fast Travel, Stash
Snow Shwalda Outpost	Medium	500 XP, Population, Village Resources	1250 XP for stealth, Fast Travel, Stash
Fallen Tashla Outpost	Hard	500 XP, Population, Village Resources	1500 XP for stealth, Fast Travel, Stash
Platu Cave Outpost	Hard	500 XP, Population, Village Resources	1500 XP for stealth, Fast Travel, Stash
Ring Wall Outpost	Hard	500 XP, Population, Village Resources	1500 XP for stealth, Fast Travel, Stash
Tushwarha Outpost	Hard	500 XP, Population, Village Resources	1500 XP for stealth, Fast Travel, Stash
Twarsha Cave Outpost	Hard	500 XP, Population, Village Resources	1500 XP for stealth, Fast Travel, Stash
Kaba Blade Outpost	Very Hard	500 XP, Population, Village Resources	1750 XP for stealth, Fast Travel, Stash
Kwacha Stone Outpost	Very Hard	500 XP, Population, Village Resources	1750 XP for stealth, Fast Travel, Stash
Nada Swamp Outpost	Very Hard	500 XP, Population, Village Resources	1750 XP for stealth, Fast Travel, Stash
Nasan Horn Outpost	Very Hard	500 XP, Population, Village Resources	1750 XP for stealth, Fast Travel, Stash
Rotten Lake Outpost	Very Hard	500 XP, Population, Village Resources	1750 XP for stealth, Fast Travel, Stash

KAPAL OUTPOST

DIFFICULTY	Easy
TRIBE	Udam
AWARDS	500 XP, Population, Village Resources
SPECIAL	1000 XP for Stealth, Fast Travel, Stash
STATIONARY ALARMS	0
ENEMIES	2 Archers, 2 Slingers, 1 Warrior, 1 Villagers
WAVE REINFORCEMENT	None

This outpost has no reinforcements due to its lack of a Stationary Alarm or Elite Slinger. Take the high road in from the north, and line yourself up to take a shot at the animal cage, freeing the Wolf inside.

Prioritize any enemies attacking the Wolf, this allows you to remain in your position while the Wolf does all of the footwork chasing down enemies and finishing them off.

Follow the path around toward the waterfall and take up a position at the base of the large mossy log and begin raining down arrows on your enemies.

If the Wolf dies, take the quick way down and jump into the water below, before emerging to finish off the remaining enemies. Make sure to remain hidden to secure the 1000 XP undetected bonus in this easy Outpost.

SWARAS OUTPOST

WELCOME

SURVIVING
THE WILD

LAND OF OROS

TAKKAR'S JOURNEY

◆ MAJOR LANDMARKS

OUTPOSTS

BONFIRES

LOCATIONS

VILLAGE
CONSTRUCTION

ENEMY TRIBES

WILDLIFE

GEAR

SKILLS

FOOD RECIPES

RESOURCES

COLLECTIBLES

TROPHIES/
ACHIEVEMENTS

THE ART OF OROS

DIFFICULTY	Easy
TRIBE	Udam
AWARDS	500 XP, Population, Village Resources
SPECIAL	1000 XP for Stealth, Fast Travel, Stash
STATIONARY ALARMS	3
ENEMIES	2 Archers, 1 Spearman, 1 Warrior, 2 Villagers
WAVE REINFORCEMENT	2 Warriors, 2 Spearmen

Reinforcements can easily be stopped by eliminating the Stationary Alarms before entering the base as there is no Elite Slinger to call for reinforcements.

Start out north of the base. The entrance that leads northeast out of the base will allow an easy shot on two of the three stationary alarms. Take them out with your arrow, and kill the Warrior nearby, then move clockwise around the outside of the base. The next entrance you come across will give an easy shot on the third alarm.

XP BONUS
Destroying all three alarms grants you a small XP bonus even if you end up getting spotted.

Pick off the closest Archer then cross the road taking out the Spearman hiding in the tents. The last Archer is on the west side of the camp. He may come running down to you when you begin killing his allies on the east side of the camp. If he doesn't, move up the road with your bow drawn and be ready to eliminate him or send your beast out to do the dirty work for you. Sending your beast prevents you from being spotted.

PAYSKA RIVER OUTPOST

DIFFICULTY	Medium
TRIBE	Izila
AWARDS	500 XP, Population, Village Resources
SPECIAL	1250 XP for Stealth, Fast Travel, Stash
STATIONARY ALARM	1
ENEMIES	2 Archers, 2 Spearmen, 2 Elite Slingers, 2 Villagers, 1 Elite Archer
WAVE REINFORCEMENT	3 Archers, 3 Spearmen

Enter from the water to the southeast of the outpost, quickly killing the Archer that patrols the south side of the camp. With the Archer down, look east into the camp toward the Stationary Alarm and use a spear to take down the Elite Archer with shot to the head. Then quickly use a rock or shot from your bow to destroy the Stationary Alarm.

An Elite Slinger patrols up to the location of the Stationary Alarm, wait for him to get close, then quickly kill him with a spear as well.

Continue around the outskirts of the camp, picking off the Archers and Spearmen around the camp with takedowns or a few well-placed arrows.

The second Elite Slinger stays near the middle of the camp, mostly circling the campfire unless something else has caught his attention. This makes him less of a priority since you are more likely to get noticed sneaking in to kill him than you are killing everybody around him first.

Killing the Elite Slinger will most likely draw the attention of any enemies you may have missed, so it's best to make sure you're in a concealed location and have disabled the alarm to avoid losing your stealth bonus.

PIKI MEAT OUTPOST

WELCOME

SURVIVING
THE WILD

LAND OF OROS

TAKKAR'S JOURNEY

◆ MAJOR LANDMARKS

OUTPOSTS

BONFIRES

LOCATIONS

VILLAGE
CONSTRUCTION

ENEMY TRIBES

WILDLIFE

GEAR

SKILLS

FOOD RECIPES

RESOURCES

COLLECTIBLES

TROPHIES/
ACHIEVEMENTS

THE ART OF OROS

DIFFICULTY	Medium
TRIBE	Udam
AWARDS	500 XP, Population, Village Resources
SPECIAL	1250 XP for Stealth, Fast Travel, Stash
STATIONARY HORNS	1
ENEMIES	3 Warriors, 2 Archers, 2 Villagers, 2 Elite Slingers
WAVE REINFORCEMENT	3 Archers, 2 Spearmen, 1 Warrior

Enter the Camp from the north, sticking to the high ground. You encounter two Warriors on the outskirts of the base, these are easy targets for takedowns or arrows since they are so far away from the rest of their allies.

With them dead, use your higher elevation to land a shot on the Stationary Alarm, disabling it. Then enter the camp from the east side, killing the single Warrior that guards that entrance.

Slowly move into the camp, heading toward the disabled Stationary Alarm. Two Archers will be in between you and the Elite Slingers. They are far enough from each other and the Elite Slingers to prevent raising the alarm from killing either of them.

This part is a little tricky as the two Elite Slingers like to stay together in the Outpost. Ready a spear and then call in your beast on one of the Elite Slingers and throw your spear for a headshot on the remaining one to clear the outpost.

175

SNOW SHWALDA OUTPOST

DIFFICULTY	Medium
TRIBE	Udam
AWARDS	500 XP, Population, Village Resources
SPECIAL	1250 XP for Stealth, Fast Travel, Stash
STATIONARY HORNS	1
ENEMIES	3 Archers, 2 Scourge, 2 Villagers, 1 Spearman, 1 Warrior, 1 Caged Wolf
WAVE REINFORCEMENT	4 Spearmen, 2 Archers

Enter from the south, leading through a small cavern. Just before you get to the Outpost climb up the vines on the rocks to the right, then follow the path north up into the back side of the Outpost. On your way north, take a look into the camp and shoot the Stationary Alarm with your bow.

Climb down the large vines in the north side of the camp, being careful to not attract the attention of the Scourge or Elite Slinger near the campfire. Call in your beast and have them take out the Elite Slinger while you kill the Scourge. Now that you've eliminated all the alarms, you have guaranteed a "No Alarms" bonus. Remain undetected to get the full bonus.

Move west into the camp, killing the Warrior and Archer. Hold your position once you begin firing, keeping yourself concealed from the two Spearmen that will likely come looking for you. Kill the Spearmen then retreat back up the vines that you took down into the camp.

Once you're back at the south entrance, kill off the Archer if he is still guarding the entrance, and move in to kill the Spearmen if they weren't drawn out by the death of the other Udam. If you remained concealed, you'll have a hefty 1250 XP bonus waiting for you upon completion!

FALLEN TASHLA OUTPOST

DIFFICULTY	Hard
TRIBE	Izila
AWARDS	500 XP, Population, Village Resources
SPECIAL	1500 XP for Stealth, Fast Travel, Stash
STATIONARY ALARMS	2
ENEMIES	3 Spearmen, 3 Villagers, 2 Warriors, 2 Elite Slingers, 1 Elite Chieftain, 1 Elite Warrior
WAVE REINFORCEMENT	2 Elite Spearmen, 2 Warriors, 1 Elite Slinger

This Outpost has multiple stealth entries due to its multi-leveled layout. The bottom level is uninhabited by enemies, unless something grabs their attention, allowing you the move stealthily through the outpost.

UNDERWATER CAVE

A waterfall to the north conceals an underwater cave that allows for a stealth water entry. It is complicated by the darkness of the underwater caves that you need to navigate in order to get there, but as long as you pick the right option at every fork, you navigate to the Grappling Point in time without drowning. This point brings you to the backside of an Elite Chieftain allowing for a quick takedown if you have learned the Heavy Takedown skill.

Start on the north side of the camp. This path is patrolled by a Spearman so hang out in the bushes along the path until they come in close enough for a takedown.

With the Spearman down, move up the path and use your bow to take out the Stationary Alarms. The Stationary Alarm in the cave has a Warrior nearby; take them out with another shot from your bow. Eliminate the Stationary Alarm to the west by lighting the attached hut on fire. This not only disables the alarm, but the fire forces enemies out of the area, allowing you to pick them off one by one. After you've killed the remaining Spearmen and Warriors that fled the fire, take out the Elite Slinger on the north side of the camp with your beast. Stay away from the cave while you move south to eliminate the remaining Elite Slinger.

Once you've taken down the last Elite Slinger make sure your beast is healed and head toward the cave to face an Elite Warrior and Elite Chieftain. Try to separate them by throwing rocks, dividing their attention to two locations. Depending on your success of separating them, you may be able to sneak up to the Elite Warrior and perform a takedown. If sneaking up is not possible, call in your beast to take out the Elite Warrior for you.

Use rocks to keep the Elite Chieftain out of the fight while your beast takes out the Elite Warrior. Once the battle is over, switch from rocks to Spears and help your beast take down the Elite Chieftain and claim the Outpost for the Wenja.

PLATU CAVE OUTPOST

DIFFICULTY	Hard
TRIBE	Udam
AWARDS	500 XP, Population, Village Resources
SPECIAL	1500 XP for Stealth, Fast Travel, Stash
STATIONARY ALARMS	2
ENEMIES	3 Spearmen, 2 Elite Scourge, 2 Elite Slingers, 2 Elite Chieftains, 2 Villagers
WAVE REINFORCEMENT	4 Archers, 2 Warriors, 1 Elite chieftain, 1 Scourge

Find the south entrance to the cave and be ready to encounter an Elite Chieftain. Sneaking up behind him and using your Heavy Takedown skill is the easiest way to kill him and gain entry, but if you do not have that skill, lure him out and use your Two Handed Club, only performing heavy hits. Attacking with heavy hits keeps the Elite Chieftain off balance and prevents him from attacking or calling his allies.

With the Elite Chieftain dead, use your bow and arrow to pick off the Stationary Alarm and the two Spearmen nearby.

Carefully continue through the cave and perform a takedown on the Elite Scourge before using your bow to disable the second Stationary Alarm.

Sneak to the north side of the cave, leaving the two Villagers and Spearman alone while you work your way around into position to perform takedowns on each of the Elite Slingers that resides on the upper level. As you take down the second Elite Slinger you'll be in position just in front of an Elite Scourge and Elite Chieftain. Using your beast here likely results in them being knocked down and killed.

Throw some rocks to attract the attention of the Elite Chieftain and Elite Slinger, separating them enough for you to perform a quick takedown. Sneak around to the Elite Chieftain and perform a takedown if possible, if you are unable to do this, use your spears to weaken the Elite Chieftain then finish him off with some arrows.

At this point you only have a Spearman to deal with, that you've left behind down by the Villagers. Follow the path back out toward the entrance you took to get into the cave. Turn back toward the Villagers for an easy shot on the Spearman. Once he is down the cave is clear, no need to kill the Villagers.

RING WALL OUTPOST

DIFFICULTY	Hard
TRIBE	Udam
AWARDS	500 XP, Population, Village Resources
SPECIAL	1500 XP for Stealth, Fast Travel, Stash
STATIONARY ALARMS	2
ENEMIES	2 Spearmen, 1 Elite Archer, 1 Elite Slinger, 2 Elite Chieftains, 2 Villagers, 2 Warriors, 1 Archer
WAVE REINFORCEMENT	2 Warriors , 1 Archer, 1 Elite Slinger, 1 Elite Scourge

Search for the south entrance to the caverns, move past the first grappling point you see and follow the path into the cavern. After a short walk you find a lower grappling point which, when used, allows you to pull yourself into range of another higher grappling point.

This point effectively pulls you up into the back side of the Outpost.

Your first enemy will be an Elite Archer, wait for him to look away from the last ledge then quickly perform a takedown and line yourself up to shoot out the two Stationary Alarms with your bow. Remember, you can destroy them by lighting an attached object on fire. This approach is a little higher profile and will cause enemies to change positions.

Wait for the Elite Slinger to move into one of the tents containing a female Villager. He will be "distracted" there for a while. With the Elite Slinger distracted, move to the north side of the camp and take down the two Spearmen and then move into position to perform a Heavy Takedown on the Elite Chieftain.

LOCATION, LOCATION, LOCATION
Make sure you perform the takedown on the Elite Chieftain in a concealed place, or the body may be discovered by a patrolling Warrior.

Work clockwise around the camp and use your arrows to take down the two Warriors that patrol the outside of the camp. Another Elite Chieftain is at the south side of the camp. Stay crouched and throw rocks to distract him, allowing you to easily sneak up for the takedown.

All that's left now is the enemy Elite Slinger who has been "distracted" by the female Villager inside of one of the tents in the Outpost. Stay crouched and sneak in for an easy takedown to finish clearing the Ring Wall Outpost for the Wenja.

TUSHWARHA OUTPOST

DIFFICULTY	Hard
TRIBE	Izila
AWARDS	500 XP, Population, Village Resources
SPECIAL	1500 XP for Stealth, Fast Travel, Stash
STATIONARY ALARMS	2
ENEMIES	2 Spearmen, 3 Archers, 2 Scourges, 2 Elite Slingers, 2 Villagers
WAVE REINFORCEMENT	2 Warriors, 2 Slingers, 3 Archers

Grappling points to the east of the Outpost allow for easy access into the area. Once at the top of the Grappling Point, you are in great position to handle both of the Stationary Alarms; quickly take them out with your bow.

Your next objective is to take out both of the Elite Slingers which are located near the two now broken Alarms. This is complicated by three Archers who patrol a circle around the Outpost, so be sure to look around before performing a takedown on either Elite Slinger. Eliminate the Archers with a headshot from your bow if they are within range.

Once you've eliminated both Elite Slingers finish off the any of the patrolling Archers and move into the outpost to kill the remaining Scourge and Spearmen. The Scourge and Spearmen are spread far enough to not be aware of their allies being eliminated with stealth, so choose a direction, then work around in a circle killing them off one by one. You can use your beast to cut the time in half, sending him to attack the next enemy while you sneak up on yours.

Once all of the enemies are eliminated, the outpost is yours.

TWARSHA CAVE OUTPOST

WELCOME

SURVIVING
THE WILD

LAND OF OROS

TAKKAR'S JOURNEY

◆ MAJOR LANDMARKS

OUTPOSTS

BONFIRES

LOCATIONS

VILLAGE
CONSTRUCTION

ENEMY TRIBES

WILDLIFE

GEAR

SKILLS

FOOD RECIPES

RESOURCES

COLLECTIBLES

TROPHIES/
ACHIEVEMENTS

THE ART OF OROS

DIFFICULTY	Hard
TRIBE	Udam
AWARDS	500 XP, Population, Village Resources
SPECIAL	1500 XP for Stealth, Fast Travel, Stash
STATIONARY ALARM	2
ENEMIES	2 Scourge, 2 Archers, 2 Villagers, 1 Elite Slinger, 1 Slinger, 1 Warrior
WAVE REINFORCEMENT	2 Warriors, 1 Archer, 1 Spearman

Enter from the northern-most entrance into the cave.

Once inside you are greeted by a Scourge that you can quickly kill with a headshot from your bow. Push a little further into the cave, looking for the Archer in the south part of the cave, near the water.

Take the Archer out with your bow, then turn right and look into the northern part of the cave. Use another shot from your bow to release the caged animal, which will most likely run straight for the Elite Slinger. While the Udam are fighting off the animal, take out the first alarm near the water, then move across the water heading to the west side of the cave. Take out the Scourge that is guarding the entrance on that side, then climb up and head into the northern part of the cave. If you've done this quickly enough, they may still be fighting the animal, making it very easy to line up a shot on the Stationary Alarm.

After the alarm is down, you face a Slinger and a Archer. Remain hidden behind the rocks, and take them out without getting noticed to secure the maximum reward for this outpost.

SPEED RUN

If you're looking to speed run this Outpost without getting the stealth bonus, and have the ability to ride a Mammoth, grab a Mammoth from nearby and charge it straight into the caves! Charging circles around the cave kills all of the enemies and any reinforcements that come in an extremely short time.

KABA BLADE OUTPOST

DIFFICULTY	Very Hard
TRIBE	Izila
AWARDS	500 XP, Population, Village Resources
SPECIAL	1750 XP for Stealth, Fast Travel, Stash
STATIONARY ALARM	2
ENEMIES	2 Spearmen, 2 Elite Slingers, 1 Scourge, 2 Chieftains, 1 Archer, 1 Elite Scourge, 3 Villagers, 1 Caged Bear
WAVE REINFORCEMENT	2 Spearmen, 2 Scourges, 2 Chieftain, 2 Archers

First take out the stationary alarms. The two in the north side of the camp can be shot with a bow from the west entrance; the remaining one can easily be shot from the south entrance.

Have your spears equipped and head into the outpost from the southwest corner. Call in your beast on one of the Elite Slingers while you take the other one down with your spears.

Use your bow to take out the Scourge nearby, then wait for any other enemies to come your way, making sure to recall your beast

after it kills the Elite Slinger so that it doesn't move east into the camp and attack the Elite Chieftain before you've eliminated the other enemies.

Retreat back out of the camp and then infiltrate the camp again from the west side. The enemies should have moved to the south. The first enemy you encounter is the Elite Scourge that may still be on his small tower to the left of the west entrance. Take him down with a spear or a couple of arrows before moving into the camp and picking off any remaining Spearmen and the Archer, if they did not get pulled into the initial fight with the Elite Slingers.

Once you've isolated the Elite Chieftain in the east side of the camp, free the caged Brown Bear when the Elite Chieftain is nearby. Throw some rocks to get the Elite Chieftain in a good position between you and the Bear. If you don't have him close enough to the freed Bear, you may end up facing the Elite Chieftain and the Brown Bear at the same time.

Stun the Elite Chieftain with rocks from a distance and let the bear deal damage to him. This prevents you from being spotted and gives you an easy victory over this outpost.

KWACHA STONE OUTPOST

DIFFICULTY	Very Hard
TRIBE	Izila
AWARDS	500 XP, Population, Village Resources
SPECIAL	1750 XP for Stealth, Fast Travel, Stash
STATIONARY ALARM	3
ENEMIES	3 Warriors, 4 Elite Slingers, 1 Elite Archer, 1 Archer, 1 Spearman, 1 Elite Chieftain
WAVE REINFORCEMENT	2 Archers, 2 Warriors

At first glance, this outpost looks incredibly challenging with seven potential opportunities for reinforcements to be called. Don't let the reinforcements scare you as they are relatively weak compared to the other Very Hard rated outposts.

First things first, keep your distance, and move your way around the perimeter of the camp. Use your bow to take out the three Stationary Alarms through the openings. With those alarms down, now focus on releasing the four caged animals using the same method.

STAY DOWN

Be sure to stay crouched as you move around the camp. Sprinting or standing makes you stand out to the four Elite Slingers watching over the outpost.

Slowly work your way in a circle, staying inside the camp, and use your beast to pick off enemies without revealing yourself. If you aren't sure of the enemy's location, discretely retreat from the camp and call in your Owl to get a bird's eye view of the area. With that knowledge you can choose a new entry point to give you the upper hand on any remaining enemies.

Once you've freed the animals, move in from the west side of the base. With your spears equipped, begin to slowly move into the camp looking for the four Elite Slingers if the animals haven't already killed them. Use your spears to quickly kill off the Elite Slingers, be sure to stay concealed as you move through the camp as a few enemies may have stayed away from the animals.

More likely than not, the only remaining enemy after the caged animals are released is the Elite Chieftain. The easiest way to take him down is using the Upgraded Takedown ability from your Owl while you search the camp for enemies.

Once you've killed all of the enemies, the camp is yours!

NADA SWAMP OUTPOST

DIFFICULTY	Very Hard
TRIBE	Izila
AWARDS	500 XP, Population, Village Resources
SPECIAL	1750 for Stealth, Fast Travel, Stash
STATIONARY ALARM	3
ENEMIES	2 Warriors, 2 Elite Warriors, 2 Spearmen, 2 Elite Slingers, 2 Chieftains, 2 Villagers
WAVE REINFORCEMENT	3 Archers, 2 Spearman, 2 Slingers, 1 Chieftain

Both Elite Slingers are located near each other in the northwest corner of the camp. Stay hidden in the trees and tall brush as you approach the camp from the north.

Use some rocks to attract the attention of the Slinger nearest to the large tent closer to you, then perform a takedown on them out of view of the other enemies.

With one Elite Slinger down, use your bow to take out the three Stationary Alarms; all of them are easily seen from the east side of the large tent. Shoot them from inside the tent, preventing you from accidentally being spotted by the other hostiles in the camp

Quickly kill the Elite Slinger with a spear or two quick headshots from your bow. Order your beast to take down the Elite Warriors, helping it finish them off once you've killed the Elite Slinger.

Move around the north side of the camp, working your way clockwise around the perimeter, and use your bow to pick off the Warriors and Spearmen.

As you reach the East side of the camp, you face the Elite Chieftain. Use the different huts and tall grass to stay hidden, launching your assault from a distance. Alternatively, you can use the Heavy Takedown skill to make short work of this foe.

NASAN HORN OUTPOST

DIFFICULTY	Very Hard
TRIBE	Udam
AWARDS	500 XP, Population, Village Resources
SPECIAL	1750 XP for Stealth, Fast Travel, Stash
STATIONARY ALARMS	3
ENEMIES	3 Scourge, 1 Slinger, 2 Warriors, 1 Spearman, 1 Elite Spearman, 2 Villagers, 2 Elite Chieftains, 1 Elite Slinger, 1 Caged Cave Lion
WAVE REINFORCEMENT	3 Warriors, 1 Slinger, 1 Archer, 1 Scourge

Enter from the high ground looking out into the camp from the south. There are multiple grappling points in the area, allowing you to change your elevation, giving you clear shots on all of the Stationary Alarms.

Once you've taken out all of the alarms, you have two choices. You can either attempt to take down the Elite Slinger from above with a Spear, which allows you to take them down with a Head Shot, or move away and back down the rocks and enter from the East, putting you right next to a Scourge and the Elite Slinger.

Once you've eliminated the Elite Slinger quickly kill the Scourge and then hide behind the tent nearby and take out the approaching Warrior and the Scourge to the west.

Continue up the path toward the Elite Chieftain, killing the nearby Slinger, before making a move toward the Elite Chieftain. If you have the Heavy Takedown skill, sneak up behind the Elite Chieftain and perform a takedown. If not, leave the Elite Chieftain alive until you've cleared out more enemies, so you don't get overrun.

Retreat back down toward the area where you killed the Elite Slinger. From there look east and use your bow to take down the Spearman and Warrior near the caged Cave Lion.

Release the Cave Lion with a ranged shot, this draws the attention of the Elite Chieftain and Elite Spearman on the east side of the camp. Quickly kill the Elite Spearman then throw rocks at the Elite Chieftain to keep him stunned while the Cave Lion Finishes him off. Keep your distance on the off chance that the Cave Lion is not able to kill the Elite Chieftain.

If you weren't able to takedown the initial Elite Chieftain, work your way to his side of the campsite for your final showdown before clearing the outpost.

ROTTEN LAKE OUTPOST

DIFFICULTY	Very Hard
TRIBE	Izila
AWARDS	500 XP, Population, Village Resources
SPECIAL	1750 XP for Stealth, Fast Travel, Stash
STATIONARY ALARMS	2
ENEMIES	2 Archers, 2 Elite Warriors, 1 Scourge, 1 Elite Scourge, 3 Elite Slingers, 1 Spearman, 2 Villagers
WAVE REINFORCEMENT	2 Warriors, 3 Spearmen, 2 Archers

Sneak into the Outpost from the high ground to the west of it. Once you're in a nearby concealed position, call in your Owl to locate the enemies.

Two Elite Slingers should be close by to the north; they will be your first targets.

Stay on the upper path and work your way past the Archer to the furthest Elite Slinger. If the Elite Slinger begins to walk back toward the camp, let them go, and stay hidden until they pass. Once they have moved back into the camp, sneak down to the Elite Slinger on the upper level and perform a quick takedown. Use your bow to quickly kill the Archer to the north before moving back into the camp and taking down the second Elite Slinger that is now facing west in the south side of the camp.

With two Elite Slingers down, move back to the high ground on the West side and use your bow to take out the two Stationary Alarms in the middle of the camp.

This attracts the attention of the Elite Slinger and Archer that are near the fire in the center of the camp. As you move up, throw some rocks over their heads to distract them from your movement. Perform a takedown on the Archer, and then quickly take down the Elite Slinger.

At this point there is no way for reinforcements to be called. Retreat back to your insertion point and then work your way around the camp in a circle. Take out the remaining enemies one by one, using rocks to separate them if they come together.

TAR PITS

Be sure to stay out of the bubbling pits to the south, they begin inflicting damage on you the moment you set foot in them.

BONFIRES

Successfully lighting a bonfire and clearing out all of the enemies awards Takkar with a varying amount of XP and Population (depending on difficulty), a Fast Travel point, a Spawn Point, and access to his Stash.

The level of difficulty does not change in respect to the player's current level or progress in the story. For example, a highly leveled and well-equipped player can easily accomplish a Hard rated bonfire, while a newer player with a less diverse skill set may struggle.

SECURING THE BONFIRE CAMP

Scout the area out with your Owl making sure to locate the Elite Slingers first. These are the priority target as taking them out prevents reinforcements from being called.

YOUR CHOICE

Stealth is optional when clearing out Bonfires as there is no XP bonus for completing them with no alarms or undetected.

If you have learned Owl Attack II from the Beast Master Skill Tree, you can take down the Elite Slingers without even entering the camp!

You don't need to kill caged animals and enemy Villagers to complete the bonfire.

Bonfires have fewer enemies guarding them in comparison to Outposts, making night or day raids fairly easy.

LIGHTING THE FIRE

You can light the fire at any point during your attack, but doing so attracts the attention of the enemies. This is the easiest objective of the raid, and in general should be accomplished once all enemies are eliminated.

Light the tall pillar of wood by carrying fire with any of your melee weapons over to the wood. Hold **(R2/RT)** to hold your weapon out and light the Bonfire. You can also light one of your arrows on fire with Animal Fat or one of the local fire sources (lit torch or campfire) and shoot the lit arrow into the stack of wood. Using an arrow prevents you from causing damage to your melee weapons.

BONFIRE LIST

Name	Difficulty	Awards	Special
Roaring Falls Bonfire	Easy	400 XP, 3 Villagers	Fast Travel, Spawn Point, Stash
Stone Watch Bonfire	Easy	400 XP, 3 Villagers	Fast Travel, Spawn Point, Stash
Burning Spear Bonfire	Hard	900 XP, 3 Villagers	Fast Travel, Spawn Point, Stash
High Cliff Bonfire	Hard	900 XP, 3 Villagers	Fast Travel, Spawn Point, Stash
Hold Rock Bonfire	Hard	900 XP, 3 Villagers	Fast Travel, Spawn Point, Stash
Shaha Bush Bonfire	Hard	900 XP, 3 Villagers	Fast Travel, Spawn Point, Stash
Stone Beak Bonfire	Hard	900 XP, 3 Villagers	Fast Travel, Spawn Point, Stash
Sun Daughter Bonfire	Hard	900 XP, 3 Villagers	Fast Travel, Spawn Point, Stash
Gwarashnar Bonfire	Medium	600 XP, 3 Villagers	Fast Travel, Spawn Point, Stash
Night Watch Bonfire	Medium	600 XP, 3 Villagers	Fast Travel, Spawn Point, Stash
Stone Galu Bonfire	Medium	600 XP, 3 Villagers	Fast Travel, Spawn Point, Stash
Yagi Arrow Bonfire	Medium	600 XP, 3 Villagers	Fast Travel, Spawn Point, Stash
Hisu Sister's Bonfire	Very Hard	1200 XP, 3 Villagers	Fast Travel, Spawn Point, Stash
Mamsa Saja Bonfire	Very Hard	1200 XP, 3 Villagers	Fast Travel, Spawn Point, Stash
Sajas Hill Bonfire	Very Hard	1200 XP, 3 Villagers	Fast Travel, Spawn Point, Stash

NAKUTI BONFIRE

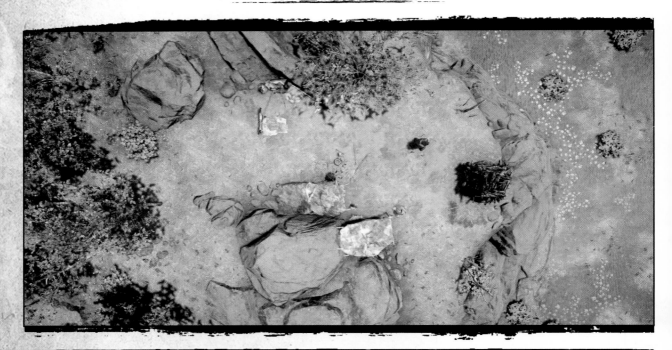

DIFFICULTY	Easy
TRIBE	-
AWARDS	400 XP, 3 Villagers
SPECIAL	Fast Travel, Spawn Point, Stash
ENEMIES	None
WAVE REINFORCEMENT	None

This one serves as an introduction to bonfires. Found at a high point northeast of the village, on your way to your first encounter with Tensay the Shaman. Simply light the fire with no fear of retaliation. It is yours.

ROARING FALLS BONFIRE

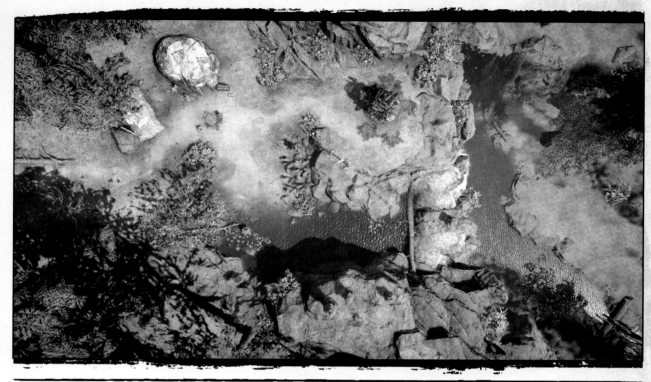

DIFFICULTY:	Easy
TRIBE:	Udam
AWARDS:	400 XP, 3 Villagers
SPECIAL:	Fast Travel, Spawn Point, Stash
ENEMIES:	1 Spearman, 1 Archer, 1 Elite Slinger
WAVE REINFORCEMENT:	1 Warrior, 1 Archer

Use the grappling point just north of the bonfire. This grappling point leads you up to the isolated Elite Slinger, allowing you to easily take him down with a couple of arrows or your beast companion.

Once you've eliminated the Elite Slinger, shift your focus onto the Spearmen. If only one of the Spearman is visible, check the tent. If you find the spearman asleep, perform a quick takedown **(R3)** then turn around and take out the last spearman that is facing the water. If there is no Spearman in the tent, take out the one by the water first, then follow the path past the tents and finish off the last spearman.

STONE WATCH BONFIRE

DIFFICULTY:	Easy
TRIBE:	Udam
AWARDS:	400 XP, 3 Villagers
SPECIAL:	Fast Travel, Spawn Point, Stash
ENEMIES:	2 Warriors, 1 Spearman
WAVE REINFORCEMENT:	None

The Stone Watch Bonfire is the only bonfire that does not have a Slinger to call for backup. This means that even if you get noticed by the enemies, they cannot call for reinforcements.

The enemies are grouped up, surrounding the Bonfire. Sometimes one of the Spearmen moves west to a smaller campfire.

Throw a rock to pull them away from each other. Once they've separated, use your bow to take them down while remaining hidden behind the tents and larger bushes.

Optionally, you can light the fire by using a lit arrow; this causes confusion in the group and they begin searching the nearby area. Let them separate, then pick the Udam off one by one.

GWARASHNAR BONFIRE

WELCOME

SURVIVING
THE WILD

LAND OF OROS

TAKKAR'S JOURNEY

MAJOR LANDMARKS

OUTPOSTS

BONFIRES

LOCATIONS

VILLAGE
CONSTRUCTION

ENEMY TRIBES

WILDLIFE

GEAR

SKILLS

FOOD RECIPES

RESOURCES

COLLECTIBLES

TROPHIES/
ACHIEVEMENTS

THE ART OF OROS

DIFFICULTY:	Medium
TRIBE:	Udam
AWARDS:	600 XP, 3 Villagers
SPECIAL:	Fast Travel, Spawn Point, Stash
ENEMIES:	1 Scourge Elite, 1 Spearman Elite, 1 Elite Slinger
WAVE REINFORCEMENT:	1 Warrior, 2 Archer

Climb up the two ledges north of the bonfire, then use the hanging vines to pull yourself the rest of the way up to the bonfire. Once there, the Elite Slinger will be to the right of you, while the Elite Spearman and Elite Scourge will be next to a small campfire in front of you.

Gaining line of sight on the Elite Slinger is a bit hard at first, so throw a rock to pull them away from cover opening them up for a ranged attack, or call your beast in to do the dirty work for you.

The next move is up to you, attacking the Elite Slinger draws the attention of the Elite Spearman and Elite Scourge. Taking out the Elite Scourge is a better option at first, this prevents you from getting poisoned, however it does expose you to devastating spears being thrown by the Elite Spearman. Strafe left to right to avoid the spears while eliminating the Elite Scourge from range. Then move in and take down the Elite Spearman and light the bonfire to claim it.

191

NIGHT WATCH BONFIRE

DIFFICULTY:	Medium
TRIBE:	Izila
AWARDS:	600 XP, 3 Villagers
SPECIAL:	Fast Travel, Spawn Point, Stash
ENEMIES:	1 Spearman, 1 Chieftain Elite, 1 Elite Slinger
WAVE REINFORCEMENT:	1 Archer, 1 Warrior, 1 Spearman

Use the grappling point that is slightly east of the bonfire, right next to the southern path that leads up to the bonfire. The Elite Slinger faces away from you, looking off the cliff. Take a quick shot with your arrow to the back of his head to knock his mask off, then quickly follow up with another shot to kill him, preventing reinforcements from showing up.

If you stayed hidden while taking out the Elite Slinger, you can take out the Spearman in the north side of the encampment leaving you only the Elite Chieftain. If you get knocked down and need to heal, you can quickly run down either path or circle around the tents to give yourself enough space to heal before attacking again.

Izila sun walkers.

STONE GALU BONFIRE

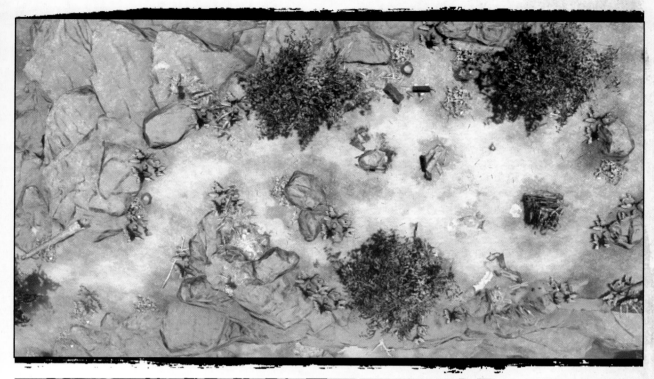

DIFFICULTY:	Medium
TRIBE:	Izila
AWARDS:	600 XP, 3 Villagers
SPECIAL:	Fast Travel, Spawn Point, Stash
ENEMIES:	3 Spearman, 1 Elite Slinger
WAVE REINFORCEMENT:	3 Spearman

The Stone Galu Bonfire has three routes leading into it, a grapple point on the north and south end, as well as a land route heading up from the west.

Use your Owl to scout the enemy locations before using the southern grappling point. Pull yourself up and you are in a nice position behind the bonfire, concealed by a rock. Use your bow to take out the first enemy to the east, making sure to keep yourself hidden from the Elite Slinger located on the high ground to the right.

Stay along the edge of the cliff, without entering the huts, moving to the right until you find a small spot to climb up. Once you've pulled yourself back up, stay crouched and move yourself into a good position to take out the Elite Slinger. With the Elite Slinger down you are free to take out the remaining Spearman however you see fit, without worrying about potential reinforcements.

YAGI ARROW BONFIRE

DIFFICULTY:	Medium
TRIBE:	Udam
AWARDS:	600 XP, 3 Villagers
SPECIAL:	Fast Travel, Spawn Point, Stash
ENEMIES:	1 Elite Slinger, 1 Spearman, 1 Archer
WAVE REINFORCEMENT:	1 Warrior, 1 Archer

The Yagi Arrow bonfire is the easiest of all the Medium rated Bonfires due to its low enemy count and number of Elites.

Climb up the long vines to the south of the Bonfire. This puts you right next to the Elite Slinger. Quickly crouch to remain hidden in the bushes. Depending on the position of the Elite Slinger you may be able to start a takedown from the bushes.

With the Elite Slinger down, the only enemies left are an Archer and a Spearman. Use your bow to dispatch them quickly, taking the Spearman down, then looking towards the campfire to take out the unsuspecting Archer. With all the enemies down, you should still be right next to the bonfire, light it and claim this spawn point for the Wenja.

BURNING SPEAR BONFIRE

WELCOME

SURVIVING
THE WILD

LAND OF OROS

TAKKAR'S JOURNEY

MAJOR LANDMARKS

OUTPOSTS

BONFIRES

LOCATIONS

VILLAGE
CONSTRUCTION

ENEMY TRIBES

WILDLIFE

GEAR

SKILLS

FOOD RECIPES

RESOURCES

COLLECTIBLES

TROPHIES/
ACHIEVEMENTS

THE ART OF OROS

DIFFICULTY:	Hard
TRIBE:	Izila
AWARDS:	900 XP, 3 Villagers
SPECIAL:	Fast Travel, Spawn Point, Stash
ENEMIES:	1 Archer Elite, 1 Spearman Elite, 1 Warrior Elite, 1 Elite Slinger
WAVE REINFORCEMENT:	1 Spearman Elite, 1 Warrior Elite, 1 Archer Elite

Enter the camp using the Path that leads in from the north. Once you've closed the distance, stay hidden in the bushes to the north side of the camp while moving towards the bonfire.

An Elite Archer may be on top of a small shelter acting as a lookout. Use a rock to distract him, allowing you to sneak by without being detected.

Depending on the Elite Slinger's location, you may be able to lure him into the bush for a takedown. If the Elite Slinger has started to head down the southern path, use your beast to take him out, disabling their ability to call for reinforcements.

While your beast is attacking the Elite Slinger take out the Elite Archer in the camp.

The remaining Elite Spearman and Elite Warrior are down the southern path, patrolling the area. Focus on taking out the Elite Warrior from range with your bow or spears, and send your beast to attack the Elite Spearman to prevent yourself from fighting two enemies at once.

Once that fight is complete the camp is clear for your taking.

HIGH CLIFF BONFIRE

DIFFICULTY:	Hard
TRIBE:	Izila
AWARDS:	900 XP, 3 Villagers
SPECIAL:	Fast Travel, Spawn Point, Stash
ENEMIES:	2 Spearman, 1 Elite Chieftain, 1 Elite Slinger
WAVE REINFORCEMENT:	None

Climb the vines leading up to the platform on the east side of the camp. This puts you directly underneath the Elite Slinger. Once there, use a rock to distract the Elite Slinger off of the platform, bringing him close enough for a takedown.

If you didn't alert any enemies, maintain your cover and use your bow to take down the two Spearman allowing you to then focus on a one-on-one fight with the Elite Chieftain. There is plenty of high ground available in this area, so using ranged weapons is a great option.

Be careful if you run to the west of the bonfire as there is a small camp that is sometimes inhabited by more Izila tribe members. Once all the enemies are down, light the fire.

HOLD ROCK BONFIRE

WELCOME

SURVIVING
THE WILD

LAND OF OROS

TAKKAR'S JOURNEY

◆ MAJOR LANDMARKS

OUTPOSTS

BONFIRES

LOCATIONS

VILLAGE
CONSTRUCTION

ENEMY TRIBES

WILDLIFE

GEAR

SKILLS

FOOD RECIPES

RESOURCES

COLLECTIBLES

TROPHIES/
ACHIEVEMENTS

THE ART OF OROS

DIFFICULTY:	Hard
TRIBE:	Izila
AWARDS:	900 XP, 3 Villagers
SPECIAL:	Fast Travel, Spawn Point, Stash
ENEMIES:	2 Elite Archers, 2 Elite Spearman, 1 Elite Slinger, 1 Caged Animal
WAVE REINFORCEMENT:	1 Elite Spearman, 1 Scourge, 2 Archers

The enemies in this bonfire stay spread out across the camp. If you are patient and remain concealed, you can use a takedown on each enemy.

Take the vines on the south side of the bonfire. They are located on the east side of the path that takes you directly into the bonfire. From there, sneak up on the Elite Slinger and perform a takedown. An Elite Spearman is your next target, located next to a small campfire on the left. Stay in the bushes and take them down.

Work your way around to the north side of the Bonfire area, staying in the bushes, then perform a takedown on the next Elite Spearman. The two Elite Archers tend to patrol the path within the camp, leading down towards the caged animal.

Use your bow to free the caged animal while one of the Elite Archers is nearby. With the now-free Wolf attacking one of the Elite Archers, sneak up on the other and perform a takedown.

Be ready for the Wolf to come attack you as it most likely is still alive. The Wolf should be weakened from its encounter with the enemy, making this an easy kill with a few well-placed arrows, or a strike from your spear.

With all the enemies down, the Hold Rock Bonfire is yours.

SHAHA BUSH BONFIRE

DIFFICULTY:	Hard
TRIBE:	Udam
AWARDS:	900 XP, 3 Villagers
SPECIAL:	Fast Travel, Spawn Point, Stash
ENEMIES:	1 Spearman Elite, 1 Archer Elite, 2 Chieftain Elite, 1 Elite Slinger, 1 Caged Animal
WAVE REINFORCEMENT:	1 Warrior Elite, 2 Archer Elite, 1 Chieftain Elite

A grappling point to the south of the Bonfire helps you get up to the path if you aren't already at the correct elevation. From there, stay to the left of the path leading into the bonfire, heading for the high ground of the rock that protrudes into the camp itself.

Killing the Elite Slinger without detection is crucial in this Bonfire, as allowing them to sound the alarm results in more Elite enemies coming your way.

Stay concealed in brush on top of the rock while you wait for an opportune time to strike the Elite Slinger You can either distract other enemies away from the Elite Slinger with some rocks, or, wait until the Elite Slinger crosses in front of the caged Jaguar.

The Jaguar may not attack the Elite Slinger when it is released from the cage, so be ready with a couple of arrows to take them down while the other enemies are distracted.

Having the Heavy Takedown skill is extremely useful in this camp, allowing you to make short work on the two Chieftain Elites. If you have not learned the Heavy Takedown Skill (located in the Fighting Skills tree), try your best to keep the two Elite Chieftains Separate while killing off the Elite Spearman and Elite Archer. If you attracted the attention of both Chieftains at once, run away and come back around behind them.

Once you're behind them, use some rocks to divide their attention, opening them up to be attack separately. You can also use a Sting Bomb to temporarily hold one of the Elite Chieftains at bay while you fight the other.

After you've killed all the enemies, light the bonfire and claim it for the Wenja.

STONE BEAK BONFIRE

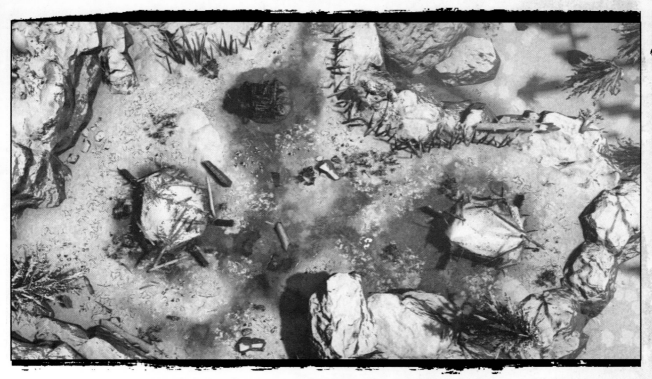

DIFFICULTY:	Hard
TRIBE:	Udam
AWARDS:	900 XP, 3 Villagers
SPECIAL:	Fast Travel, Spawn Point, Stash
ENEMIES:	1 Elite Chieftain, 1 Elite Slinger, 2 Elite Spearman
WAVE REINFORCEMENT:	3 Archers

Look for the two grapple points leading up to the large rock that protrudes from the mountain pointing directly north.

These points take you up to the bonfire, practically dropping you on top of the Elite Slinger, allowing you to make quick work of him

however you see fit. The Elite Spearman and Elite Chieftain are located nearer to the tents and the bonfire. Stay hidden behind the tents and take out the two Elite Spearman first. If you aren't in a good position, you can head back down the cliff via the grapple and latch on to the west grapple point. Coming up from the west gives you an easy flank on the enemies, especially if you have directed their attention back towards the campsite.

Try to engage the Elite Chieftain while you are hidden away. This allows you to quickly take down his health before he gets close enough to deal damage.

SUN DAUGHTER BONFIRE

DIFFICULTY:	Hard
TRIBE:	Izila
AWARDS:	900 XP, 3 Villagers
SPECIAL:	Fast Travel, Spawn Point, Stash
ENEMIES:	2 Elite Spearman, 1 Elite Chieftain, 1 Elite Slinger, Caged Animal
WAVE REINFORCEMENT:	2 Archer Elite, Spearman Elite

Use the grappling point to the south of the bonfire. Climbing from the grapple point places you right next to the bonfire, lining you up for a clear shot on the caged animal.

Use your bow and arrow to shoot the cage open. Simply shooting the front of the cage breaks the door open, freeing the Cave Lion. As long as there is an enemy nearby, the lion begins to attack them.

Once the Cave Lion starts attacking the Izila, use the confusion to quickly kill the Elite Slinger. The freed Cave Lion should have killed at least one enemy by now, use your Hunter Vision to detect the remaining enemies.

Use arrows from behind the bonfire to kill off the two Spearman and the Elite Chieftain. If you get overrun, run down the path and use the grappling spot to pull yourself back up to the bonfire, then begin your attack again from behind them.

HISU SISTER'S BONFIRE

WELCOME

SURVIVING
THE WILD

LAND OF OROS

TAKKAR'S JOURNEY

◆ MAJOR LANDMARKS

OUTPOSTS

BONFIRES

LOCATIONS

VILLAGE
CONSTRUCTION

ENEMY TRIBES

WILDLIFE

GEAR

SKILLS

FOOD RECIPES

RESOURCES

COLLECTIBLES

TROPHIES/
ACHIEVEMENTS

THE ART OF OROS

DIFFICULTY:	Very Hard
TRIBE:	Izila
AWARDS:	1200 XP, 3 Villagers
SPECIAL:	Fast Travel, Spawn Point, Stash
ENEMIES:	1 Spearman Elite, 1 Chieftain Elite, 1 Archer Elite, 2 Elite Slinger
WAVE REINFORCEMENT:	3 Warrior, 1 Chieftain Elite

Get yourself in position to use the Grappling point to the west of the camp, near the bonfire. Make sure you have a Beast companion ready, and call in your Owl.

Use your Owl to scout out the enemies, then when you are ready to attack, call in your Beast on the Elite Slinger farthest from the grappling point.

Quickly climb up and perform a takedown on the other Elite Slinger while the enemies all begin to focus on your Beast. Quickly move around, and perform a takedown on the Elite Archer and Elite Spearman before focusing your attention on the Elite Chieftain.

Depending on the outcome, you may want to quickly run over and revive your beast to avoid using Red Leaf.

Use Heavy attacks to keep the Elite Chieftain stunned while finishing him off and claiming the Hisu Sister's Bonfire from the Wenja.

 MAMSA SAJA BONFIRE

The Mamsa Saja Bonfire is part of the Into the Udam Land mission, check the Mission walkthrough to complete this Bonfire.

SAJAS HILL BONFIRE

DIFFICULTY:	Very Hard
TRIBE:	Izila
AWARDS:	1200 XP, 3 Villagers
SPECIAL:	Fast Travel, Spawn Point, Stash
ENEMIES:	2 Spearman, 1 Chieftain Elite, 2 Elite Slingers
WAVE REINFORCEMENT:	3 Archers

After scouting out the enemies with your Owl, work your way to the southeast side of the encampment and locate the grappling point. Grapple up, and then climb up the vines to get to the same level of the encampment. From there, you are hidden behind a rock, so there is no immediate danger to you.

Locate the first Elite Slinger to your left, carefully moving within striking distance while avoiding the gaze of the nearby Elite Chieftain.

WELCOME

SURVIVING
THE WILD

LAND OF OROS

TAKKAR'S JOURNEY

◆ MAJOR LANDMARKS

OUTPOSTS

BONFIRES

LOCATIONS

VILLAGE
CONSTRUCTION

ENEMY TRIBES

WILDLIFE

GEAR

SKILLS

FOOD RECIPES

RESOURCES

COLLECTIBLES

TROPHIES/
ACHIEVEMENTS

THE ART OF OROS

SIC 'EM!

Use one of your powerful Beast Companions to take down the Elite Slinger without raising alarm, and then call it back to your side before anybody notices.

With one Elite Slinger down, your focus now shifts to sneaking to the other side of the camp to take down the remaining Elite Slinger. Head back toward the grapple you used to come up, still making sure to not attract the attention of the Elite Chieftain or either of the Spearmen. Once you've safely navigated to the other side, use your beast to take down the Elite Slinger. The Spearman may see this attack happen so have your bow and arrow ready to take them out while remaining concealed in the bushes.

If any Spearman are alive at the end of this encounter, quickly eliminate them with takedowns or a few well-placed arrows. With the Spearmen dead, all that's left is killing the Elite Chieftain. There are plenty of cover spots available if you need to heal during the fight. In extreme cases you can climb down the vines you originally climbed and take the path back up to the camp, allowing you to easily flank the Elite Chieftain

When all the enemies are dead, light the bonfire and the encampment is yours!

LOCATIONS

From the icy, mountainous north wastes to the southern marshlands, Oros is an extraordinary, lively world and it begs to be explored. A variety of fauna and flora produces an array of resources, necessary for building a Wenja village and crafting gear. During your travels you discover new locations. Caves, campfires, and unknown locations earn you XP as well as a few perks. Navigate or fight your way through Lost Caves to find two types of collectibles, Daysha Hands and Cave Paintings. Doing so completes the cave and earns a decent amount of XP. Discovered campfires act as spawn points; die and you respawn at the closest one. Unknown locations earn you bonus points just for walking through a new area.

LEGEND

1	Cave of Bones	12	Gwashtru Cave
2	Cave of Hasari	13	Hagwi Drink Cave
3	Cave of Strength	14	Hungry Walkwa Cave
4	Cave of Sun Walkers	15	Marsa Cave
5	Chanting Cave	16	River Bagwi Cave
6	Charnga Cave	17	Shanma Cave
7	Chishta Cave	18	Sharp Stone Cave
8	Cold Swim Cave	19	Shayu's Cave
9	Cut Mamaf Cave	20	Split Rock Cave
10	Dangu Cave	21	Wisya Hurt Cave
11	Freezing Caves	22	Yachawha Cave

LOST CAVES

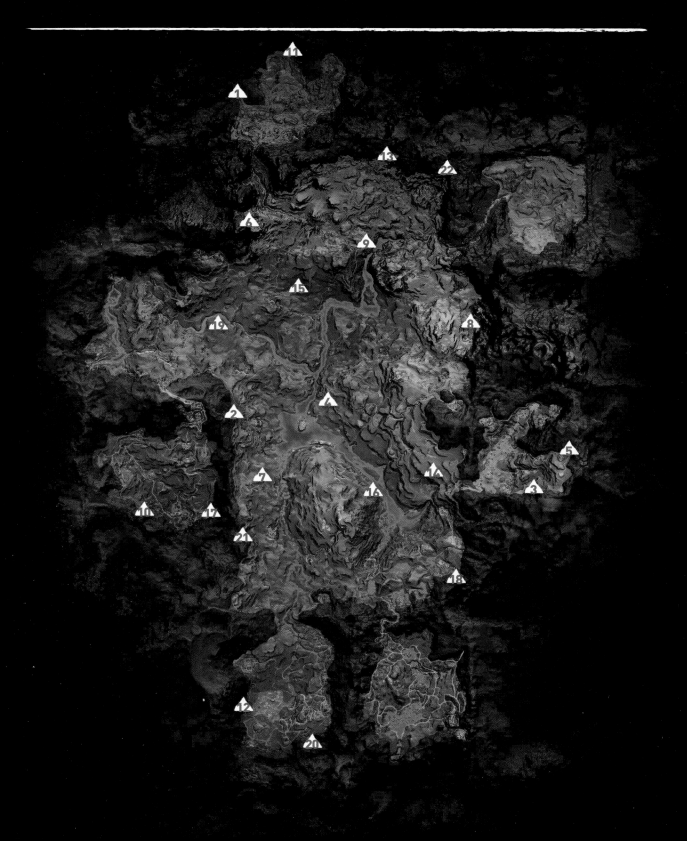

Lost Caves come in two varieties, navigation and combat. The former tends to be more complex, requiring you to find your way through a maze in order to gather the two collectibles. A fire in the first main room signifies the start of your exploration, as tricky jumps and grappling points challenge your platforming skills. The latter is just as it sounds, fight your way to the items. Udam, Izila, and/or wildlife occupy the cave. Using stealth or straight-up combat, find the Daysha Hand and Cave Painting to complete the cave and earn XP.

PREPARE

It is a good idea to stock up on supplies before entering a cave. Some are big, complex systems that require a lot of time to explore. Clubs and Animal Fat are used to light your way while weapons are required to destroy stalactites, weak walls, and ivy that block the paths. Some caves require a grappling claw to navigate, while having a supply of Antidote is recommended to limit damage in rot fume areas. Sprinting through the poison gas also works, but remember to heal when needed.

LIGHTING THE WAY

Fire is an important asset inside the Lost Caves. Here are some valuable tips for using fire in the dark interiors:

▶ Light campfires and flammable materials inside the caves to provide more light and a source of fire for your weapons.

▶ Lighting floating wood offers a much-needed light when swimming in the murky waters below.

▶ Lit weapons are put out when entering water, but tossing the weapon onto dry land before getting wet maintains the fire.

▶ Thorny ivy blocks entryways and paths, but setting it ablaze opens the way. Icicles that get in your way are melted with fire arrows.

▶ Send a fire arrow across a big cavern to get a better look. Just be sure you have the spare materials to burn.

CLUES

Look for clues as you hunt for Daysha Hands and Cave Paintings. Hunter Vision highlights clues, such as footprints, in red as they lead you the correct way. There are plenty of resources to collect too, so it can still be worthwhile to go off course.

Fireflies indicate important and useful locations. Arrows on the ground often mean you need to shoot something. Some grappling points are only accessible from a coil of rope on the ground. Always be aware of the clues around you.

OBSTACLES

Many obstacles block your path inside the caves. Thorns can be burnt down with fire. Icicles covering grappling points are melted with a fire arrow. Some big stalactites can be destroyed with a thrown club. Weak walls marked with three white marks and ice walls are knocked down with your club.

ENEMIES

Inside fighting caves, enemy tribespeople or aggressive wildlife occupy the area. Human enemies do not necessarily need to be fought to complete a cave. There are often ways to sneak by without a fight. Animals appear randomly inside the caves. One time through, you may not see any wildlife. The next time though may see half a dozen Dholes.

CAVE OF BONES

TYPE	Combat
ENEMIES	Udam Warriors, Udam Slingers, Udam Spearmen, Udam Elite Scourge, Udam Elite Spearman, Udam Elite Warrior

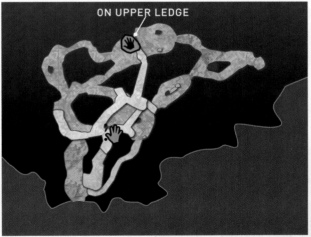

ON UPPER LEDGE

THE CAVE

Find Cave of Bones to the far north on the west side of the wastes next to Totems of the Old Ones. The Udam inhabit the cave, but they only occupy the main floor. They can be avoided altogether by climbing onto the right pathway from the entrance and following the narrow ledges to the back of the cave. Exit the same way without any confrontation. Though it is fun to get Death from Above Takedowns from the narrow ledges.

DAYSHA HAND

Reach the upper ledges in the main room and follow the north corridor. At the very back of the cave, the Daysha Hand rests on a narrow bridge above a fire.

CAVE PAINTING

From the cave entrance, climb up the ledges on the right and follow the path straight until you reach the big room. Study the Cave Painting on the right wall, next to the pots.

CAVE OF HASARI

TYPE	Combat
ENEMIES	Wolves, Jaguars, Cave Bear, Dholes

THE CAVE

There are two entrances to the cave, one on a ledge above the other. Wolves, Jaguars, Dholes, or a Cave Bear can spawn inside the lair, but you are also likely to find nothing. This small, straightforward cave has three big chambers connected by a narrow tunnel and breakable wall.

DAYSHA HAND

Enter the upper cave entrance and make an immediate left. Burn down the thorns on the left to reveal a small corridor. The Daysha Hand sits in the back.

CAVE PAINTING

Find the painting in the big room closest to the lower entrance. Make your way inside and hug the right wall to find a group of thorns. Burn them down to access the Cave Painting. To reach it from the upper entrance you must bust through the weak wall in the first room. Then follow the path through the second room on into the final room.

CAVE OF STRENGTH

TYPE	Navigation
REQUIRED	Grappling Claw

THE CAVE

Located at Twisted Path Climb, this fairly complex cave requires skillful use of the grappling claw and platform jumping. Two tips before navigating this cave, look for the red footprints that lead to the collectibles and spot the fireflies when you are not sure where to go.

1. The first big room includes platforms on the middle column along with ledges on the outside. Make your way to a tunnel above with some running jumps. Use Hunter Vision to spot the red footprints.

2. An intersection is blocked by thorns on the left, stones in the middle, and a ledge to the right. The latter path is not necessary to complete the cave. Set the hanging thorns ablaze to reveal a grappling point. By attaching to this point, you can swing to the ledge ahead. If you hold the rope too low, you hit the wall; too high and you cannot reach when detached.

3. In the next big cavern, water floods the bottom around a huge column. Many of the ledges around the outside are only accessible by grappling claw. Before going right, jump over to a platform on the left wall and find the thorns that block the path to the southeast. Set them on fire and return to the room entrance.

4. Clear the thorns to the right, swing to the next platform, and then jump into the far corner. Climb the ivy, turn around, and swing across the series of hooks, detaching onto the platform that was blocked by ivy. You can now climb up the far wall to reach the upper tunnel.

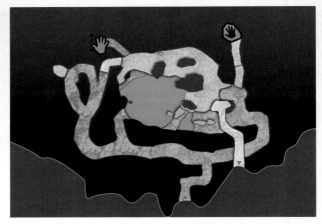

5 Following the path beyond the Daysha Hand leads you back outside to a secret access above the main entrance.

DAYSHA HAND

After swinging around the big cavern, follow the right ledge to a grappling point. Climb up to the upper level to find the Daysha Hand.

CAVE PAINTING

When the path splits three ways, burn the thorns down and enter the left. Attach to the grapple above, but do not climb all the way up. Swing into the mid-way tunnel and then hop onto the small platform to find the Cave Painting.

THE CAVE

You may have already explored the Cave of Sun Walkers if you completed the Tribal Clashes. In the secondary quest, you burn down the Izila camp inside. Those Izila still hide out within the cave, so explore cautiously. Besides the main entrance, a second stealth opening is found on top of the cave, slightly to the east. Avoid enemy contact from the main entrance by sticking to the right, completing the collectibles, and slipping back out. Find your way to the upper level to find long ivy that leads to the secret exit.

CAVE OF SUN WALKERS

TYPE	Combat
ENEMIES	Izila archers, Izila Spearmen, Izila Warriors, Izila Scourge, Wolves, Jaguars, Sabretooth Tigers, and a Cave Bear

DAYSHA HAND

From the main entrance, hug the right wall all the way into the big cavern. Continuing on the right side, climb onto the ledge and bust open the weak wall. The Daysha Hand sits at the end of the hall.

CAVE PAINTING

Inside the main room, find the flooded area and follow the water to the north to find thorns blocking a room. Burn them down to access the painting on the back wall.

THE CAVE

In far eastern Oros find a cave just behind a circle of standing stones. The Izila occupy the grotto, but there is no need to pick a fight. Tag the enemies whenever possible, while using pillars and water to break line of sight. Immediately after entering the cave, look for a path on the right. Dive underwater to find a water tunnel that connects to the main room. Access the ivy from this water and climb up to the two collectibles. This allows you to complete the cave without worrying about the enemy.

CHANTING CAVE

TYPE	Combat
ENEMIES	Izila Warriors, Izila Elite Spearman, Izila Elite Archer, Izila Scourges
REQUIRED	Grappling Claw

DAYSHA HAND

Follow the cave until you reach the water on the right, spot the ivy on the back wall, and climb to the upper ledge. Hop and grapple up to a higher level. Walk toward the waterfall and cross the rock bridge to the left. Hop over to the platform on the right and climb up to the Daysha Hand.

CAVE PAINTING

Find the ivy that climbs out of the water on the right side and take it up to the ledge. Grapple up to a higher level and look straight ahead to spot the Cave Painting.

CHARNGA CAVE

TYPE	Navigation
ENEMIES	Bitefish
REQUIRED	Grappling Claw, Antidote

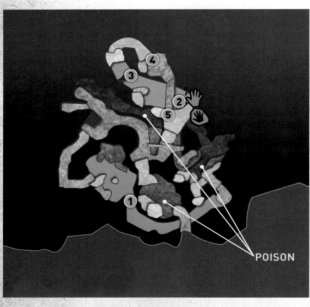

POISON

THE CAVE

Just inside snowy north Oros, find Charnga Cave on the west edge. There are a few general tips for the ice caves. Icicles often block your path and must be shattered with your club or melted with a fire arrow. Sprinting through or taking an Antidote can minimize the effect of the poisonous gas. A couple of flooded rooms require time in the water, but be careful of a Bitefish that can appear.

1. At the first flooded room, shoot a burning arrow at the floating wood to set it on fire. This allows you to see while swimming underwater. Just past this point, descend into the rot fumes to gather the Daysha Hand.

2. At the second flooded room, spot more wood debris floating in the water ahead. Light it on fire and swim around to the far side of it.

3. After climbing out of the second flooded room, look for a frozen grappling point at a rock point. Hit the ice with a burning arrow and then use the grappling claw on it. Swing and detach on the other side.

④ A deep valley offers a quick death if you don't make the jump to the other side. Get a running start and be sure you jump before the edge.

⑤ After the long jump, you reach a split with ice blocking both paths. The Cave Painting is on the left and right leads back to the exit.

DAYSHA HAND

Find the grapple point after swimming under the first pile of burning wood. Take an Antidote if available and descend into the rot fumes. Move through the gas to find the Daysha Hand sitting in the back of the room.

CAVE PAINTING

After the long jump, you reach a split with ice blocking both paths. Drop down and shatter the left blockade. Study the painting on the far wall before exiting the cave.

CHISHTA CAVE

TYPE	Navigation
ENEMIES	Brown Bear
REQUIRED	Grappling Claw, Antidote (side path)

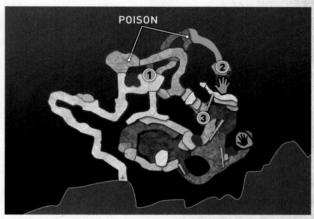

THE CAVE

In the southern wetlands, find the entrance to Chishta Cave west of the river and northeast of Nasan Run Valley. This one has many side paths, but if you stick to the clues, it is fairly straightforward. Trees litter the underground cavern; use them to reach the various levels.

① Just after the initial fire, the path splits into three routes. It is best to follow the footprints along the middle path.

② At the flooded room, light up the floating wood and dive underneath. Watch out for the possibility of a Brown Bear in the lower room with the Cave Painting.

③ After grabbing the Daysha Hand, hop down and follow the footprints. Climb up the log and follow the path until you reach a breakable wall. Look up and grapple to the upper tunnel. Follow this to the exit.

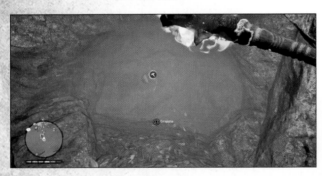

DAYSHA HAND

After the Cave Painting, climb up the log to spot the Daysha Hand on the ledge above. Squeeze through the narrow path behind you and continue up another log. Jump over to the platform and collect your prize.

CAVE PAINTING

Follow the middle path from the starting fire, bust through the weak wall, and continue down into the lower room. Light the floating wood with a burning arrow and dive underwater. Prepare your spear as you pass through the waterfall, since a Brown Bear may spawn in the room. Find the Cave Painting on a central rock and study it.

COLD SWIM CAVE

TYPE	Navigation
REQUIRED	Grappling Claw

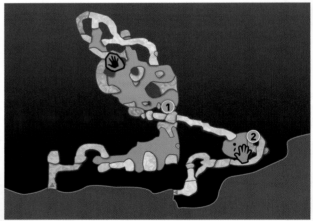

THE CAVE

Head to the lake in the southeast corner of icy Oros and jump in. Swim to the entrance, located on the west side of the body of water, to find Cold Swim Cave.

(1) Passing through the icy waterfall places you inside the main cave room. Rocks jutting out of the flooded cavern provide stepping-stones for crossing the water. Light up the floating piles of wood for extra light and another fire source. The Daysha Hand shines brightly on a high platform to the left. The Cave Painting can be found down the other path by grappling to the top of the waterfall.

(2) After studying the painting, use the grappling claw to reach the upper tunnels and then use it again to reach a second exit on a rock outcrop high above the north end of the lake. Icy stalactites that hang in your way are easily taken out with a weapon; be careful that you don't end up with a sharp icicle in your eye.

DAYSHA HAND

As you pass through the waterfall into the main room, look up to the left to spot the Daysha Hand shining bright on an upper ledge. Find an iced-in grappling point on the ceiling and free the ice with an arrow. Attach your claw and swing toward the bright glow. Detach at the platform, slipping under the stalactites, and collect the hand. There is ivy located on the other side of the Daysha Hand that can also be used to access the platform.

CAVE PAINTING

Follow the upper path to the grappling point and break the surrounding ice if you have not already done so. Swing to the top of the waterfall and break the ice wall ahead. Slide down to the lower cave room and study the painting on the far wall.

CUT MAMAF CAVE

TYPE	Combat
ENEMIES	Udam Chieftain, Udam Hunters, Udam Spearmen, Udam Warriors, Udam Scourge, Leopard, Rare Black Jaguar, Cave Bear, Brown Bear, Black Lion

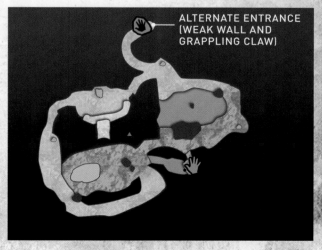

ALTERNATE ENTRANCE
(WEAK WALL AND
GRAPPLING CLAW)

THE CAVE

Just inside northern Oros, an Udam camp hides a small entrance into an underground lair. Udam and predators are found inside and out, so you must sneak or fight your way to this opening. A second stealth entrance can be found on top of the cave, just to the northwest. Udam litter the interior, but for the most part, they are easily avoided.

DAYSHA HAND

Drop into the lair through the main entrance, head right and then take an immediate left. Follow the corridor back to find the Daysha Hand. A grappling point above leads straight to the alternate entrance.

DANGU CAVE

TYPE	Navigation
REQUIRED	Grappling Claw

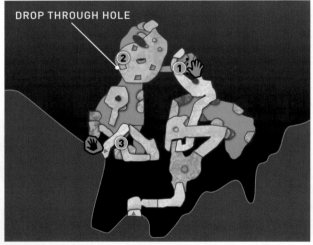

DROP THROUGH HOLE

CAVE PAINTING

From the main entrance, drop inside, immediately head left, and enter the small pool of water. Dive and follow the water tunnel northeast to find the Cave Painting. Burn the thorns to clear the way and study the picture. This room can also be accessed through a weak wall to the northwest.

THE CAVE

In southwest Oros, a cave runs through the mountain west of a small lake. Thorns block many of your paths out of the flooded rooms. Dry locations must be found from which you can shoot burning arrows. Arrows on the ground often signify the best spots. A second exit can be reached with your grappling claw, leaving you high above the lake.

1. After studying the Cave Painting, use your club to knock out the stones that block the east path and dive underwater. Swim south to reach a big room. Spot the fireflies on the right and climb onto the rock. Continue up to reach an upper rock floor, where a few openings lead back into the water. Drop into the east hole to continue through the cave.

2. After grappling to the upper level, bust through the stones and head left. Grapple up two more grappling points to find the exit above the lake. Swing from another grappling point to jump into the water.

3. After grappling to the upper level, bust through the stones and head left. Grapple up two more grappling points to find the exit above the lake. Swing from another grappling point to jump into the water.

 Players should not miss the various cave networks!

— *Vincent Pontbriand, Senior Producer*

DAYSHA HAND

As you emerge from the upper exit, the Daysha hand sits on the side of the platform. Grab it before jumping to the grappling point above the lake.

CAVE PAINTING

Burn the thorns that block the path before jumping across the gap. Continue up the corridor and attach to the grappling point ahead. Lower yourself to the bottom platform or hop down the series of ledges to find the Cave Painting.

FREEZING CAVES

TYPE	Navigation
REQUIRED	Grappling Claw

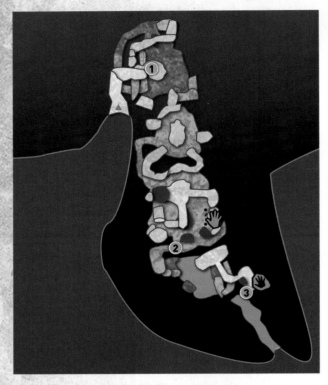

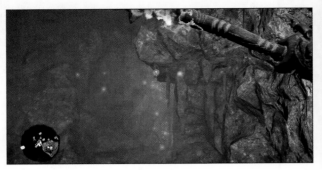

② After getting the Cave Painting in the second room, follow the red footprints west to a narrow tunnel. Inside the next room, the glow from the Daysha Hand can be seen on the platform ahead.

③ Continue past the Daysha Hand to find a waterfall. Jump into the water to exit the cave, well south of where you entered.

DAYSHA HAND

In the third room, the Daysha Hand can be seen ahead. Drop down to find coils of rope. Swing east and detach at the far side. If you miss, just swim back to a lower platform on the south side and reattach to the grappling point. Use another grappling point to reach the upper level, turn around, and grab the hand ahead.

THE CAVE

A campfire sits just outside Freezing Caves, located at the northern tip of Oros, which is good since the deep caverns have seen its share of deaths from falling. Some grappling points can only be used where you see the coil of rope.

① From the start, descend from the grappling point onto the small platform. There are resources to collect in this first room, but they are not necessary. Hop, grapple, and climb to the southeast corner. From there are a few ways into the second room.

GWASHTRU CAVE

TYPE	Navigation
REQUIRED	Grappling Claw

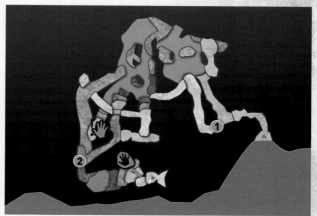

CAVE PAINTING

Inside the second room, climb onto the upper, north ledge to find coils of rope. Face southeast and use the two grappling points to swing onto the far ledge where the Cave Painting is found. Study it before dropping to the lower level.

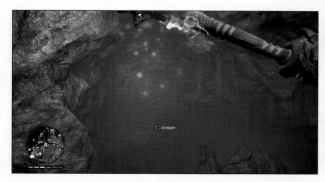

THE CAVE

To the far south, west of the Praying Stones, Gwashtru Cave sits on the north side of a small lake. Break up the stones that block the small opening. This cave requires a lot of jumping to navigate your way through.

A second exit emerges on the cliff above the west side of the lake.

1. At the first fire, burn the pile of hay on the left to gain access to the main room. A few platforms provide a way across this flooded room with ivy leading back up in case you fall in.

2. Follow the footprints through the tunnels and bust your way through the stones that block your path to reach a small body of water. Swing across and climb toward the light to find the exit.

DAYSHA HAND

Swing toward the exit and climb up the natural steps to a log. Cross it to find the Daysha Hand.

CAVE PAINTING

After crossing the first flooded room, hop to the left platform and look right to spot a glow under a rock wall. Dive underneath and climb the ivy to reach the platform where the Cave Painting is found.

HAGWI DRINK CAVE

TYPE	Navigation
REQUIRED	Grappling Claw, Antidote

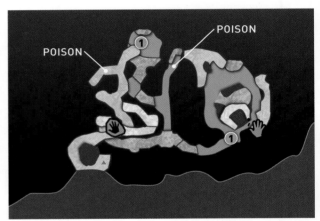

THE CAVE

Travel to Hunter's Shelter in far north Oros and grapple up the cliff-side to the north to reach a path high above. Follow it east to another grappling point, cross a log, and climb up another two grapples to finally reach Hagwi Drink Cave. Slip through the narrow opening on the left to enter. Note that there is no campfire on this cliff, so if you die, you must climb all the way back up.

1 Just past the fire, dive into the deep shaft to find a flooded cave. Be sure to drop straight down or else you may die hitting the rock walls. Shatter ice walls to open the paths and burn the thorns to light the way. Take an Antidote and dive underwater to reach the main room.

2 On the west side of the main room, light the floating wood and dive underneath. Follow the path through a weak wall and up two grappling points—melting the ice to gain access. Drop into the hole to return to the cave start.

CAVE PAINTING

After passing through the rot fumes and entering the big room, jump onto the middle rock island and then over to the far side. Study the painting on the south side of the room.

DAYSHA HAND

Light the floating wood and dive underneath. Follow the path to the end where a couple fish heads lie. Melt the ice from the grappling point above and pull yourself up to find the Daysha Hand.

HUNGRY WALKWA CAVE

TYPE	Navigation
REQUIRED	Grappling Claw, Antidote (side path)

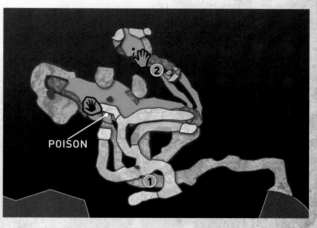

POISON

THE CAVE

Just north of Great Prashrawa in southeast Oros, the Hungry Walkwa Cave is found on a shelf north of the big waterfall. This cave doesn't require tricky jumps or swinging on grappling points, just follow the clues through the flooded cavern. Watch out for the possible snake though.

1. The cave immediately branches three ways. Follow the footprints up the left path, climbing the ivy and then grappling to reach the top tunnel.

CAVE PAINTING

After collecting the Daysha Hand, back out and follow the right path. Use the two grappling points to descend into the lower depths of the cave. Light the floating wood and swim underneath. This path leads you straight to the Cave Painting.

2. After collecting the Daysha Hand and Cave Painting, dive into the water and quickly swim underwater. Follow any tunnel to reach the exit.

DAYSHA HAND

From the start, take the left path. Climb the ivy and grappling point to reach the top tunnel. Take the first left and burn the thorns ahead to find a short corridor. At the other end is the Daysha Hand.

MARSA CAVE

TYPE	Combat
ENEMIES	Udam Spearman, Udam Warrior, Udam Scourge, Wolves, Cave Lion, Black Lion, Brown Bear, Rare Black Jaguar

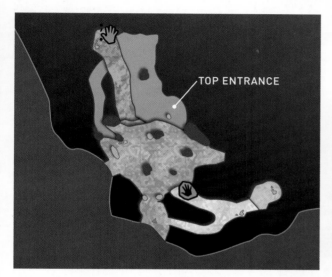

TOP ENTRANCE

THE CAVE

Find Marsa Cave a short distance from your village to the northeast. There are three entrances, two adjacent entrances in the front and another stealth entrance accessible above by grappling claw near the waterfall. The cave is relatively small, requiring only a little combat to clear it out. Watch out for various wildlife that may attack, especially the Brown Bear that will dive into the water with you. Drop in from above to avoid the Udam.

DAYSHA HAND

On the south side of the cave, climb onto the ledge and follow the path to a breakable wall. Bust through to find the Daysha Hand.

CAVE PAINTING

From the waterfall, swim underwater north and west through the tunnel. Exit at the first opening to find the Cave Painting behind thorns. Burn them down to reach the collectible.

My favorite beast companion is the Jaguar because it's a super stealthy animal. I like seeing my beast crouch like me and go kill enemies at my command.

— *Jean-Christophe Guyot, Creative Director*

RIVER BAGWI CAVE

TYPE	Navigation
ENEMIES	Crocodile, Udam Warriors, Udam Scourge
REQUIRED	Grappling Claw, Antidote

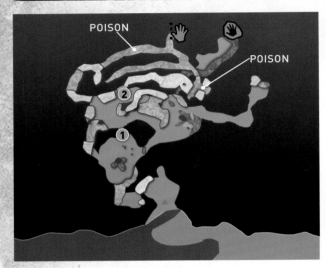

THE CAVE

Flooded by the nearby waterway, River Bagwi Cave is situated on the river, west of the big waterfall. This is a navigation cave, but there is a possibility of finding a Crocodile in the flooded areas and Udam Warriors in the upper tunnels.

1 Set the floating wood on fire in the main room and swim underneath. Climb onto the left rock and grapple to the ledge above.

2 Turn right from the grapple and follow the path into the upper tunnels, where Udam Warriors may be present.

DAYSHA HAND

At the main room, run through the waterfall on the right and then burn the ivy that blocks the small hole on the far side. The Daysha Hand sits at the back of the next room.

CAVE PAINTING

In the upper tunnels, throw your club into the stalactite that hangs in your way and jump across. Use the grappling claw to lower yourself away from the rot fumes. Set the blocking ivy on fire and then follow the right path to find the Cave Painting.

SHANMA CAVE

TYPE	Combat
ENEMIES	Udam Slinger, Udam Warriors, Udam Archer, Udam Elite Spearman, Udam Scourge, Udam Elite Slinger

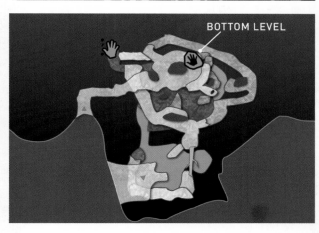

BOTTOM LEVEL

THE CAVE

In the southwest region of Oros, find a big bone tree marking an Udam lair in the southeast corner. Several Udam occupy Shanma Cave, including an Elite Slinger, so reinforcements can be called. Southwest of the main entrance, a waterfall offers an alternate way in by grappling claw. A long water tunnel connects this area to small pools on the north and south sides of the main room.

Just inside the main entrance you find your easiest takedown, a Slinger with his back turned. Peek around every corner and tag every enemy you can. Try to move Udam bodies to inconspicuous locations so as not to be discovered. Use the changes in elevation to your advantage.

DAYSHA HAND

The Daysha Hand sits in the east corner of the main room. Enter the cave at the waterfall and swim through the water tunnel to the south side of the main room. Sneak along the east side of the room and gather the collectible.

CAVE PAINTING

From the main entrance, turn left at the first opportunity and climb onto the left ledge, quietly moving behind the Warrior so not to alert him. Use your grappling claw to descend into the hole to find the Cave Painting.

SHARP STONE CAVE

TYPE	Combat
ENEMIES	Izila Elite Chieftain, Izila Hunters, Izila Spearmen, Izila Warriors, Rare Black Jaguar, Black Lion (All Outside Cave)

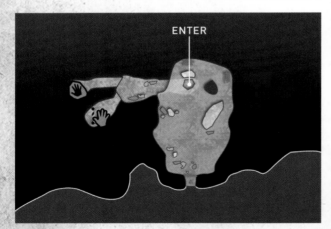

ENTER

THE CAVE

This very small cave is hidden in the back of an Izila camp in the southeast corner north of the Izila Homeland and is by far the quickest Lost Cave to complete. Izila may occupy the area just in front of the cave entrance. Two rare felines roam the area as well, so be ready with your bait if you haven't nabbed them yet. Call your Owl to scout the area to see when entry is safe. Drop into the hole to enter the cave.

DAYSHA HAND

Drop into the cave, bust open the breakable wall, and collect the Daysha Hand inside.

CAVE PAINTING

Burn the thorns that block the second opening. Move inside and study the Cave Painting to complete the cave.

SHAYU'S CAVE

TYPE	Navigation

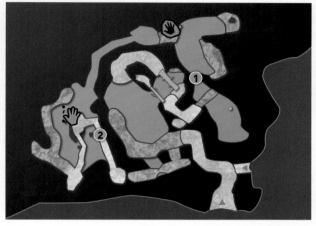

THE CAVE

Shayu's Cave is the nearest Lost Cave to your village so it is likely your first. It if fairly short for a navigation cave and does not require a grappling claw or Antidote. Follow the clues to find your way through the maze.

1 Set floating wood on fire to light your path and swim in the dark waters.

2 After studying the Cave Painting, cross a rock bridge and descend into the lower tunnel. Burn the vines to reach the first cave room.

DAYSHA HAND

Light the floating wood with a burning arrow and dive into the water. Swim under the debris, climb onto the ledge on the other side, and collect the Daysha Hand.

CAVE PAINTING

From the Daysha Hand, set more wood on fire and swim underneath. In the big cavern, climb up the right ledges and follow the path to find the Cave Painting.

SPLIT ROCK CAVE

TYPE	Combat
ENEMIES	Izila Slingers, Izila Archer, Izila Warriors, Izila Spearman, Izila Elite Spearmen, Izila Elite Scourge, Izila Elite Archer
REQUIRED	Grappling Claw (to access upper level)

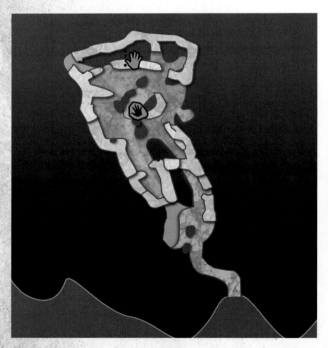

THE CAVE

In the southernmost regions of Oros, an Izila lair sits at the base of the southern mountains. The starting passage accesses a big cavern with high ledges and platforms around the outside and a big pillar in the middle. Water on the left side of the entryway connects to a couple of pools around the outside of the main room. Follow the water tunnels all the way back for easy access to the south ledge where the Cave Painting is found. The water also allows for an escape if things go bad.

Climb the ledges just beyond the first water and follow the path to ivy, which leads you up to the east ledge of the main room—giving you easy access to both collectibles. A variety of Izila fighters are found throughout the interior, including a couple who patrol the ledges. Tag them as you explore to keep track of their movements.

DAYSHA HAND

The Daysha Hand rests atop the central pillar in the main room. It is accessible by jumping from the grappling point on the east ledge or a rock platform to the west.

CAVE PAINTING

Find the Cave Painting on a narrow ledge on the south side of the main room. It is accessible from the east and west along the walkways. Follow the suggested path to the east ledge or follow the water tunnels all the way back and follow the path up to the south ledge.

WISYA HURT CAVE

TYPE	Navigation
REQUIRED	Grappling Claw, Antidote

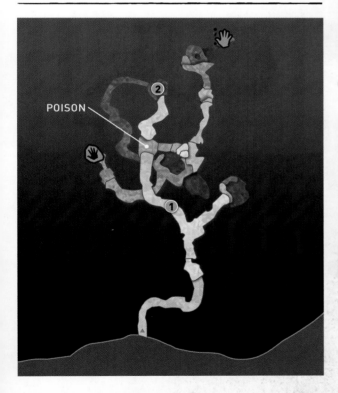

THE CAVE

Wisya Hurt Cave sets on a cliff right off the road south of Nasan Run Valley and west of Rotten Lake Outpost. Follow the clues to find the main cave room. From there the two collectibles and the exit are all accessible. Watch for possible snakes in the lower cave tunnels.

(1) Follow the footprints down the left path at the split and use the grappling point to swing over the poison pit.

(2) Use the grappling claw to descend into the lower depths. Bust through the weak rock wall and continue into the main room.

③ Climb the vines in the main room and grapple to reach the upper tunnels. Burn the vines that block the path to reach the main tunnel.

TYPE	Navigation
REQUIRED	Grappling Claw, Antidote

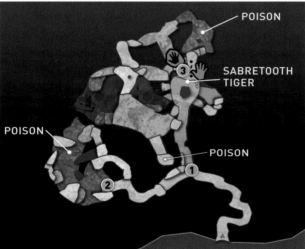

DAYSHA HAND

Once you reach the main cave room, follow the right tunnel to the rot fumes. Eat an Antidote if available and smash through the weak wall. Find the Daysha Hand inside.

CAVE PAINTING

From the main cave room, climb up the stone pillar. Follow the corridor past the breakable wall and descend into the snake pit to find the Cave Painting.

THE CAVE

North of Big Darwa Fort, Yachawba Cave requires some climbing to reach the entrance, similar to Hagwi Drink Cave. It is accessible from the south or west across log bridges and grappling points. The southern route requires swinging between two points to reach a distant rock ledge. Watch out for the possible Udam who camp outside the cave entrance.

1 On your way to the starting point, look for a tunnel to the right. Enter to possibly find a Sabretooth Tiger. Tame it, get an easy kill and skin, or ignore the room altogether.

2 At the split, follow the left path across the rock platforms. Knock down the icicles and use the grappling point to swing to the other side.

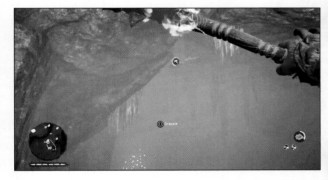

3 After studying the painting, break the stalactites and swing on the other side of the waterfall. Use the grappling claw to return to the upper cave level. Climb the vines and break the ice to return to the main corridor.

DAYSHA HAND

After swinging across the gap, descend into the lower area with another grappling point. Continue down by following the clues and grapple again to descend to the lowest depths. Shatter the ice in the waterfall room and collect the Daysha Hand before continuing down the left corridor.

CAVE PAINTING

Burn the bushes that block the path and move through the poison ahead. Continue up the ledges and bust down the ice wall. Study the Cave Painting inside.

CAMPFIRES

Look for the white Campfire icons on
your mini-map to find places to rest.
A white icon means the Campfire has
not been discovered yet, black means
undiscovered. Each Campfire gives you
the following perks:

- ▶ **Earn XP:** Gain 100 XP for discovery

- ▶ **Rest until Dawn or Nightfall:** Use the sleeping fur and then select when you want to wake up.

- ▶ **Reward Stash:** Access your Reward Stash in case you wish to move resources into your pack.

- ▶ **Spawn Point:** When you die, you respawn at the closest discovered Campfire, so it is well worth the effort to approach as
  many of these camps as possible.

- ▶ **Fast Travel:** a few Campfires also offer Fast Travel. These are designated with an asterisk on our map.

- ▶ **Light a Fire:** The Campfire can be lit using a certain wood, which differs based on the region of Oros.

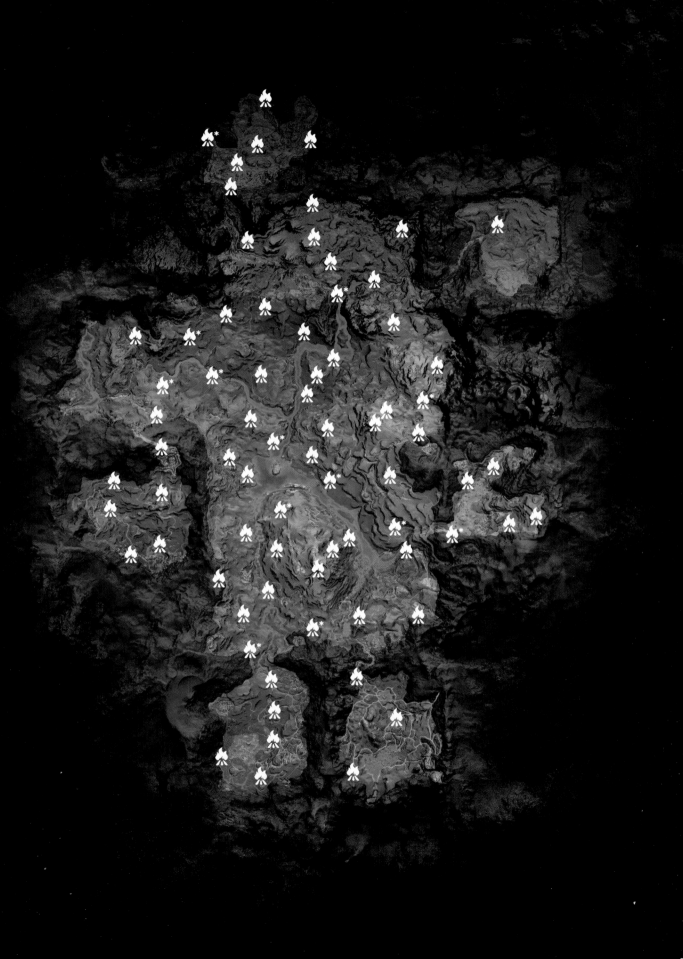

UNKNOWN LOCATIONS

Unknown locations give you 100 XP when discovered. There are many regular locations and 10 Major Locations. If a question mark appears nearby, go ahead and steer close enough to get the XP, but it isn't worth going too far out of the way.

MAJOR LOCATIONS

 Altar of Suxli

 Blajiman Stones

 Cut Mamaf Cave

 Great Prashrawa

 Mamaf Graveyard

 Mash Baya Rocks

 Nasan Run Valley

 Prashrawa's Birth

 Praying Stones

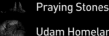 Udam Homeland

MINOR LOCATIONS

#	Location	#	Location	#	Location	#	Location
1	Hungry Hollow	40	Mamaf Scout Camp	79	Forgotten Crater	118	Sweet Water Totem
2	Totems of the Old Ones	41	Silent Camp	80	Lone Spear Camp	119	Kalni Grave
3	Yagi Canyons	42	Chayhi Shelter	81	Daywa Snake Path	120	Forest Tomb
4	Hot Springs	43	Baydaya Hut	82	Rock Tooth Pass	121	Beast Bone Waterfall
5	Courage Rock	44	Bone Break Pit	83	Dry Fish Camp	122	Kashatigri's Home
6	Chalta Camp	45	Minash Peak	84	Naymin of Spirits	123	Bloodfang Den
7	Mouth of Galay	46	Long Sleep Cliffs	85	Gwardu Camp	124	Hunter's Refuge
8	Nasan Shelter	47	Bone Finders Camp	86	Broken Arm Dwaray	125	Shanhima Totem
9	Tashtan Cliffs	48	Eagle Cry Peak	87	Singing Water Rest	126	Stone Hill Camp
10	Last Dajri Refuge	49	Mansi Rest	88	Twarshi Basin	127	Hiding Hole
11	Parkun Foot Lake	50	Den of Walkwa	89	Udam Mashashman	128	Burning Tree Grotto
12	Snayshaw Rocks	51	Lost Camp	90	Still Water Dwaray	129	Patash Rock
13	Greedy Pardal's Camp	52	Stone Fingers	91	Strong Jaw Cave	130	Stone Bowl Camp
14	Chalta Rest	53	Warha Cliffs	92	Stone Doorway	131	Great Scar Bear Den
15	Hunter's Shelter	54	Chasa Hills	93	Kumba Perch	132	Brama of the Bear
16	Mamaf Walk Pond	55	Tarshta Stones	94	Bandu Blood Stone	133	Tashla Island
17	Hidden Padisu Shelter	56	Watcher's Pool	95	Forgotten Shwalda	134	Hars Valley
18	Shwadari Fight Den	57	Padurgi Refuge	96	Kawti Shelter	135	Gathering Tree
19	Crack Skull Camp	58	Fashna's Grove	97	Pardal's Perch	136	Twisted Path Climb
20	Padisu Shelter	59	Mamaf Foot Pond	98	Burning Sun Circle	137	Blood Gate
21	Widu Rest	60	Marsa Cave	99	Sleeping Galun Tomb	138	Walkwa Den
22	Bayabar Rock Shelter	61	Fishing Rest	100	Mayta Wenja Camp	139	Pishcha Waters
23	Forgotten Grave Rest	62	Shelter of the Lost	101	Jasari Pond	140	Tomb of Teeth
24	Wood Danti Camp	63	Warm Pelt Shelter	102	Fallen Watcher Rest	141	Pushra Path
25	Hasar Likarta	64	River Bend Camp	103	The Tall Watchers	142	Gwada Stones
26	Dantan's Den	65	Mother Jaysta Hill	104	Sun Walker Ring	143	Digway Camp
27	Hut of Shasti	66	Twisted Grove	105	Drowning Huts	144	Stone Tusks
28	Blood Snow Totem	67	Stuck Foot Brothers	106	Pur Tanhin Rocks	145	Stone Damshi Island
29	White Hiswan Shelter	68	Piki Pond	107	Flat Rock Waterfall	146	Sinking Tashla
30	Jaysta Watch Pass	69	Raw Flesh Camp	108	Split Water	147	Gwijara Camp
31	Danti Walk Hill	70	Bayabar Hunter Totem	109	Dead Mamaf Hill	148	Forsaken Altar
32	Goat Hoof Peaks	71	Halchi Hunt Run	110	Mamaf Island	149	Kala Island
33	Horned Pond	72	Walkwa River Stones	111	Sun Walker's Hatra	150	Darcha Watch
34	Stone Mother Camp	73	Fadasi Hollow	112	Pig Sikari Camp	151	Reflecting Stone
35	Dead Tree Camp	74	Stones of the Lost	113	Putila Crying Stones	152	Dakru Pit
36	Goat Fall Valley	75	Whispering Grotto	114	Howling Tomb	153	Danchapays Water
37	Lawka Hunting Camp	76	Torn Flesh Retreat	115	Sleeping Hill Grave	154	Den of Klapi
38	Wailing Cliffs	77	Forgotten Glade	116	Chawda Tomb	155	Temple of Batari
39	Mi-Mamsa Falls	78	Parku Wood Shelter	117	Stone Shadow Camp	156	Mazga Pit

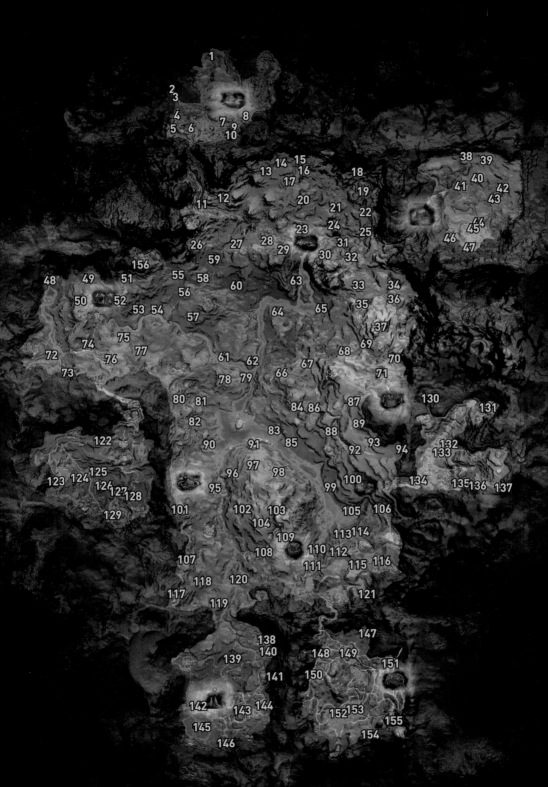

VILLAGE CONSTRUCTION

Reaching the promised land that is Oros starts a process of rebuilding the long lost tribe of Wenja. This involves finding fellow tribespeople, bringing them back to the village, and building new huts for them—a cave for yourself and seven huts for the specialists. As you progress through the game, capture locations, and complete quests; more Wenja join the village. The specialists offer special skills and gear, while the other villagers give you an XP boost.

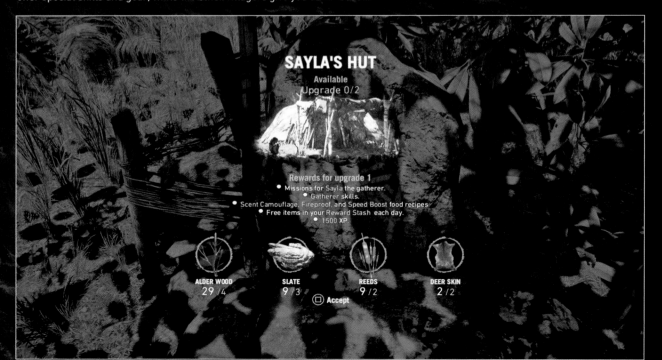

SAYLA'S HUT
Available
Upgrade 0/2

Rewards for upgrade 1
• Missions for Sayla the gatherer.
• Gatherer skills.
• Scent Camouflage, Fireproof, and Speed Boost food recipes.
• Free items in your Reward Stash each day.
• 1500 XP.

ALDER WOOD 29/4   SLATE 9/3   REEDS 9/2   DEER SKIN 2/2

☐ Accept

HOW IT WORKS

Complete Tensay's Beast Master mission to unlock the ability to build your village. Talk to Sayla and Tensay before constructing their huts. Next, stand in front of each stone marker to see the resource requirements and hold the interact button to create the shelter. Their locations show up on the mini-map as an icon showing the specialist. XP, unlocked skills, and more are rewarded for each one. All eight structures that make up your village have two upgrades, the initial build and an improved version. Below we list what is required and awarded for each upgrade.

The upgraded huts are tougher to get **done** since they all require a specific rare skin. That means spending time hunting for rare versions of the wildlife that can be found throughout the world to receive the rare skin. Refer **to our** Resources chapter for an idea of where to **find all of the materials.**

TRIBE POPULATION REWARDS

As your village population grows, you earn extra bags of weapon resources and bonus XP. The added 2% XP for every 10 rescued tribespeople really adds up and maxes out at 48% bonus— allowing you to grab skills at a faster pace. Add Wenja to your village by completing missions, secondary quests, and major landmarks whenever possible. It is possible to lose population too. Accidently killing a Wenja or taking too long rescuing someone can result in a loss. Notifications of additions and subtractions are given on the left side of the HUD.

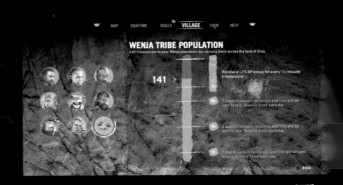

POPULATION REWARDS

POPULATION	REWARD
20	1 bag of weapon resources and food sent to Reward Stash each day
40	2 bags of weapon resources and food sent to Reward Stash each day
60	3 bags of weapon resources and food sent to Reward Stash each day
Each 10 above 60	Receive a +2% XP bonus for every 10 rescued

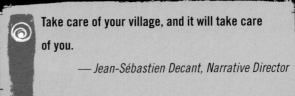

Take care of your village, and it will take care of you.

— *Jean-Sébastien Decant, Narrative Director*

TAKKAR'S CAVE

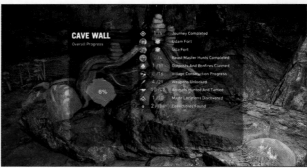

AVAILABLE	Complete Beast Master mission, then talk to Sayla
LEVEL 1 REQUIREMENTS	4 Alder Wood, 3 Slate, 2 Reeds, 4 Goat Skins
LEVEL 1 REWARDS	Survival Skills, Bow upgrade, Club upgrade, Sting Bomb throwable, 1500 XP
LEVEL 2 REQUIREMENTS	35 Alder Wood, 25 Slate, 10 Reeds, 4 Badger Skins, 40 Villagers
LEVEL 2 REWARDS	3000 XP

Takkar needs a place to stay and he decides to build in the cave. A sleeping fur and Reward Stash are provided nearby for easy access. Using the village Fast Travel puts you inside this location.

Game progression is given on the Cave Wall deeper inside. Approach the stones in the middle of the cavern for Overall Progress. Examine the outside wall to find detailed progression for Beasts, Collectibles, Weapons, Major Locations, Outposts and Bonfires, Journey completion, and Village construction. For the completionist, these lists give a quick rundown on what has been done and how many of each item have not yet been discovered or completed.

SAYLA'S HUT

AVAILABLE	Complete Beast Master mission, then talk to Sayla
LEVEL 1 REQUIREMENTS	4 Alder Wood, 3 Slate, 2 Reeds, 2 Deer Skins
LEVEL 1 REWARDS	Sayla missions, Gathering Skills, Food Recipes (Scent Camouflage, Fireproof, Speed Boost), Free items in Reward Stash, 1500 XP
LEVEL 2 REQUIREMENTS	35 Alder Wood, 20 Slate, 20 Reeds, 4 Mammoth Skins, 40 Villagers
LEVEL 2 REWARDS	Food Recipes (Full Health and Ultimate Boost), Rare items in Reward Stash, 3000 XP

Sayla asks for your help with building a new village, so give her a hut to stay in. Combine this with a hut for Tensay to unlock the Attack of the Udam mission, which is required to progress in the game. Sayla also teaches the more noteworthy food recipes. Unlike most huts, the reward for upgrading to level 2 is more than XP—unlocking two more recipes and rare items in your Reward Stash.

TENSAY'S HUT

AVAILABLE	Complete Beast Master mission, then talk to Tensay
LEVEL 1 REQUIREMENTS	2 Alder Wood, 2 Slate, 2 Reeds, 2 Wolf Skins
LEVEL 1 REWARDS	Tensay missions, Beast Master skills, 1500 XP
LEVEL 2 REQUIREMENTS	38 Alder Wood, 15 Slate, 16 Reeds, Rare Black Lion Skins, 40 Villagers
LEVEL 2 REWARDS	3000 XP

Tensay's hut is necessary to move the story along, unlocking the Attack of the Udam mission if Sayla already has a home. Tensay has a few missions that are required to finish the story, so you become very familiar with his hut. His Beast Master skills are well worth spending XP on, allowing you to tame better beasts.

WOGAH'S HUT

AVAILABLE	Complete Blood of Oros mission, then talk to Wogah
LEVEL 1 REQUIREMENTS	3 Alder Wood, 3 Slate, 3 Reeds, 2 Jaguar Skins
LEVEL 1 REWARDS	Crafting Skills, Club Belt, Spear Belt, Pack, Hunter Belt, Throwing Shard Belt, Trap, Berserk Shard, 1500 XP
LEVEL 2 REQUIREMENTS	20 North Cedar, 15 North Black Rock, 10 North Clay, 3 Cave Bear Skin, 40 Villagers
LEVEL 2 REWARDS	Bomb Belt, 3000 XP

> We wanted the Wenja to be grounded in the realities of the Stone Age. Life was simpler but far more deadly than today. People were hunters, crafters, and fighters. Everyone bore violent scars of one kind or another.
>
> — *Kevin Shortt, Lead Writer*

Convince Wogah you are Wenja in Trapped and then collect the precious stones in Blood of Oros to convince the crafter to join your Wenja village. Wogah offers quite a few useful items—including packs, bombs, shards, traps, and the extremely useful grappling claw.

WELCOME

SURVIVING
THE WILD

LAND OF OROS

TAKKAR'S JOURNEY

MAJOR LANDMARKS

LOCATIONS

VILLAGE
CONSTRUCTION

ENEMY TRIBES

WILDLIFE

GEAR

SKILLS

FOOD RECIPES

RESOURCES

COLLECTIBLES

TROPHIES/
ACHIEVEMENTS

THE ART OF OROS

JAYMA'S HUT

AVAILABLE	Complete On the Hunt mission, then talk to Jayma
LEVEL 1 REQUIREMENTS	5 Alder Wood, 4 Slate, 3 Reeds, Brown Bear Skin
LEVEL 1 REWARDS	Hunting Skills, Sling, Long Bow, 1500 XP
LEVEL 2 REQUIREMENTS	45 South Maple, 30 South Stone, 15 South Rock Dust, 2 Rare White Deer Skins, 40 Villagers
LEVEL 2 REWARDS	Double Bow, 3000 XP

After defeating the Attack of the Udam, Jayma appears on the mini-map to the southeast. Complete her On the Hunt mission and she comes by the village. Build her hut to unlock the sling and long bow in the crafting menu. The level 2 upgrade rewards you with her double bow. Jayma offers some valuable Hunting skills.

KAROOSH'S HUT

AVAILABLE	Complete Brother in Need mission, then talk to Karoosh
LEVEL 1 REQUIREMENTS	4 Alder Wood, 5 Slate, 2 Reeds, 4 Wolf Skins,
LEVEL 1 REWARDS	Fighting skills, Two-Handed Club, Winter Clothing, 1500 XP
LEVEL 2 REQUIREMENTS	30 North Cedar, 35 North Black Rock, 20 North Clay, Rare Stripe Wolf Skins, 40 Villagers
LEVEL 2 REWARDS	3000 XP

Finding Karoosh and completing the Brother in Need mission brings the warrior back to the village. Building his hut unlocks Fighting skills, the flashiest of the available talents. A variety of takedowns and beast riding skills give you a few satisfying ways of killing your foes. Karoosh also unlocks the extremely valuable Winter Clothing, allowing you to last longer in cold temperatures.

DAH'S HUT

AVAILABLE	Complete Wenja Welcome mission, then talk to Dah
LEVEL 1 REQUIREMENTS	15 North Cedar, 15 North Black Rock, 15 North Clay, Rare Black Dhole Skins, 40 Villagers
LEVEL 1 REWARDS	Udam skills, 1500 XP
LEVEL 2 REQUIREMENTS	35 North Cedar, 25 North Black Rock, 20 North Clay, Rare Two Horn Rhino Skin, 50 Villagers
LEVEL 2 REWARDS	3000 XP, unlocks a mission for Dah

Capture the Big Darwa Fort and complete the Wenja Welcome mission to bring this unwelcome guest back to the village. After talking to Dah, you can build his hut. The Berserk Bomb and Udam skills unlock with his arrival and hut build. His Melee Resistance skills can be a life saver against Chieftains.

ROSHANI'S HUT

AVAILABLE	Complete Seeds of the Sun mission then talk to Roshani
LEVEL 1 REQUIREMENTS	25 South Maple, 20 South Stone, 15 South Rock Dust, 2 Rare Red Elk Skin, 40 Villagers
LEVEL 1 REWARDS	Izila Skills, 1500 XP
LEVEL 2 REQUIREMENTS	50 South Maple, 40 South Stone, 30 South Rock Dust, 2 Rare Red Bitefish Skins, 50 Population
LEVEL 2 REWARDS	3000 XP

After capturing the Fire Screamer Fort, complete Roshani's Seeds of the Sun mission. Now you can build the Izila commander's hut. Bringing him back to the village unlocks the devastating Fire Bomb. Building his hut unlocks Izila skills, five extremely valuable fire abilities. Work toward these skills as soon as you get the him in your village.

WELCOME

SURVIVING THE WILD

LAND OF OROS

TAKKAR'S JOURNEY

MAJOR LANDMARKS

LOCATIONS

VILLAGE CONSTRUCTION

ENEMY TRIBES

WILDLIFE

GEAR

SKILLS

FOOD RECIPES

RESOURCES

COLLECTIBLES

TROPHIES/ ACHIEVEMENTS

THE ART OF OROS

ENEMY TRIBES

Two hostile tribes call Oros their home, Udam and Izila, and they both cause their share of trouble for the Wenja. The Udam are proficient with poison while the Izila have mastered fire. They both possess the same types of enemies: Warriors, Archers, Hunters, Spearmen, Slingers, Scourges, and Chieftains. All but the Chieftains have two versions, regular and elite. Typically Elite troops are the same as their counterpart but with head armor that must be broken before you can get a headshot. Their attributes differ slightly between the two clans, but their roles basically remain the same.

UDAM TRIBE

Making their base in the north snowy mountains, these Neanderthals have become fierce killers with a taste for human flesh. As they die out from disease, the Udam have recently started to move away from the comfort of their caverns, wreaking havoc on enemy tribes. Ull, their brutal leader, can't just sit back while his tribespeople perish. He declares war on those who encroach on his land and sets out to find a better future for his people.

The Udam use poison to block access to their homeland and valuables. They also use it in a poison bomb that eats away at your health. Fortunately, you also get a chance to use it on your enemies—causing them to attack each other. You can also counter their poison attacks by eating an Antidote.

ARCHER

ROLE	Primal Assaulter
HP	Medium
DAMAGE	Low
ATTACK FREQUENCY	Medium
RANGE	Medium/Long
MOVEMENT SPEED	Medium
SPECIAL	-
ELITE CHARACTERISTICS	Breakable Helmet

Archers are equipped with a bow, but their range is not that great. They shoot from cover, so getting a shot on them can be tough, but it's nothing a quick beast or lobbed bomb can't take care of.

CHIEFTAIN

ROLE	Anti-Beast Tank
HP	Very High
DAMAGE	Very High
ATTACK FREQUENCY	Slow
RANGE	Melee
MOVEMENT SPEED	Slow/Charge
SPECIAL	Elite only, Takedown requires Heavy Takedown skill
ELITE CHARACTERISTICS	Indestructible Helmet, Roar Charge

The powerful Chieftain takes and dishes out a lot of damage. In order to perform a takedown on him, you must purchase the Heavy Takedown skill. Outside of the Commander and Leader, these guys are the strongest members of the tribe with the ability to knock you down. Take them out early with stealth or your Owl. They do have the easiest time against your beast, so be sure to help when sending your companion after the foe. A Bear is a good match for these guys, allowing you to fight from longer range while it draws the enemy's focus. Chieftains are melee fighters, but they do have the ability to use throwables.

HUNTER

ROLE	Stealth
HP	Low
DAMAGE	Low
ATTACK FREQUENCY	Medium
RANGE	Medium/Long
MOVEMENT SPEED	Medium
SPECIAL	Poison Arrows
ELITE CHARACTERISTICS	Breakable Helmet

Hunters are much like Archers, but they are equipped with long-range bows and poison arrows—making them a much bigger threat. They tend to hide, so lob a sting bomb or fire bomb their way to drive them out. With their low health, they go down fairly easy, but if left standing too long, they pick away at your health from afar. If you get close, the Hunter pulls out his knife and takes a swing.

SCOURGE

ROLE	Area of Effect Unit
HP	High
DAMAGE	Low
ATTACK FREQUENCY	Slow
RANGE	Medium/Melee
MOVEMENT SPEED	Medium
SPECIAL	Poison Bomb
ELITE CHARACTERISTICS	Breakable Helmet

The Scourge lobs poison bombs from a medium range. The explosive does not need to hit you, as it has an area of effect. Making contact with the rot fumes poisons you, causing your health to slowly drain. This can be a problem unless you have the Antidote food recipe, which negates the effects of these projectiles.

SLINGER

ROLE	Primal Sniper
HP	Low
DAMAGE	Low
ATTACK FREQUENCY	Medium
RANGE	Long
MOVEMENT SPEED	Slow
SPECIAL	-
ELITE CHARACTERISTICS	Breakable Helmet, Blow Horn (to call for reinforcements)

Slingers are equipped with a sling that they use to great effect. flinging projectiles your way from a long distance. They are often positioned in guard positions such as on top of huts or watchtowers. The damage they cause is minimal, but it does add up. The Elite version becomes a much bigger threat when given a blow horn that can be used to call in reinforcements once danger is detected. These guys should be your first priority when taking on an outpost, bonfire, or fort. If there are multiple Slingers in an area, take them out as quietly as possible to prevent being spotted by the others. When close, the Slinger strikes with the sling.

SPEARMAN

ROLE	Melee/Range Hybrid
HP	Medium
DAMAGE	Medium
ATTACK FREQUENCY	Slow
RANGE	Melee/Medium
MOVEMENT SPEED	Medium
SPECIAL	Charge with Spear
ELITE CHARACTERISTICS	Breakable Helmet

The Spearman can be dangerous from a short distance and up close. They often sit back and throw their spear at you, but they can charge with their weapon for a melee attack. Watch out, as they have the ability to knock you down with this ability. The elite version only differs in that it wears breakable head armor. This must be destroyed before you can kill them with a headshot—unless, of course, you have the Precision Sling skill which allows the sling to pierce headgear.

WARRIOR

ROLE	Melee Unit
HP	Medium
DAMAGE	Low
ATTACK FREQUENCY	Fast
RANGE	Melee
MOVEMENT SPEED	Fast
SPECIAL	Throw Shard
ELITE CHARACTERISTICS	Breakable Helmet, Ambush

Warriors are the standard melee troops. They charge in with their clubs and start hacking away. They do throw a shard if they cannot get to you, but the cudgel is their weapon of choice. Pick them off as they approach or switch to your club and beat them down.

DAH - UDAM COMMANDER

Dah is a proud, ferocious, and sickly Udam war chief. One of the strongest fighters in the tribe, Dah commands the respect of all who follow him as he coordinates raiding parties and guards the gateway to the Udam homeland. Like all Udam, Dah fights to save his dying tribe from extinction—and he respects displays of dominance and strength above all else. He prides himself as the only Udam to have survived a duel with the tribe leader, Ull—a fight that won him great power and respect among his tribe.

Dah's strength has waned in recent months as crippling "skull fire" fevers sap his strength. This disease is one of many that afflict the Udam, the result of generations of inbreeding. The skull fires will eventually kill Dah, but until then he is determined to fight the contemptible Wenja softbloods and the fire-wielding sun walkers, two rival tribes that stand in the way of the Udam's survival.

WELCOME

SURVIVING THE WILD

LAND OF OROS

TAKKAR'S JOURNEY

MAJOR LANDMARKS

LOCATIONS

VILLAGE CONSTRUCTION

ENEMY TRIBES

UDAM

IZILA

WILDLIFE

GEAR

SKILLS

FOOD RECIPES

RESOURCES

COLLECTIBLES

TROPHIES/ ACHIEVEMENTS

THE ART OF OROS

ULL - UDAM LEADER

Ull is the leader of the Udam tribe. He commands the respect and fear of all Udam. He is a fierce brute with limbs of timber and severe fire burns across most of his body. His nose and ears have melted away, leaving him with a mottled mask. These hideous scars came from the deadly fire arrows of the Izila tribe.

He bears a heavy heart over the future of his people. It's clear that the Udam are dying. They suffer constant sickness, many Udam die young. He doesn't know why they are dying but he knows that rival tribes are not suffering in the same way and he wants them all wiped out. Anyone who encroaches on Udam land is an enemy who's taking advantage of Udam weakness.

The survival of his people is foremost in his mind as he marches through Oros, desperately fighting for more plentiful lands and to earn his people a chance to recover from their hard years deep in the frozen mountains.

 Ull is very primitive and really showcases the more primitive and animal aspect of human kind. Once you get to know him, you'll realize his motivations are deeper and more interesting than what you'll get from the beginning of the game. He is a strong antagonist.

— *Jean-Christophe Guyot, Creative Director*

IZILA TRIBE

The more advanced Izila live in the southern marshlands of Oros with fertile land ideal for farming. The tribe also has a firm grasp on everything fire. Their belief that they are superior to all other tribes leads them to enslave members of the Wenja and Udam. It is up to the Wenja to take the fight to the Izila and remove their leader before more of their tribe is taken. Their fire bomb is a devastating weapon which you gain late in the game.

Izila troops tend to have higher HP and damage than the Udam, requiring better weapons. This should be the case though as the story takes you to Izila territory later in the game when you are more powerful.

ARCHER

ROLE	Primal Assaulter
HP	High
DAMAGE	Medium
ATTACK FREQUENCY	Medium
RANGE	Medium/Long
MOVEMENT SPEED	Medium
SPECIAL	-
ELITE CHARACTERISTICS	Breakable Helmet

Unlike the Udam, the Izila use women in their army, as the Archers and Hunters. Archers shoot from cover so bring them out of hiding by sending in your beast or tossing a bomb. Of course it is better to kill them quietly with a headshot or takedown before being detected. The Izila Archers have more HP than their Udam counterparts so they may take more to kill.

CHIEFTAIN

ROLE	Anti-Beast Tank
HP	Very High
DAMAGE	Very High
ATTACK FREQUENCY	Slow
RANGE	Melee
MOVEMENT SPEED	Slow/Charge
SPECIAL	Elite only, Takedown requires Heavy Takedown skill
ELITE CHARACTERISTICS	Indestructible Helmet, Roar Charge, Fire Ground Strike

An elite-only troop, these guys are very similar to the Udam; they have a strong melee attack and are tough to kill. The Heavy Takedown skill is required to score a takedown. There is also a skill available for the Owl that allows it to eliminate a Chieftain. Make these guys an early priority, just after Elite Slingers and alarms. The stronger beasts, such as Bears or Tigers, are best against these foes; they beat down lesser animals with ease. This Izila carries a big, fire-lit torch that he slams against the ground for a devastating fire attack.

HUNTER

ROLE	Stealth
HP	Medium
DAMAGE	Medium
ATTACK FREQUENCY	Medium
RANGE	Medium/Long
MOVEMENT SPEED	Medium
SPECIAL	Fire Arrows
ELITE CHARACTERISTICS	Breakable Helmet

Hunters are similar to Archers except they shoot fire arrows and hide from their target. They are not as prevalent as Archers, stationed mostly at later locations. They do not light every arrow, shooting a few regular projectiles before igniting another. Watch out for their deadly attacks, breaking line of sight whenever possible. When up close, Hunters swing with their knives.

WELCOME

SURVIVING THE WILD

LAND OF OROS

TAKKAR'S JOURNEY

MAJOR LANDMARKS

LOCATIONS

VILLAGE CONSTRUCTION

ENEMY TRIBES

UDAM

IZILA

WILDLIFE

GEAR

SKILLS

FOOD RECIPES

RESOURCES

COLLECTIBLES

TROPHIES/ ACHIEVEMENTS

THE ART OF OROS

SCOURGE

ROLE	Area of Effect Unit
HP	High
DAMAGE	High
ATTACK FREQUENCY	Slow
RANGE	Medium/Melee
MOVEMENT SPEED	Medium
SPECIAL	Fire Bomb
ELITE CHARACTERISTICS	Breakable Helmet

The Izila Scourge lobs fire bombs. This makes them a much bigger threat than their Udam equivalent, since there is not an easy way to counter the attack like the Antidote. Their bomb sets an area on fire with the ability to spread quickly. Navigate away from the area when you notice one incoming. Scourge may not be as large a threat as the Chieftain or Slinger, but they do pose a danger.

SLINGER

ROLE	Primal Sniper
HP	Medium
DAMAGE	Medium
ATTACK FREQUENCY	Medium
RANGE	Long
MOVEMENT SPEED	Slow
SPECIAL	-
ELITE CHARACTERISTICS	Breakable Helmet, Blow Horn (to call for reinforcements)

In its regular form, the Slinger poses a relatively minor danger. Their sling does cause decent damage from a long distance, but as long as you break line of sight, they cannot hurt you. Elite Slingers possess a blow horn though, giving them the ability to call in reinforcements whenever they detect an enemy. They are great targets for your Owl. Make these guys a high priority. Remember that alarms are just as dangerous and anyone can use them.

SPEARMAN

ROLE	Melee/Range Hybrid
HP	High
DAMAGE	High
ATTACK FREQUENCY	Slow
RANGE	Melee/Medium
MOVEMENT SPEED	Medium
SPECIAL	Charge with Spear
ELITE CHARACTERISTICS	Breakable Helmet

Izila Spearmen are fairly dangerous with high HP and damage, though their attacks are less frequent than others. They usually sit back and throw spears your way, but will charge in for a melee attack when given the chance. Elite Spearmen only differ in that they wear headgear that must be destroyed before you can get a headshot.

The Mesolithic Age was a period of great change. Humans were settling and forming tribes, language was becoming more advanced, and wars emerged between tribes. We wanted our tribes to reflect these changing times. The Udam reflect the past, the Wenja live in the present, at one with Nature, while the Izila consider themselves the future— a dark, unforgiving future.

—Kevin Shortt, Lead Writer

WARRIOR

ROLE	Melee Unit
HP	High
DAMAGE	Medium
ATTACK FREQUENCY	Fast
RANGE	Melee
MOVEMENT SPEED	Fast
SPECIAL	Throw Shard
ELITE CHARACTERISTICS	Breakable Helmet, Ambush, Dodge

The Izila Warriors fight primarily at close range with their club, but they do throw a shard if you are not reachable. Their high HP makes them tough to pick off as they charge, so be ready to switch to your melee weapon. Elite Warriors are more advanced. Besides their breakable headgear, they attempt to ambush their target and dodge your attacks.

ROSHANI - IZILA COMMANDER

Roshani is a proud but paranoid Izila Commander. He leads an impressive Izila fortress that has never suffered any threats from rival tribes. Like many Izila, Roshani has prideful faith in the Izila's place in the world. He's led a sedentary life and has limited combat experience. He earned his command through charm and manipulation. He can easily talk his way out of troubles or into new opportunities.

Roshani has made enemies among the Izila over the years. He's known as a man who puts himself before all else, including his own people. It's a reputation that could catch up with him one day soon—and he knows it.

BATARI - IZILA LEADER

Batari is the divine matriarch of the Izila tribe. Zealous, vindictive, and arrogant, she has ushered her people into a new age of agrarian prosperity with the harsh but benevolent hand of a spiritual leader. Batari has enjoyed the reverence of the Izila ever since she was born during a solar eclipse and deemed a descendant of the sun goddess, Suxli. The Izila people now venerate her as the "sun daughter," a divine savior who will protect them from danger.

Like the Izila sun goddess, Batari presents herself as an icon of warmth, nourishment, and fertility. But beneath her warm exterior burns the heart of a prideful tyrant consumed by vanity and paranoia. She is obsessed with superiority—first over her fellow tribespeople, and second over the inhuman Wenja and Udam pests that populate other tribes.

Only one name haunts the Izila matriarch: Krati, the name of her beloved son. He betrayed Batari's trust many years ago and sparked a revolt, forcing Batari to burn him alive for his crimes. She uses the myth of Krati the Destroyer to keep the Izila under her thumb, but deep down she fears her son will one day return to kill her.

WILDLIFE

A variety of wildlife makes Oros their home. From the venomous Adders to the giant Elder Mammoths, animals of all types wander the land and many present a danger, but not all. Always beware of the animals around you, as some tend to come out of nowhere and attack. There are a number of ways to lessen the danger. Take along a beast to protect you from surprise attacks; eat a scent camouflage to lessen the likelihood of being detected; or tame a Badger to scare the creatures away.

The health and damage ratings of each animal found in Oros, as well as whether they are tamable, are given in the following table. Skinning animals can give animal fat, meat, and animal hide. Plus most animals give a specific skin, which is used in crafting and upgrading. The skin received and difficulty to hunt each animal is also given. Stats are based on a ranking system of 0 to 5. For example, a "-" in damage translates to an animal that does not hurt you. A health of "1" means one hit kills it. A "5" is given to the most powerful beasts and means you need a plan and possibly a tough beast companion to take it out. The Notes column gives extra details for the wildlife.

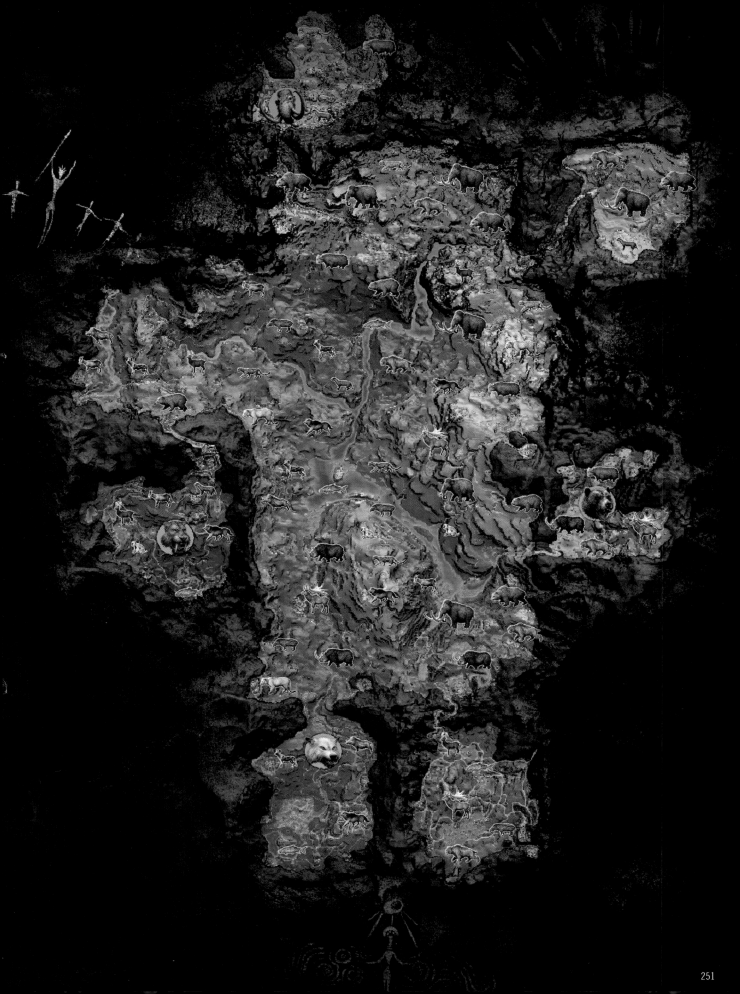

OROS FAUNA

ANIMAL NAME	SKIN	HUNTING DIFFICULTY	HEALTH	DAMAGE	TAMABLE?	NOTE
Adder	-	Very Easy	1	2	No	Snakes are tough to spot unless Hunter Vision is enabled. They poison if allowed to attack.
Badger	Badger Skin	Hard	3	2	Yes	Catch a Badger and take it along on your hunts to keep unwanted predators at bay. These guys are tough for their size so do not underestimate them. They do not fear fire.
Beehive	Bee Cluster	Very Easy	1	2	No	Beehives are only an issue if you decide to attack. If the bees swarm you, hold the Heal button to shoo them away. Simply interact with the hive to grab a bee cluster for your resources.
Bitefish	Bitefish Skin	Medium	2	2	No	Scan water before going for a swim to avoid being bitten by a Bitefish. Use a spear on the fish and then dive in for the skin.
Bloodfang Sabretooth	Sabretooth Tiger Skin	Very Hard	5	5	Yes	Tame this powerful beast after completing the Bloodfang Sabretooth Hunt. Once tamed, it may never leave your side.
Bloodtusk Mammoth	Mammoth Skin	Very Hard	5	5	No	The Bloodtusk Mammoth is the only Beast Master Hunt that doesn't result in a tamed beast. Refer to our Secondary Quests chapter for details on the hunt.
Brown Bear	Brown Bear Skin	Hard	4	3	Yes	The Brown Bear is another great addition as a beast, but it does pose a danger for low to medium level players. They can swim and are not afraid of fire.
Boar	Boar Skin	Medium	2	2	No	Boars will attack unprovoked, but they are fairly easy kills.
Cave Bear	Cave Bear Skin	Very Hard	5	4	Yes	Tame the Cave Bear at first chance for a strong beast companion. If you decide to fight it, bring along a strong animal of your own. They can swim and do not fear fire.
Cave Lion	Cave Lion Skin	Hard	3	3	Yes	These felines are quick so be ready to switch to your melee weapon when one approaches. They are able to climb short ledges.
Crocodile	-	Easy	2	3	No	Crocodiles lie in wait in bodies of water. Use Hunter Vision to make sure there isn't one in your path. Shoot an arrow in its big head to get an easy kill and collect the skin.
Deer	Deer Skin	Medium	2	-	No	Deer are fairly easy kills and they do not attack, but they are quick to flee a scene. Sic your fast cat on it or take a Scent Camouflage to sneak up on it.
Dhole	Dhole Skin	Easy	1	1	Yes	Dholes are also quick, but they are even easier takedowns. Just one or two hits with your club will do it. They are aggressive and come to you. Early on though, packs of Dholes can be overwhelming.
Eagle	Feather	Medium	1	2	No	Eagles only bother you at high locations. If you hear its screech, spot it in the air and ready your bow or club. Time your shot to knock it out of the air. Dealing with these guys is a must for The Peak of Oros mission.
Elder Mammoth	Mammoth Skin	Very Hard	5	5	No	Do not provoke the Elder Mammoths unless you are ready for a big fight. Take along a powerful beast like a Bear or Sabretooth. They do not fear fire.

ANIMAL NAME	SKIN	HUNTING DIFFICULTY	HEALTH	DAMAGE	TAMABLE?	NOTE
Fish	-	Very Easy	1	-	No	Besides the Bitefish, the fish in the waterways are passive.
Goat	Goat Skin	Easy	1	-	No	Goats are found everywhere in Oros. They do not attack and are easy kills.
Great Scar Bear		Very Hard	5	5	Yes	Complete this hunt quest to tame the beast. This animal is a very powerful asset.
Gull	Feather	Very Easy	1	-	No	
Jaguar	Jaguar Skin	Medium	2	2	Yes	Jaguars are quick and stealthy. Be ready to quickly switch to your club if one attacks. They can also climb.
Leopard	Leopard Skin	Hard	3	2	Yes	Leopards are tougher kills than Jaguars. Be ready for their attacks. Having the Badger beside you or taking the Scent Camouflage helps keep them away. They are very stealthy and can climb.
Lizard	-	Very Easy	1	-	No	
Mammoth	Mammoth Skin	Hard	4	3	No	Similar to the Elder Mammoth but they are smaller, have less health, and less damage. These young Mammoths are able to call an Elder Mammoth for help, so beware. They do not fear fire. They can be ridden with the Mammoth Rider skill.
Monkey	Monkey Skin	Easy	1	-	No	Monkey skins are required for an upgrade, so you need to kill a few of these guys. They quickly run away, so try a stealthy approach.
Rare Black Jaguar	Rare Black Jaguar Skin	Medium	3	3	Yes	The rare version of the Jaguar. Look for it in packs of the regular cats.
Rare Black Lion	Rare Black Lion Skin	Hard	3	3	Yes	The rare version of the Cave Lion.
Rare Dhole	Rare Black Dhole Skin	Easy	2	1	Yes	Look for the Rare Dhole in packs of the dogs.
Rare Red Bitefish	Rare Red Bitefish Skin	Easy	2	3	No	The Rare Red Bitefish is the subject of The Biter in the Deep mission. The skin gained from that quest helps in building Roshani's hut.
Rare Red Elk	Rare Red Elk Skin	Very Hard	4	3	No	The rare version of the Tall Elk, required for Roshani's hut.
Rare Stripe Wolf	Rare Stripe Wolf Skin	Medium	3	3	Yes	Search for this rare canine in Wolf packs. The Wolf Beast Kill quest guarantees at least one.

ANIMAL NAME	SKIN	HUNTING DIFFICULTY	HEALTH	DAMAGE	TAMABLE?	NOTE
Rare Two Horn Rhino	Rare Two Horn Rhino Skin	Hard	4	4	No	Look for this rare Rhinoceros in packs of the Rhinos. Look out for its charge attack which can do serious damage with its two horns. Jump out of the way to avoid it.
Rare White Deer	Rare White Deer Skin	Medium	2	-	No	The rare version of the Deer is just as easy to kill as the regular one, but you may have to chase it down.
Rare White Wolf	Rare White Wolf Skin	Medium	2	3	Yes	Another rare Wolf, found within packs of the canines. Your first tamed beast is a White Wolf in the Beast Master mission.
Rare White Yak	Rare White Yak Skin	Medium	3	2	No	Just like the regular Yak, the rare white one is weak, but it does take a few hits with a spear to take it down.
Rat	-	Very Easy	1	-	No	Rats are tiny targets and only supply meat upon their death.
Raven	Feather	Very Easy	1	-	No	A Raven kill is necessary in the Fly Like a Bird mission. Otherwise, they can be ignored...unless you need feathers.
Sabretooth Tiger	Sabretooth Tiger Skin	Very Hard	4	4	Yes	The Sabretooth Tiger is the most powerful regular feline. Watch out for its pounce and tame one right away. They are able to climb, so keep that in mind when fleeing their attack.
Small Bitefish	Bitefish Skin	Easy	1	2	No	A smaller Bitefish, but it can still hurt you with its bite. Use Hunter Vision to spot them in the water.
Snowblood Wolf	Wolf Skin	Very Hard	4	4	Yes	Another epic animal that must be defeated in a Beast Master Hunt quest. It attacks with a big pack of Wolves, so be ready with your torch.
Snow Bird	Feather	Very Easy	1	-	No	A Snow Bird kill is necessary in the Fly Like a Bird mission. Otherwise, they can be ignored...unless you need feathers.
Tapir	Tapir Skin	Easy	2	-	No	These boar-like mammals are passive and do not flee very fast, making them a very easy kill. These animals only come out at night.
Tall Elk	Tall Elk Skin	Very Hard	3	3	No	The Tall Elk is hunted in Jayma's second mission. Its charge attack does serious damage and it takes some abuse. Pull out the spear for this one and send your beast after it. It will flee, so use Hunter Vision to pick up its trail if necessary. Watch out as it switches between passive and aggressive very quickly.
Tortoise	-	Very Easy	1	-	No	Tortoises are very easy kills with your club, though they tend to hide in their shell. A few hits knock it out even through the armor. They only provide meat, so not a required kill, except for Fly Like Bird quest.
Wolf	Wolf Skin	Medium	2	2	Yes	Wolves tend to run around in packs, but each one is an easy kill with the club. They are easily tamed.
Woolly Rhino	Woolly Rhino Skin	Hard	4	4	No	Get out your spear for this beast. He is relatively passive until provoked, so be careful. His horn can cause some damage and he does not fear fire.
Yak	Yak Skin	Medium	2	2	No	Yaks are fairly weak for their size, but can still do some damage with their charge.

A BEAST BY YOUR SIDE

Beasts that have a "Yes" in the tamable column above can be added to your beast roster with a piece of bait. Toss the bait nearby and wait for the animal to show interest. Hold the interact button to tame it. If a beast is killed, you can heal it with a piece of meat before the timer runs out. Beyond that, you must revive it from the Beast menu with a certain number of Red Leaves.

▶ **CALL BEAST**   Press Right on the D-Pad to open the Beasts Menu, highlight a beast, and then confirm to call the selected animal. Stats and special abilities are listed when highlighting a beast.

▶ **REVIVE**   When your beast dies, press Right on the D-Pad to open the Beasts Menu, highlight the beast and then confirm on its picture to revive it. There is a cost for this action, so pay attention to your supplies.

▶ **COMMAND**   Hold the Aim button and press the Throwable button to send the beast to a destination or after an enemy.

▶ **RECALL BEAST** Hold Right on the D-Pad and the beast returns to your side.

Beasts are a powerful addition to your attacks, plus they have unique abilities that can help out in other aspects of play. Some are better at stealth, while others excel at damage. Dholes skin their kills. Bears collect resources when idle. Select the beast that best assists in your current endeavor.

CANINES

REQUIRED SKILL   Tame Canines

DHOLE

STRENGTH	1
SPEED	2
STEALTH	4
REVIVE COST	Red Leaf
PASSIVE ABILITY 1	Skins carcasses and gathers resources for you after making a kill.

Dholes are available just after completing the Beast Master mission. Take one along for the convenience in collecting skins.

RARE DHOLE

STRENGTH	2
SPEED	2
STEALTH	4
REVIVE COST	Red Leaf
PASSIVE ABILITY 1	Skins carcasses and gathers resources for you after making a kill.

The Rare Dhole is a little stronger than the regular Dhole, making it a slightly better choice as a companion. Dholes are resistant to fire.

WOLF

STRENGTH	1
SPEED	3
STEALTH	3
REVIVE COST	Red Leaf
PASSIVE ABILITY 1	Growls to warn of nearby enemies or predators.
PASSIVE ABILITY 2	Reveals 350 feet of terrain around you in the Map menu. Reveals more territory on your mini-map.

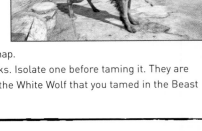

Wolves can be found across most of Oros, but they tend to hunt in packs. Isolate one before taming it. They are weak, but fast. It's not really worth calling in a Wolf when you can get the White Wolf that you tamed in the Beast Master mission.

WHITE WOLF

STRENGTH	2
SPEED	3
STEALTH	3
REVIVE COST	Red Leaf
PASSIVE ABILITY 1	Growls to warn of nearby enemies or predators.
PASSIVE ABILITY 2	Reveals 350 feet of terrain around you in the Map menu. Reveals more territory on your mini-map.

The first beast tamed is the White Wolf in Tensay's Beast Master mission. He is a decent first beast, but is quickly replaced. Keeping it by your side clears out the map fog quicker.

RARE STRIPE WOLF

STRENGTH	3
SPEED	3
STEALTH	3
REVIVE COST	Red Leaf
PASSIVE ABILITY 1	Growls to warn of nearby enemies or predators.
PASSIVE ABILITY 2	Reveals 350 feet of terrain around you in the Map menu. Reveals more territory on your mini-map.

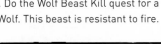

The Rare Stripe Wolf can sometimes be found with a pack of Wolves. Do the Wolf Beast Kill quest for a guaranteed sighting. As a companion, it is very similar to the White Wolf. This beast is resistant to fire.

WILDCATS

WELCOME

SURVIVING
THE WILD

LAND OF OROS

TAKKAR'S JOURNEY

MAJOR LANDMARKS

LOCATIONS

VILLAGE
CONSTRUCTION

ENEMY TRIBES

WILDLIFE

GEAR

SKILLS

FOOD RECIPES

RESOURCES

COLLECTIBLES

TROPHIES/
ACHIEVEMENTS

THE ART OF OROS

REQUIRED SKILL   Tame Wildcats

JAGUAR

STRENGTH	2
SPEED	4
STEALTH	5
REVIVE COST	Red Leaf
PASSIVE ABILITY 1	Attacks unsuspecting targets without alerting nearby enemies.

Jaguars are found in western and southern Oros. They are ideal for stealth situations with the ability to take down unsuspecting foes without alerting others. Take one along when capturing outposts for added support. They also have great speed, allowing them to chase down any target.

RARE BLACK JAGUAR

STRENGTH	3
SPEED	4
STEALTH	5
REVIVE COST	Red Leaf
PASSIVE ABILITY 1	Attacks unsuspecting targets without alerting nearby enemies.

Find the Rare Black Jaguar mixed in with other Jaguars. Just like the Jaguar, it excels at stealth and speed. Be sure to tame it as soon as you get a chance; it is a very handy beast to have at your beck and call. The Rare Black Jaguar is resistant to fire.

LEOPARD

STRENGTH	3
SPEED	4
STEALTH	4
REVIVE COST	Red Leaf
PASSIVE ABILITY 1	Tags nearby animals within a small radius.

The Leopard is the fastest feline, allowing it to chase down any fleeing animals. It also has the ability to move quietly; if you crouch, it crouches.

CAVE LION

STRENGTH	3
SPEED	3
STEALTH	3
REVIVE COST	Red Leaf x2
PASSIVE ABILITY 1	Tags nearby enemies within a small radius.

The Cave Lion is the most balanced of the wildcats. With decent speed and stealth, it is a decent choice for hunting and capturing an enemy location. The ability to tag nearby animals makes it the ultimate hunting companion.

RARE BLACK LION

STRENGTH	4
SPEED	3
STEALTH	3
REVIVE COST	Red Leaf x2
PASSIVE ABILITY 1	Tags nearby enemies within a small radius.

The Black Lion is tough to find, but it does make appearances where Cave Lions are found. It shares similar stats to the Cave Lion, making it a good companion for most situations. It is resistant to fire.

APEX PREDATORS

REQUIRED SKILL   Tame Apex Predators

BROWN BEAR

STRENGTH	4
SPEED	3
STEALTH	2
REVIVE COST	Red Leaf x2
PASSIVE ABILITY 1	Draws enemy attacks in battle.
PASSIVE ABILITY 2	Uncovers and gives you nearby resources when you stand idle.

The Brown Bear is found all across Oros, so pick one up soon after learning the Tame Apex Predators skill. It is very strong with decent speed. It acts as a tank, drawing an enemy's attacks, plus it collects nearby resources when you stand idle. It is a great choice when taking on the bigger, slower wildlife.

SABRETOOTH TIGER

STRENGTH	4
SPEED	5
STEALTH	3
REVIVE COST	Red Leaf x4
PASSIVE ABILITY 1	The fastest predator in Oros.

The Sabretooth Tiger roams throughout Oros and is one of the better standard beasts that can be tamed. It has good strength, speed, and stealth. It takes down its prey mercilessly, climbing on top of the bigger predators and bringing them to the ground. Try out a Tiger on a hunt or capture and you may never use another beast. This beast is ridable (requires the Beast Rider skill).

My favorite beast? The Sabretooth Tiger, he is the king of the jungle!

— *Jean-Sébastien Decant, Narrative Director*

CUNNING BEASTS

WELCOME

SURVIVING
THE WILD

LAND OF OROS

TAKKAR'S JOURNEY

MAJOR LANDMARKS

LOCATIONS

VILLAGE
CONSTRUCTION

ENEMY TRIBES

WILDLIFE

GEAR

SKILLS

FOOD RECIPES

RESOURCES

COLLECTIBLES

TROPHIES/
ACHIEVEMENTS

THE ART OF OROS

REQUIRED SKILL   Tame Cunning Beasts

BADGER

STRENGTH	3
SPEED	1
STEALTH	3
REVIVE COST	Red Leaf x2
PASSIVE ABILITY 1	A fearless beast that can revive itself from death once.
PASSIVE ABILITY 2	Terrifies all wildlife in Oros.

The Badger, found between the western and southern forests of Oros, is extremely handy as a companion. It is not very fast and is only moderately strong, but its ability to ward off wildlife is huge when hunting. It goes down fairly quickly, but it does revive itself once. The Badger is immune to poison.

> My favorite beast companion is the Honey Badger; he is the most vicious animal. It's very funny that one of the smallest animals in the food chain survived among bigger beasts. Each player should try to pet one a few times.
>
> — *Fabien Govini, Level Design Director*

CAVE BEAR

STRENGTH	5
SPEED	3
STEALTH	1
REVIVE COST	Red Leaf x4
PASSIVE ABILITY 1	Draws enemy attacks in battle.

Cave Bears are mostly found to the north, but do make appearances elsewhere. It is the strongest of the regular beasts and surprisingly quick. This beast is great against higher-health enemies, but do not plan to go undetected with it by your side. Its ability to draw an enemy's attacks and high health make it a great tank.

GREAT BEASTS

REQUIRED SKILL None

SNOWBLOOD WOLF

STRENGTH	4
SPEED	3
STEALTH	4
REVIVE COST	Red Leaf x3
PASSIVE ABILITY 1	Growls to warn of nearby enemies or predators.
PASSIVE ABILITY 2	Reveals +350 feet of terrain around you in the Map menu. Reveals more territory on your mini-map.

Complete the Snowblood Wolf hunt to tame this canine. Its stats are well balanced. Like other dogs, it warns of nearby enemies by growling. It also reveals a wider range in the mini-map and Map menu. Its lack of stealth make it a poor choice when trying to go undetected.

BLOODFANG SABRETOOTH

STRENGTH	5
SPEED	5
STEALTH	3
REVIVE COST	Red Leaf x5
PASSIVE ABILITY 1	Very fast predator.

To get the Bloodfang Sabretooth, you must hunt it down in the Beast Master Hunt quest. It is a good choice for almost any situation. It isn't the strongest or stealthiest, it isn't even the fastest, but it still does a great job in all three areas. It can take down the biggest and strongest foes, chase down most wildlife, and still fight by your side against an enemy tribe—remaining undetected.

GREAT SCAR BEAR

STRENGTH	5
SPEED	3
STEALTH	2
REVIVE COST	Red Leaf x5
PASSIVE ABILITY 1	Draws enemy attacks in battle.

The Great Scar Bear must be defeated as part of the Beast Master Hunts before gaining access to the beast. The Bear is very powerful and relatively fast for its size, though leave this one at home if you wish to remain undetected. It does a good job as the tank, drawing the focus of the enemy while you pick them off from afar. It can go longer between feedings than other beasts, but still keep an eye on its health.

GEAR

As you progress through the story and bring back specialists, weapons, bags, and tools become available in the Crafting menu. Weapon upgrades make you more effective in combat. Bags allow you to carry more resources and weapons. A few tools are required to take advantage of what Oros has to offer. Note resources needed for later upgrades and seek them out in Oros.

 This is the first Far Cry to move away from guns, but it retains its FPS feel. What challenges did this create for the team?

We knew that going back to the Stone Age meant reinventing our core gameplay loop. Without access to guns or vehicles, we had tons of work to do! We created new mechanics as part of this, first and foremost; the ability to tame all the predators in the world and use them as weapons. This alone will add new ways to engage with your enemy; this is what we like to call "The Beast Master". We also looked at the life of people in the Stone Age and translated that into our new core mechanics. This includes everything from the ability to track animal blood trails, to new combat styles with, among many other things, clubs, spears, and bows while having the option of combining those with fire if you are up for it.

—Clark Davies, Lead Game Designer

WEAPONS

Weapons crafted with the materials found around Oros come in four varieties: bows, clubs, spears, and throwables. This latter category includes bombs, shards, and traps. Bait is also considered a throwable, but it is definitely no weapon. Though it does work to distract a hungry animal.

SLING

UNLOCKED FOR CRAFTING

UPGRADE 1	Build Jayma's Hut

CRAFTING REQUIREMENTS

SLING	South Maple x4, South Stone x2, Animal Hide x8

CONTROLS Hold Down on the D-Pad to prepare the sling. Release to throw.

The sling throws rocks faster, farther, and with more damage. Headshots can kill enemies. With unlimited damage, this is a great choice when picking off unsuspecting foes from a distance. Get the Precision Sling skill to pierce enemy headgear.

BOW

UNLOCKED FOR CRAFTING

UPGRADE 1	Unlocked during Path to Oros
UPGRADE 2	Build Takkar's Cave

CRAFTING REQUIREMENTS

UPGRADE 1	Alder Wood x5, Slate x2, Reeds x2
UPGRADE 2	South Stone x6, South Rock Dust x8

STATS

BOW	Damage	Accuracy	Rate of Fire
UPGRADE 1	3	6	5
UPGRADE 2	4	7	8

WEAPON WHEEL REQUIREMENTS Hardwood per Arrow

The bow is a balanced and versatile long-range weapon with great accuracy. The second upgrade adds rapid fire capability, loading and firing arrows very quickly. The bow has better range than the sling, so use this when farther out. The bow is great for headshots on regular enemies. Collect your spent arrows when possible or you could use up Hardwood reserves in a hurry.

LONG BOW

UNLOCKED FOR CRAFTING

UPGRADE 1	Build Jayma's Hut

CRAFTING REQUIREMENTS

UPGRADE 1	North Cedar x14, North Black Rock x12, North Clay x10

STATS

WEAPON	Damage	Accuracy	Rate of Fire
UPGRADE 1	5	9	4

WEAPON WHEEL REQUIREMENTS Hardwood per Arrow

The long bow is slow to draw, but provides increased damage and aim zoom for unmatched long range precision. It is slower than the regular bow, but its improved damage and accuracy make it better in stealth situations.

DOUBLE BOW

UNLOCKED FOR CRAFTING

UPGRADE 1	Upgrade Jayma's Hut to Level 2

CRAFTING REQUIREMENTS

DOUBLE BOW	Rare North Cedar x5, Rare South Maple x5, Rare Reeds x5

STATS

WEAPON	Damage	Accuracy	Rate of Fire
DOUBLE BOW	6	8	6

WEAPON WHEEL REQUIREMENTS Hardwood per Arrow

The double bow offers fast performance, loading and firing two arrows at once. It has the best damage of the bows, but it spends twice as many arrows. The cost for crafting is fairly steep, at three rare resources, but easily doable as you explore the far reaches of Oros.

CLUB

UNLOCKED FOR CRAFTING

UPGRADE 1	Reach campfire in Path to Oros
UPGRADE 2	Build Tensay's and Sayla's Huts
UPGRADE 3	Build Takkar's Cave
UPGRADE 4	Upgrade 3

CRAFTING REQUIREMENTS

UPGRADE 1	Alder Wood x3
UPGRADE 2	Build Sayla's Hut and Tensay's Hut
UPGRADE 3	South Maple x12, South Rock Dust x6, South Stone x4
UPGRADE 4	Rare South Maple x3, Rare South Stone x2

STATS

WEAPON	Damage	Durability	Agility
UPGRADE 1	3	4	4
UPGRADE 2	4	4	5
UPGRADE 3	6	6	6
UPGRADE 4	7	8	8

WEAPON WHEEL REQUIREMENTS   Hardwood x2, Flint x2, Animal Hide

Clubs are powerful and fast attacking weapons with high durability. Throw them to stun your enemy and then rush in with a follow up attack. With a club you can hit multiple enemies in one swing. Hold the attack button for a heavy attack, though you are vulnerable during this charge time. This is your best option for close combat, so always have it ready.

TWO-HANDED CLUB

UNLOCKED FOR CRAFTING

UPGRADE 1	Build Karoosh's Hut
UPGRADE 2	Upgrade 1

CRAFTING REQUIREMENTS

UPGRADE 1	North Cedar x8, Bone x8
UPGRADE 2	Rare North Cedar x2, Blood of Oros x2, North Clay x10

STATS

WEAPON	Damage	Durability	Agility
UPGRADE 1	5	5	1
UPGRADE 2	9	8	4

WEAPON WHEEL REQUIREMENTS   Hardwood x2, Flint x2, Animal Hide

Two-handed clubs deal great damage when swung or thrown. They are heavy and slow, so pace yourself and prepare your attacks. Swing to hit multiple enemies, can kill enemies when thrown.

BLOOD SHASTI CLUB

UNLOCKED FOR CRAFTING

UPGRADE 1	ULC

A bloodstained cudgel of bone and teeth wielded by Ull, the vicious leader of the Udam. It is also unbreakable but consumed by fire.

SPEAR

UNLOCKED FOR CRAFTING

UPGRADE 1	Complete Deep Wounds mission
UPGRADE 2	Upgrade 1
UPGRADE 3	Upgrade 2
UPGRADE 4	Upgrade 3
UPGARDE 5	Upgrade 4

CRAFTING REQUIREMENTS

UPGRADE 1	Alder Wood x4, Slate x2, Reeds
UPGRADE 2	North Cedar x6, Reeds x6, Bone x6
UPGRADE 3	North Cedar x12, North Black Rock x8, North Clay x6
UPGRADE 4	South Maple x10, Rare South Stone, South Stone x10
UPGRADE 5	Rare South Maple x3, Rare South Stone x3

STATS

WEAPON	Damage	Durability	Agility
UPGRADE 1	1	2	2
UPGRADE 2	2	3	2
UPGRADE 3	4	4	3
UPGRADE 4	4	5	4
UPGRADE 5	6	7	6

WEAPON WHEEL REQUIREMENTS   Hardwood x3, Flint x2, Animal Hide x2

Spears are great defensive weapons with long reach. Throw them for high damage. They are not very effective in close combat, but can be used to scare off fire-fearing wildlife if lit. The spear is great against bigger animals, especially if you can get a headshot with a throw. Grab the Weapon Agility skill to improve the spear throw.

STING BOMB

UNLOCKED FOR CRAFTING

UPGRADE 1	Build Takkar's Cave

CRAFTING REQUIREMENTS

UPGRADE 1	Animal Hide x4, Bee Cluster x2

WEAPON WHEEL REQUIREMENTS Bee Cluster, Animal Hide

Sting bombs are bags filled with angry bees. Throw at your enemies and run. Toss one or two into a group of enemies to stir things up. Great fun when dropped from your Owl. Pick up the Owl: Weapon Drop skill to do so.

BERSERK BOMB

UNLOCKED FOR CRAFTING

UPGRADE 1	Capture Udam Big Darwa Fort

CRAFTING REQUIREMENTS

UPGRADE 1	Clay Pot x6, North Yellow Leaf x12

WEAPON WHEEL REQUIREMENTS North Yellow Leaf x2, Clay Pot

Throw berserk bombs at human enemies to drive them berserk, making them attack others. Increase your odds by pitting the enemy against itself. Pick up the Owl: Weapon Drop skill to drop poison from the sky.

FIRE BOMB

UNLOCKED FOR CRAFTING

UPGRADE 1	Capture Izila Fire Screamer Fort

CRAFTING REQUIREMENTS

UPGRADE 1	Clay Pot x4, Animal Fat x12

WEAPON WHEEL REQUIREMENTS Animal Fat x2, Clay Pot

Fire bombs are thrown and shatter on impact, igniting enemies and animals. Fire is great against enemies and many wildlife. The Izila are strong against the element, but otherwise fire is the way to go. The Owl: Weapon Drop allows for dropping fire on unsuspecting foes below. Fire Takedown adds a fire bomb to a standard takedown, igniting nearby enemies too.

STONE SHARD

UNLOCKED FOR CRAFTING

UPGRADE 1	Complete Blood of Oros mission
UPGRADE 2	Upgrade 1

CRAFTING REQUIREMENTS

UPGRADE 1	Blood of Oros x3, Animal Hide x4
UPGRADE 2	Rare South Stone x4, Animal Hide x8

WEAPON WHEEL REQUIREMENTS Flint, Animal Hide

Stone shards are thrown to damage enemies, headshots are lethal. Upgrade 2 can penetrate through most enemy masks. The Shard Takedown skill adds a second victim to your takedowns. Just after the first victim gets hit, an icon appears on a second. Tap the given button to kill him with a shard.

POISON SHARD

UNLOCKED FOR CRAFTING

UPGRADE 1	Build Wogah's Hut

CRAFTING REQUIREMENTS

UPGRADE 1	Blood of Oros x3, Animal Hide x8, Rare North Yellow Leaf

WEAPON WHEEL REQUIREMENTS Flint, North Yellow Leaf

Throw poison shards at human enemies to drive them berserk, making them attack others. Pick one of the stronger enemies to hit with the poison, turning him against his allies.

KAPALA SHARD

UNLOCKED FOR CRAFTING

UPGRADE 1	UPlay reward. Complete intro. Loading screen might be required before accessing weapon.

CRAFTING REQUIREMENTS

UPGRADE 1	UPlay reward

WEAPON WHEEL REQUIREMENTS Bones x2

A deadly throwing shard made from sharp bones. This shard is earned as part of the Ubisoft Club. Simply login and complete the intro to receive the weapon.

BAGS

The various bags in Far Cry Primal are a huge convenience as they are upgraded. They greatly increase the amount of resources, food, and weapons you can carry. Go for the upgrades that help your tendencies first. If you use a lot of arrows, increase the quiver size. If the beast companion is your favorite way to kill, improve the guts bag.

ARROW QUIVER

UNLOCKED FOR CRAFTING

UPGRADE 1	Reach Oros
UPGRADE 2	Upgrade 1
UPGRADE 3	Upgrade 2
UPGRADE 4	Upgrade 3

CRAFTING REQUIREMENTS

UPGRADE 1	Dhole Skin x3
UPGRADE 2	Feathers x2
UPGRADE 3	Brown Bear Skin x4
UPGRADE 4	Rare Feathers x4

STATS

QUIVER	# of Arrows Carried
BEFORE UPGRADE	8
UPGRADE 1	16
UPGRADE 2	24
UPGRADE 3	32
UPGRADE 4	48

Your arrow quiver holds eight arrows at first. Upgrade to increase the number of arrows that can be carried. It also allows you to carry more Hardwood, since you can immediately transfer some into arrows.

GUTS BAG

UNLOCKED FOR CRAFTING

UPGRADE 1	Reach Oros
UPGRADE 2	Upgrade 1
UPGRADE 3	Upgrade 2
UPGRADE 4	Upgrade 3

CRAFTING REQUIREMENTS

UPGRADE 1	Boar Skin x2
UPGRADE 2	Dhole Skin x4
UPGRADE 3	Yak Skin x5
UPGRADE 4	Tall Elk Skin x5

STATS

GUTS BAG	# Bait	# Meat	# Animal Fat
BEFORE UPGRADE	2	8	8
UPGRADE 1	3	12	12
UPGRADE 2	6	20	20
UPGRADE 3	8	32	32
UPGRADE 4	10	40	40

You receive the guts bag once you reach Oros. At first, it carries two Bait, eight Meat, and eight Animal Fat. The initial Guts Bag fills extremely quickly as you hunt, so upgrade with various skins as soon as possible.

CLUB BELT

UNLOCKED FOR CRAFTING

UPGRADE 1	Complete Trapped mission
UPGRADE 2	Upgrade 1
UPGRADE 3	Upgrade 2
UPGRADE 4	Upgrade 3

CRAFTING REQUIREMENTS

UPGRADE 1	Dhole Skin x3
UPGRADE 2	Jaguar Skin x3
UPGRADE 3	Leopard Skin x4
UPGRADE 4	Sabretooth Tiger Skin x4

STATS

CLUB BELT	# of Clubs
BEFORE UPGRADE	2
UPGRADE 1	4
UPGRADE 2	6
UPGRADE 3	8
UPGRADE 4	10

The club belt is available after completing the Trapped mission. Before getting this bag, you can only carry two clubs. Being able to hold more clubs is a big convenience when exploring the caves, since you tend to go through a number of torches in the darkness.

SPEAR BELT

UNLOCKED FOR CRAFTING

UPGRADE 1	Complete Trapped mission
UPGRADE 2	Upgrade 1
UPGRADE 3	Upgrade 2
UPGRADE 4	Upgrade 3

CRAFTING REQUIREMENTS

UPGRADE 1	Wolf Skin x3
UPGRADE 2	Cave Lion Skin x4
UPGRADE 3	Bitefish Skin x2
UPGRADE 4	Woolly Rhino Skin x5

STATS

SPEAR BELT	# of Spears
BEFORE UPGRADE	2
UPGRADE 1	3
UPGRADE 2	4
UPGRADE 3	5
UPGRADE 4	6

The spear belt is available after completing the Trapped mission. Before getting this bag, you can only carry two spears. The spear is the best weapon against many of the tougher enemies, so it is good to have plenty before going into these fights.

PACK

UNLOCKED FOR CRAFTING

UPGRADE 1	Build Wogah's Hut
UPGRADE 2	Upgrade 1

CRAFTING REQUIREMENTS

UPGRADE 1	Goat Skin x2
UPGRADE 2	Tapir Skin x3

STATS

PACK	Amount of Items in Pack
BEFORE UPGRADE	Standard amount
UPGRADE 1	50% more weapon resources and food
UPGRADE 2	Twice as much weapon resources and food

The pack starts out holding a standard amount of items. Two upgrades to the bags allow you to carry 50% more and then twice as many weapon resources and food.

BOMB BELT

UNLOCKED FOR CRAFTING

UPGRADE 1	Upgrade Wogah's Hut to Level 2
UPGRADE 2	Upgrade 1

HUNTER BELT

UNLOCKED FOR CRAFTING

UPGRADE 1	Build Wogah's Hut
UPGRADE 2	Upgrade 1
UPGRADE 3	Upgrade 2

CRAFTING REQUIREMENTS

UPGRADE 1	Rare White Wolf Skin x2
UPGRADE 2	Mammoth Skin x3
UPGRADE 3	Rare Black Jaguar Skin x2

STATS

HUNTER BELT	# Traps	# Sting Bombs
BEFORE UPGRADE	2	1
UPGRADE 1	4	2
UPGRADE 2	6	3
UPGRADE 3	8	4

Before upgrading the hunter belt, you are only able to carry two traps and one sting bomb.

THROWING SHARD BELT

UNLOCKED FOR CRAFTING

UPGRADE 1	Build Wogah's Hut
UPGRADE 2	Upgrade 1
UPGRADE 3	Upgrade 2
UPGRADE 4	Upgrade 3

CRAFTING REQUIREMENTS

UPGRADE 1	Goat Skin x3
UPGRADE 2	Badger Skin x3
UPGRADE 3	Monkey Skin x4
UPGRADE 4	Sabretooth Tiger Skin x4

STATS

THROWING SHARD BELT	# of Shards
BEFORE UPGRADE	2
UPGRADE 1	4
UPGRADE 2	6
UPGRADE 3	8
UPGRADE 4	10

At first, only two of each shard can be carried. Upgrade this belt to increase that number up to 10.

CRAFTING REQUIREMENTS

UPGRADE 1	Cave Bear Skin x3, Deer Skin x10
UPGRADE 2	Bitefish Skin x3, Boar Skin x10

WELCOME

SURVIVING
THE WILD

LAND OF OROS

TAKKAR'S JOURNEY

MAJOR LANDMARKS

LOCATIONS

VILLAGE
CONSTRUCTION

ENEMY TRIBES

WILDLIFE

◆ GEAR

SKILLS

FOOD RECIPES

RESOURCES

COLLECTIBLES

TROPHIES/
ACHIEVEMENTS

THE ART OF OROS

STATS

BOMB BELT	# of Berserk Bombs	# of Fire Bombs
BEFORE UPGRADE	2	4
UPGRADE 1	3	6
UPGRADE 2	4	8

When you first get the berserk bombs and fire bombs, you can only carry two and four, respectively. These upgrades allow you to double that amount. Bombs are fun for decimating a village or outpost. Pick up these upgrades to further the enjoyment.

TOOLS

A few pieces of gear do not fit in as weapons or bags. These tools are vital to your adventures in Oros.

BAIT

UNLOCKED FOR CRAFTING

UPGRADE 1	Unlocked during Beast Master mission

CRAFTING REQUIREMENTS

UPGRADE 1	Given during Beast Master mission

WEAPON WHEEL REQUIREMENTS   Meat x2

Throw bait to attract nearby animals. Some beasts attracted by bait can be tamed (requires skills). Pick up Tensay's Shaman skills to be able to tame beasts in the wild. These guys possess a variety of abilities, giving you a valuable ally in battle. Check out our wildlife chapter to see the available animals and what they do for you.

TRAP

UNLOCKED FOR CRAFTING

UPGRADE 1	Build Wogah's Hut

CRAFTING REQUIREMENTS

UPGRADE 1	Hardwood x12, Animal Hide x8, Bone x6

WEAPON WHEEL REQUIREMENTS   Hardwood x2

Place these concealed traps to surprise enemies and keep predators at bay. You could go the entire game without using a trap, but you would miss out on some easy damage. Figure out an enemy's route and place one in their way, or provoke someone who stands on the other side of it.

GRAPPLING CLAW

UNLOCKED FOR CRAFTING

UPGRADE 1	Received during Trapped mission

CRAFTING REQUIREMENTS

UPGRADE 1	Given during Trapped mission

Use the grappling claw to climb and swing across vertical terrain You receive this tool during Wogah's first mission and it is one of the most valuable items in the game. This allows you to explore the high cliffs and deep caves. If you wish to collect everything in the game, you must find Wogah and get the claw.

WINTER CLOTHING

UNLOCKED FOR CRAFTING

UPGRADE 1	Build Karoosh's Hut
UPGRADE 2	Upgrade 1

CRAFTING REQUIREMENTS

UPGRADE 1	Wolf Skin x4
UPGRADE 2	Rare White Wolf Skin x2, Rare White Yak Skin x2

STATS

WINTER CLOTHING	Minutes for Cold Meter to Drain Completely
BEFORE UPGRADE	4
UPGRADE 1	10
UPGRADE 2	Fully Protected from cold

Winter clothing is invaluable when exploring the cold north, but it does not become available until Karoosh's hut is built. Upgrade it to increase the time before you need to warm up with fire. It is always possible to warm up by igniting a weapon, but having winter clothing is a huge convenience.

SKILLS

Eight sets of skills become available as you bring specialists back to the village and build their huts. As you earn XP by completing objectives, skill points are earned which in turn can be spent on these skills. There are a variety of skills to choose from, some better than others for your play style. Some speed up resource collection and crafting, several boost your combat abilities, while many improve healing.

Access the Skills menu to see all 79 skills, how much they cost, and unlock prerequisite. The icon shows whether an ability is available for purchase.

Lines between the skill icons note paths you must take. The middle skill in the first column is always first and then it goes from left to right. Take a look at upcoming skills to see which paths you wish to take. Consider your playstyle and trouble areas. A health boost is usually a good skill for anyone to pick up. Beast Master Skills are good if you like to leave fighting up to your companion. Fighting Skills offer up some great takedowns for those who like to fight more tactically. Crafting Skills are great for getting the most out of your resources.

 A lock icon signifies the skill is unavailable, typically requiring a hut to be built.

 A gray icon means the skill is available for purchase once Skill Points are earned, but it does not mean it can be purchased next since there could be prerequisite skills ahead of it.

 White with the crafting icon shows that the skill can be purchased with the skill points you have.

 A tan icon means the skill has already been learned.

SURVIVAL SKILLS

UNLOCKED   Already Available

PRIMITIVE TAKEDOWNS

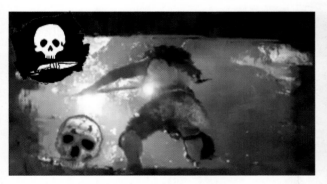

UNLOCKED FOR PURCHASE   Already Learned
SKILL REQUIREMENT   -
COST   -

Approach an enemy from behind or by cover. Press the Takedown button for a quick and silent kill. Hold the Left Stick to drag the body out of sight. This is the basic stealth takedown, performed on an unsuspecting victim.

PRIMITIVE HEAL I

UNLOCKED FOR PURCHASE   Reach Oros
SKILL REQUIREMENT   -
COST   1 Skill Point

Hold the Heal button to manually heal one health bar. More healing options are in the Food menu (Left on the D-Pad), which is a great option since it does not require any ingredients.

EXTRA HEALTH II

UNLOCKED FOR PURCHASE   Build Takkar's Cave
SKILL REQUIREMENT   Primtive Heal I
COST   2 Skill Points

Gain +1 health bars. You can have up to six in total. The more health you have, the more likely you are to survive.

HUNTER VISION

UNLOCKED FOR PURCHASE   Already Learned
SKILL REQUIREMENT   -
COST   -

Hold the Takedown button for enhanced vision. View enemies, animals, resources, and blood trails. Lasts eight seconds. Extends to your Owl companion.

PRIMITIVE HEAL II

UNLOCKED FOR PURCHASE   Build Takkar's Cave
SKILL REQUIREMENT   Extra Health II
COST   3 Skill Points

Heals +1 health bars when manually healing, up to three total.

PRIMITIVE AGILITY

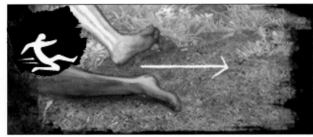

UNLOCKED FOR PURCHASE   Already Learned
SKILL REQUIREMENT   -
COST   -

Press the Sprint button to sprint, then the Crouch button to slide. Hold the Throw Throwable button to keep any throwable weapon in your hand, and release to throw it.

EXTRA HEALTH IV

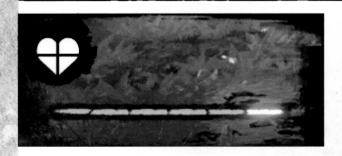

UNLOCKED FOR PURCHASE   Build Takkar's Cave
SKILL REQUIREMENT   Primitive Heal II
COST   6 Skill Points

Gain +1 health bars. You can have up to six in total.

SPRINT HEAL

UNLOCKED FOR PURCHASE	Reach Oros
SKILL REQUIREMENT	-
COST	1 Skill Point

Hold the Heal button to heal yourself while sprinting with the Sprint button. Uses the default recipe from the Food menu (Left on D-Pad). Now you can heal as you flee trouble.

SPRINT FOREVER

UNLOCKED FOR PURCHASE	Build Takkar's Cave
SKILL REQUIREMENT	Crouch Sprint
COST	3 Skill Points

Sprint forever without slowing down after running with the Sprint button. Sprint speed is permanently increased.

CROUCH SPRINT

UNLOCKED FOR PURCHASE	Build Takkar's Cave
SKILL REQUIREMENT	Sprint Heal
COST	2 Skill Points

Move faster when crouched with the Crouch button. This is a great skill for stealth players.

PRIMITIVE STEALTH

UNLOCKED FOR PURCHASE	Already Learned
SKILL REQUIREMENT	-
COST	-

Press Down on the D-Pad to throw a rock (on land) and distract enemies. Hold the Takedown button to move a dead body out of sight.

PRIMITIVE FIRE

UNLOCKED FOR PURCHASE	Already Learned
SKILL REQUIREMENT	-
COST	-

Use Hardwood to light campfires. Set your weapons on fire from the Weapon Wheel by highlighting them and pressing the Interact button. This process uses an Animal Fat.

HEALTH REGENERATION

UNLOCKED FOR PURCHASE	Build Takkar's Cave
SKILL REQUIREMENT	Extra Health I
COST	3 Skill Points

Partially drained health bars automatically regenerate much faster.

EXTRA HEALTH I

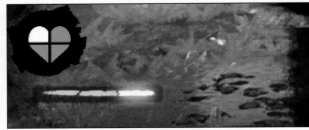

UNLOCKED FOR PURCHASE	Reach Oros
SKILL REQUIREMENT	-
COST	1 Skill Point

Gain +1 health bars. You can have up to six in total.

QUIET SPRINT

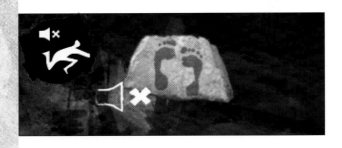

UNLOCKED FOR PURCHASE	Build Takkar's Cave
SKILL REQUIREMENT	Health Regeneration
COST	4 Skill Points

Greatly reduce the noise you make when walking and sprinting. This is a great help in stealth situations, getting you to unsuspecting foes quicker.

GATHERING SKILLS

UNLOCKED   Complete Deep Wounds

REVEAL TERRAIN I

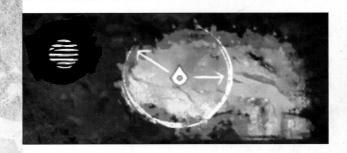

UNLOCKED FOR PURCHASE	Meet Sayla
SKILL REQUIREMENT	-
COST	1 Skill Point

Reveal 200 feet of terrain around you in the Map menu. Uncovers more activities and missions.

FIND RARE RESOURCES

UNLOCKED FOR PURCHASE	Build Sayla's Hut
SKILL REQUIREMENT	Show Resources
COST	2 Skill Points

Improved chance of finding more rare wood, stone, and reeds when gathering.

SHOW RESOURCES

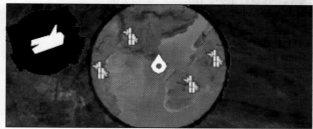

UNLOCKED FOR PURCHASE	Build Sayla's Hut
SKILL REQUIREMENT	Reveal Terrain I
COST	1 Skill Point

Wood, stone, and other village resources are displayed on your mini-map.

REVEAL TERRAIN II

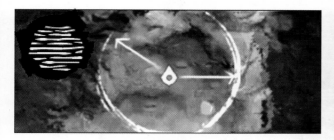

UNLOCKED FOR PURCHASE	Build Sayla's Hut
SKILL REQUIREMENT	Find Rare Resources
COST	3 Skill Points

Reveal 400 feet of terrain around you in the Map menu. Uncovers more activities and missions.

SHOW PLANTS

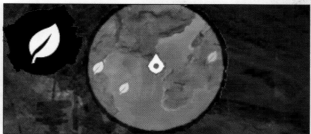

UNLOCKED FOR PURCHASE	Meet Sayla
SKILL REQUIREMENT	-
COST	1 Skill Point

Plants are displayed on your mini-map.

SEARCH TAKEDOWN

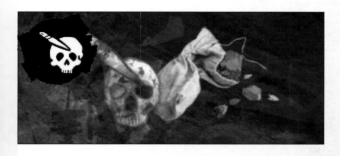

UNLOCKED FOR PURCHASE	Build Sayla's Hut
SKILL REQUIREMENT	Find Resources I
COST	2 Skill Points

Automatically search an enemy while performing a takedown. This is a huge convenience when stealthily taking down a group of enemies.

FIND RESOURCES I

UNLOCKED FOR PURCHASE   Build Sayla's Hut
SKILL REQUIREMENT   Show Plants
COST   1 Skill Point

Find more wood, stone, reeds, clay, and rock dust when gathering.

FIND RARE PLANTS

UNLOCKED FOR PURCHASE   Build Sayla's Hut
SKILL REQUIREMENT   Search Takedown
COST   2 Skill Points

Improved chance of finding more rare plant parts when gathering.

SKINNING I

UNLOCKED FOR PURCHASE   Build Sayla's Hut
SKILL REQUIREMENT   Show Plants
COST   2 Skill Points

Find +2 Meat when skinning most animals.

SKINNING II

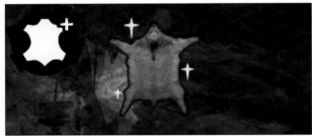

UNLOCKED FOR PURCHASE   Build Sayla's Hut
SKILL REQUIREMENT   Skinning I
COST   2 Skill Points

Find +2 Animal Fat and +2 Animal Hide when skinning most animals.

FIND RESOURCES II

UNLOCKED FOR PURCHASE   Build Sayla's Hut
SKILL REQUIREMENT   Beast Reviving
COST   2 Skill Points

Find even more wood, stone, reeds, clay, and rock dust when gathering.

BEAST REVIVING

UNLOCKED FOR PURCHASE   Build Sayla's Hut
SKILL REQUIREMENT   Skinning II
COST   2 Skill Points

Reviving your tamed beasts requires fewer Red Leaves. Grab this skill if you use beast companions a lot.

BEAST MASTER SKILLS

UNLOCKED   Find Tensay and complete Beast Master mission

TAME CANINES

UNLOCKED FOR PURCHASE   Find Tensay and complete Beast Master mission
SKILL REQUIREMENT   Owl Companion
COST   -

Now tamable: Dholes, Rare Dholes, Wolves, White Wolves, and Rare Stripe Wolves. Use bait to tame them.

TAME WILDCATS

UNLOCKED FOR PURCHASE   Build Tensay's Hut
SKILL REQUIREMENT   Tame Canines
COST   1 Skill Point

Now tamable: Leopards, Jaguars, Rare Black Jaguars, Cave Lions, and Rare Black Lions. Use bait to tame them. Wildcats are great for stealth missions, especially Jaguars who attack unsuspecting targets without alerting nearby enemies.

TAME CUNNING BEASTS

UNLOCKED FOR PURCHASE	Tame eight beasts
SKILL REQUIREMENT	Tame Apex Predators
COST	3 Skill Points

Now tamable: Cave Bears and Badgers. Use bait to tame them. Use a Cave Bear to keep enemies focused on it. A Badger revives itself once and terrifies all wildlife in Oros, keeping unwanted animals away.

TAME APEX PREDATORS

UNLOCKED FOR PURCHASE	Tame five beasts
SKILL REQUIREMENT	Tame Wildcats
COST	2 Skill Points

Now tamable: Sabretooth Tigers and Brown Bears. Use bait to tame them. These are two great additions to your beast roster; Brown Bears collect nearby resources when idle and Sabretooth Tigers skin carcasses and gather the resources after making a kill.

OWL COMPANION

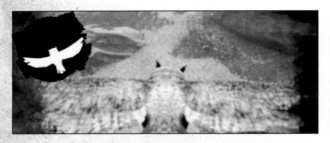

UNLOCKED FOR PURCHASE	Bring Tensay to your village
SKILL REQUIREMENT	-
COST	-

Press Up on the D-Pad to summon your Owl. Scout ahead to tag enemies.

OWL: HUNTER VISION

UNLOCKED FOR PURCHASE	Bring Tensay to your village
SKILL REQUIREMENT	-
COST	-

Hold the Takedown button to use Hunter Vision with your Owl. Other Hunter Vision skills extend to your Owl. Helps spot enemies much easier when scouting an area.

OWL: WEAPON DROP

UNLOCKED FOR PURCHASE	Build Tensay's Hut
SKILL REQUIREMENT	Owl: Hunter Vision
COST	3 Skill Points

The Owl can drop your sting bombs, berserk bombs, and fire bombs. This is great for causing chaos from above. Concentrate your fire on tougher enemies such as Chieftains.

OWL: ATTACK I

UNLOCKED FOR PURCHASE — Build Tensay's Hut
SKILL REQUIREMENT — Owl Companion
COST — 1 Skill Point

Your Owl can perform a dive attack with the Quick Attack button. This kills most regular enemies and can free caged animals. It has a 80 second cooldown time and is useful for taking out those pesky Slingers or Archers who stand guard. Finish off your recon by getting rid of an enemy.

OWL: TAGGING RANGE

UNLOCKED FOR PURCHASE — Build Tensay's Hut
SKILL REQUIREMENT — Owl: Weapon Drop
COST — 3 Skill Points

The Owl's tagging range for enemies is greatly increased. If the Tag Animals skill is learned, the tagging range for animals is also increased. Quicker recon of an area means you are quicker to the fight.

OWL: COOLDOWN I

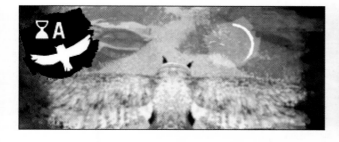

UNLOCKED FOR PURCHASE — Build Tensay's Hut
SKILL REQUIREMENT — Owl: Attack I
COST — 2 Skill Points

The Owl attack cooldown is reduced from 80s to 65s.

OWL: ATTACK II

UNLOCKED FOR PURCHASE — Build Tensay's Hut
SKILL REQUIREMENT — Owl: Cooldown I
COST — 3 Skill Points

The dive attack can now kill the large and powerful Elite enemies.

OWL: COOLDOWN II

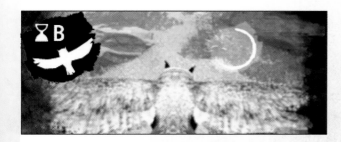

UNLOCKED FOR PURCHASE — Build Tensay's Hut
SKILL REQUIREMENT — Owl: Attack II
COST — 3 Skill Points

The Owl attack cooldown is reduced from 65s to 40s.

HUNTING SKILLS

HUNTER VISION: SACKS

UNLOCKED FOR PURCHASE   Bring Jayma to your village
SKILL REQUIREMENT   Tag Enemies
COST   1 Skill Point

Resource sacks can now be seen with Hunter Vision. This skill extends to your Owl companion.

CRAFT ARROWS I

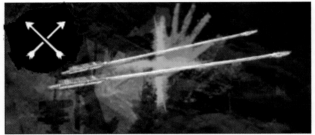

UNLOCKED FOR PURCHASE   Bring Jayma to your village
SKILL REQUIREMENT   Hunter Vision: Sacks
COST   1 Skill Point

Craft two arrows instead of one from the Weapon Wheel. Resource cost does not change. Get more arrows out of your Hardwood; great for bow experts.

CRAFT ARROWS II

UNLOCKED FOR PURCHASE   Build Jayma's Hut
SKILL REQUIREMENT   Craft Arrows I
COST   2 Skill Points

Craft four arrows instead of two from the Weapon Wheel. Resource cost does not change.

CRAFT ARROWS III

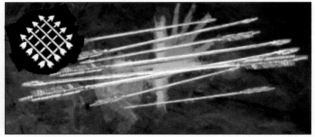

UNLOCKED FOR PURCHASE   Build Jayma's Hut
SKILL REQUIREMENT   Craft Arrows II
COST   4 Skill Points

Craft eight arrows instead of four from the Weapon Wheel. Resource cost does not change.

REDUCED FALL DAMAGE

UNLOCKED FOR PURCHASE	Build Jayma's Hut
SKILL REQUIREMENT	Tag Enemies
COST	1 Skill Point

Receive less damage when falling from a great height.

TAG ANIMALS

UNLOCKED FOR PURCHASE	Build Jayma's Hut
SKILL REQUIREMENT	Reduced Fall Damage
COST	4 Skill Points

Hold the Aim button while aiming to tag animals. Works with clubs, bows, and the spear. Tags are permanent. Your Owl companion can also tag animals. Great skill if you plan to tackle the Beast Kills quests and Beast Master Hunts.

TAG ENEMIES

UNLOCKED FOR PURCHASE	Bring Jayma to your village
SKILL REQUIREMENT	-
COST	1 Skill Point

Hold the Aim button while aiming to tag enemies. Works with clubs, bows, and the spear. Tags are permanent. Your Owl companion can also tag enemies. Tagging enemies is an extremely valuable skill. The more enemies tagged, the easier time in the fight.

ANIMAL WOUNDS

UNLOCKED FOR PURCHASE	Build Jayma's Hut
SKILL REQUIREMENT	Tag Animals
COST	6 Skill Points

Increase the amount of damage your weapons inflict on animals.

HUNTER VISION: PLANTS

UNLOCKED FOR PURCHASE	Bring Jayma to your village
SKILL REQUIREMENT	Tag Enemies
COST	1 Skill Point

Plants can now be seen with Hunter Vision. This skill extends to your Owl companion.

BOW SPRINT RELOAD

UNLOCKED FOR PURCHASE	Build Jayma's Hut
SKILL REQUIREMENT	Hunter Vision: Plants
COST	2 Skill Points

Reload any bow with a fresh arrow while sprinting. Press the Sprint button to sprint.

BOW HANDLING

UNLOCKED FOR PURCHASE	Build Jayma's Hut
SKILL REQUIREMENT	Bow Sprint Reload
COST	3 Skill Points

When aiming a bow with the Aim button, the sway is greatly reduced. Long distance shots with the bow become easier with a steadier aim.

FIGHTING SKILLS

UNLOCKED	Bring Karoosh to your village

SHARD TAKEDOWN

UNLOCKED FOR PURCHASE	Build Karoosh's Hut
SKILL REQUIREMENT	Death from Above
COST	2 Skill Points

Press the Takedown button to begin a takedown on an enemy. Then press the Quick Attack button to throw a shard at a second enemy. You must have shards to use this skill. Take out two unsuspecting foes in one fell swoop. Turn the camera to look at the second enemy or you may not get a shot at him.

HEAVY TAKEDOWN

UNLOCKED FOR PURCHASE	Build Karoosh's Hut
SKILL REQUIREMENT	Shard Takedown
COST	3 Skill Points

Press the Takedown button to takedown the large and powerful Chieftain enemies. This skill is a must have for later locations, when Chieftains become more prevalent.

DEATH FROM ABOVE

UNLOCKED FOR PURCHASE	Bring Karoosh to your village
SKILL REQUIREMENT	-
COST	1 Skill Point

Jump or fall onto an enemy below you for a quick and brutal kill. This is a very satisfying way to take out an opponent and it is cheap.

CHAIN TAKEDOWN

UNLOCKED FOR PURCHASE	Build Karoosh's Hut
SKILL REQUIREMENT	Heavy Takedown
COST	4 Skill Points

Kill multiple enemies in sequence. Start with a standard takedown. Use the Move controls as prompted to chain it between nearby enemies. Be ready with the Left Stick. Quickly press the indicated direction to keep the chain going.

MAMMOTH RIDER

UNLOCKED FOR PURCHASE	Build Karoosh's Hut
SKILL REQUIREMENT	Death From Above
COST	2 Skill Points

Approach a young Mammoth and hold the Interact button to ride it. Charge with the Sprint button. Attack enemies with the Takedown button. Use your weapons as normal. This skill is required for the Stomp Udam mission. Trample a series of enemies with the charge attack. Wipe out entire squads at outposts and bonfires by grabbing a Mammoth beforehand.

BEAST RIDER

UNLOCKED FOR PURCHASE	Build Karoosh's Hut
SKILL REQUIREMENT	Mammoth Rider
COST	2 Skill Points

This skill allows you to ride Sabretooth Tigers, Brown Bears, and the Bloodfang Sabretooth after taming them. The controls are the same as when using the Mammoth Rider skill. Hold the Interact button to mount the beast; hold the Sprint button to sprint. The Takedown button causes the beast to attack. You can attack as normal when mounted.

CLUB & SPEAR HANDLING

UNLOCKED FOR PURCHASE	Bring Karoosh to your village
SKILL REQUIREMENT	Death from Above
COST	1 Skill Point

Aiming sway is greatly reduced for clubs and spears.

WEAPON AGILITY

UNLOCKED FOR PURCHASE	Build Karoosh's Hut
SKILL REQUIREMENT	Club & Spear Handling
COST	1 Skill Point

Switching between weapons with the Heal button is much faster, even when sprinting. Aiming your weapon with the Aim button is also much faster. If you find yourself fumbling with your weapons when switching from one to the other, grab this skill to improve alternating between weapons.

USE WEAPONS WHILE MOVING BODIES

UNLOCKED FOR PURCHASE	Build Karoosh's Hut
SKILL REQUIREMENT	Club & Spear Handling
COST	1 Skill Point

While moving a dead body, you can aim and throw any club or spear. Typically, when moving a body out of sight, you are vulnerable to enemy attack. Now clubs and spears can be thrown during transport.

EXTRA HEALTH III

UNLOCKED FOR PURCHASE	Build Karoosh's Hut
SKILL REQUIREMENT	Use Weapons while Moving Bodies
COST	4 Skill Points

Gain +1 health bars. You can have up to six in total.

CRAFTING SKILLS

UNLOCKED   Bring Wogah to your village

DOUBLE CLUBS

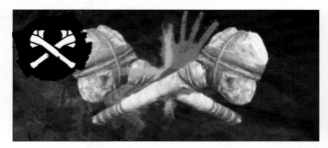

UNLOCKED FOR PURCHASE	Build Wogah's Hut
SKILL REQUIREMENT	Food Boosts I
COST	2 Skill Points

Craft two clubs instead of one from the Weapon Wheel. Applies to all club types. Resource cost does not change.

PRECISION SLING

UNLOCKED FOR PURCHASE	Build Wogah's Hut
SKILL REQUIREMENT	Vicious Traps
COST	2 Skill Points

Sling head shots pierce through enemy headgear. Headshots on Elite enemies with unlimited ammo? Yes please.

VICIOUS TRAPS

UNLOCKED FOR PURCHASE	Build Wogah's Hut
SKILL REQUIREMENT	Double Clubs
COST	1 Skill Point

Traps deal more damage when triggered by enemies or animals. A more powerful trap makes them more worthwhile in combat.

DOUBLE SPEARS

UNLOCKED FOR PURCHASE	Build Wogah's Hut
SKILL REQUIREMENT	Precision Sling
COST	3 Skill Points

Craft two spears instead of one from the Weapon Wheel. Resource cost does not change.

FOOD BOOSTS I

UNLOCKED FOR PURCHASE	Bring Wogah to your village
SKILL REQUIREMENT	-
COST	1 Skill Point

The effects of Food recipes are increased from 60s to 90s. Keep your speed boost, scent camouflage, fireproof, and poison resistance for 30 seconds longer.

DOUBLE TRAPS

UNLOCKED FOR PURCHASE	Build Wogah's Hut
SKILL REQUIREMENT	Double Sting Bombs
COST	2 Skill Points

Craft two traps instead of one from the Weapon Wheel. Resource cost does not change.

DOUBLE STING BOMBS

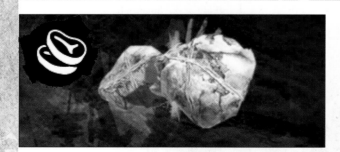

UNLOCKED FOR PURCHASE	Build Wogah's Hut
SKILL REQUIREMENT	Food Boosts I
COST	2 Skill Points

Craft two sting bombs instead of one from the Weapon Wheel. Resource cost does not change.

DOUBLE SHARDS

UNLOCKED FOR PURCHASE	Build Wogah's Hut
SKILL REQUIREMENT	Double Traps
COST	3 Skill Points

Craft two shards instead of one from the Weapon Wheel. Applies to all shard types. Resource cost does not change.

DOUBLE BAIT

UNLOCKED FOR PURCHASE	Build Wogah's Hut
SKILL REQUIREMENT	Food Boosts I
COST	1 Skill Point

Craft two bait instead of one from the Weapon Wheel. Resource cost does not change.

FOOD BOOSTS II

UNLOCKED FOR PURCHASE   Build Wogah's Hut
SKILL REQUIREMENT   Double Bait
COST   1 Skill Point

Effects of Food recipes are increased from 90s to 120s.

FOOD BOOSTS III

UNLOCKED FOR PURCHASE   Build Wogah's Hut
SKILL REQUIREMENT   Food Boosts II
COST   2 Skill Points

Effects of Food recipes are increased from 120s to 150s.

UDAM SKILLS

UNLOCKED   Bring Dah to your village

MELEE RESISTANCE I

UNLOCKED FOR PURCHASE   Bring Dah to your village
SKILL REQUIREMENT   -
COST   2 Skill Points

Receive less damage from animal attacks and enemy melee hits.
Also reduces the chance of being knocked down by enemies.

DOUBLE BERSERK BOMB

UNLOCKED FOR PURCHASE   Build Dah's Hut
SKILL REQUIREMENT   Melee Resistance I
COST   2 Skill Points

Craft two berserk bombs instead of one from the Weapon
Wheel. Resource cost does not change.

MELEE RESISTANCE II

UNLOCKED FOR PURCHASE	Build Dah's Hut
SKILL REQUIREMENT	Double Berserk Bomb
COST	4 Skill Points

Receive even less damage from animal attacks and enemy melee hits.

PRIMITIVE HEAL III

UNLOCKED FOR PURCHASE	Build Dah's Hut
SKILL REQUIREMENT	Melee Resistance II
COST	4 Skill Points

Heals +1 health bars when manually healing, up to three total. More healing options are in the Food menu (Left on D-Pad).

IZILA SKILLS

UNLOCKED   Bring Roshani to your village

FIRE RESISTANCE

UNLOCKED FOR PURCHASE	Bring Roshani to your village
SKILL REQUIREMENT	-
COST	2 Skill Points

Reduce the amount of damage you take from fire. This skill is a must have as you explore Izila territories to lessen the damage from their brutal fire attacks. Be sure to grab this one before going after Batari.

DOUBLE FIRE BOMBS

UNLOCKED FOR PURCHASE	Build Roshani's Hut
SKILL REQUIREMENT	Fire Resistance
COST	3 Skill Points

Craft two fire bombs instead of one from the Weapon Wheel. Resource cost does not change.

FIRE TAKEDOWN

UNLOCKED FOR PURCHASE   Build Roshani's Hut
SKILL REQUIREMENT   Double Fire Bombs
COST   3 Skill Points

Press the Takedown button to begin a takedown on an enemy. Then press the Throw Throwable button to smash a fire bomb onto the enemy. You must have fire bombs to use this skill. There is a possibility of nearby enemies catching on fire, making this ability even more devastating.

FIRE MASTER I

UNLOCKED FOR PURCHASE   Build Roshani's Hut
SKILL REQUIREMENT   Fire Takedown
COST   6 Skill Points

You no longer need Animal Fat to set your weapons on fire. Nab this expensive skill before exploring the Lost Caves. It is very easy to run out of Animal Fat in the bigger caves.

FIRE MASTER II

UNLOCKED FOR PURCHASE   Build Roshani's Hut
SKILL REQUIREMENT   Fire Master I
COST   4 Skill Points

If you set a weapon on fire, all subsequent weapons you equip are automatically set on fire. Press the Interact button in the Weapon Wheel to extinguish the fire at any time. This is the ultimate skill for navigating Lost Caves.

FOOD RECIPES

Basic Healing is available from the start of the game, but once you meet Sayla and build her Hut, more healing recipes become available. Besides Primitive Heal, which doesn't require any ingredients, they all need meat and a plant.

Your health starts out at two bars, but is expandable to six by purchasing skills. Hold the Heal button to use the default recipe. Press left on the D-Pad to bring up the available recipes. Select Confirm to eat the selected recipe while the Heal button sets a default for quicker use. Take into account your current location and set an appropriate recipe as the default.

Later recipes have added effects beyond healing.

▶ Speed Boost makes you sprint and swim faster, plus it lengthens how long you can hold your breath. Have this one ready in some of the cave water tunnels, in case you get lost and need that little bit of extra time.

▶ Scent Camouflage is great when hunting animals. Beast Kill quests are much easier since you can get much closer without the animals detecting you.

▶ Fireproof reduces fire damage, making it great for Izila territories. Use this food recipe as much as possible in the tougher Izila fights, such as when facing Batari.

▶ Antidote is required to get into Udam Homeland and allows you to enter poisonous gas areas without taking damage. Many rot fume clouds are small enough that you can sprint through with minimal damage, but this recipe allows you to dawdle inside the rooms. Antidote also eliminates the poison damage from Udam poison bombs and from animal attacks, such as snake bites.

▶ Ultimate Boost combines the effects of Speed Boost, Scent Camouflage, and Fireproof, while also restoring full health. As

RECIPES

ICON	FOOD	WHEN UNLOCKED	INGREDIENTS	DESCRIPTION
♥	Primitive Heal	Purchase Primitive Heal I and II skills	None	Restores 1 or 2 bars of health, depending on skill.
♥	Basic Healing	Available from start	Meat	Restores 2 bars of health.
♥	Rugged Healing	Complete Deep Wounds Mission	Meat, Green Leaf	Restores 3 bars of health.
♥	Full Health	Upgrade Sayla's Hut to Level 2	Meat, 2 Green Leaf	Restores 6 bars of health.
🦌	Speed Boost	Build Sayla's Hut	2x Meat, Blue Leaf	Restores 2 bars of health and makes you sprint and swim faster and hold your breath longer.
🦌	Scent Camouflage	Build Sayla's Hut	2x Meat, Violet Leaf	Restores 2 bars of health and makes it harder for animals to detect you.
🔥	Fireproof	Build Sayla's Hut	2x Meat, South Purple Leaf	Restores 2 bars of health and reduces fire damage.
✚	Antidote	Complete Into Udam Land and then talk to Sayla	Meat, Rare North Yellow Leaf	Restores 2 bars of health and eliminates all poison damage and effects.
💥	Ultimate Boost	Upgrade Sayla's Hut to Level 2	4 Meat, 2 Red Leaf, 4 Rare Plant Root	Restores 6 bars of health and combines the effects of Scent Camouflage, Fireproof, and Speed Boost.

RESOURCES

Resources gathered throughout Oros are essential in building your village, crafting gear, and upgrading items. Look for trees, plants, rocks, and other materials. Approach and hold the Interact button to gain resources—adding them to your pack. Killing and skinning animals also produce valuable supplies. Occasionally, you also find bonus and rare resources. Hardwood from trees and flint from rocks are examples of bonus materials. Rare versions, available with several resources, are found at a much lower rate. Enable Hunter Vision to highlight resources in yellow for easier recognition.

You are limited in the amount of each resource you can carry. Upgrade your bags to hold more. Inside your cave and at various locations in Oros, such as campfires, you can access your Reward Stash. As you progress in the game, random resources are added to this stash each day. Access it to transfer items to your pack. The following tables list the resources found in Oros along with where they are found, how they are used, and how many can be carried before upgrading your gear.

WEAPON RESOURCES

Weapon resources are needed to craft new armaments in the Weapon Wheel. Upgrade the Guts Bag to increase the amount of bait, meat, and animal that can be carried. These items are vital for keeping your beast and yourself alive. Upgrade the Pack to increase the amount of resources you can carry.

ICON	RESOURCE	INITIAL CAPACITY	LOCATION FOUND	USAGE
	Animal Fat	8	Found on almost all animals.	Set Weapons on fire, craft fire bombs in the Weapon Wheel.
	Hardwood	16	All across Oros, when collecting wood.	Craft clubs, spears, traps, and arrows in the Weapon Wheel.
	Flint	16	All across Oros, when collecting stones and rocks.	Craft clubs, spears, and shards in the Weapon Wheel.
	Animal Hide	8	Found on almost all animals.	Craft clubs, spears, shards, and sting bombs in the Weapon Wheel.
	Bone	8	Found on almost all large animals.	Upgrade items in the Crafting menu, and craft the Kapala Shard and Blood Shasti Club in the Weapon Wheel.
	Bee Cluster	4	All across Oros in hives, mostly near Bears.	Craft sting bombs in the Weapon Wheel.
	Clay Pot	4	Found on bodies of enemies.	Craft berserk bombs and fire bombs in the Weapon Wheel.

FOOD

Meat and leaves are used in the Food Recipes. Keep these items stocked up as much as possible. Once you complete the Into Udam Land mission, Rare North Yellow Leaf is occasionally found when picking North Yellow Leaf.

ICONS	RESOURCE	INITIAL CAPACITY	LOCATION FOUND	USAGE
	Meat	8	Found on almost all animals.	Craft the Basic Healing recipe in the Food menu, heal your tamed beasts, and craft bait in the Weapon Wheel. Upgrade the guts bag in the Crafting menu to carry more.
	Green Leaf	8	All across Oros.	Craft the Rugged Healing and Full Health recipes in the Food menu.
	Violet Leaf	8	All across Oros.	Craft the Scent Camouflage recipe in the Food menu.
	Blue Leaf	8	All across Oros.	Craft the Speed Boost recipe in the Food menu.
	South Purple Leaf	8	Southern region of Oros.	Craft the Fireproof recipe in the Food menu.
	North Yellow Leaf	8	Northern region of Oros.	Craft the berserk shard and berserk bomb in the Weapon Wheel.
	Rare North Yellow Leaf	8	Complete Into Udam Land mission to unlock this resource. Small chance to receive it when collecting North Yellow Leaves.	Craft the Antidote recipe in the Food menu.
	Red Leaf	8	All across Oros.	Revive beasts in the Beasts menu, and craft the Ultimate Boost recipe in the Food menu.
	Rare Plant Root	8	Small chance to receive it when collecting any plant.	Craft the Ultimate Boost recipe in the Food menu.

VILLAGE RESOURCES

Village Resources are not only used in the construction of your village but also in crafting weapons and items. Blood of Oros is not found when mining north black rock until the Blood of Oros mission is complete.

WELCOME

SURVIVING
THE WILD

LAND OF OROS

TAKKAR'S JOURNEY

MAJOR LANDMARKS

LOCATIONS

VILLAGE
CONSTRUCTION

ENEMY TRIBES

WILDLIFE

GEAR

SKILLS

FOOD RECIPES

RESOURCES

WEAPON
RESOURCES

FOOD

VILLAGE
RESOURCES

ANIMAL SKINS

COLLECTIBLES

TROPHIES/
ACHIEVEMENTS

THE ART OF OROS

ICONS	RESOURCE	INITIAL CAPACITY	LOCATION FOUND	USAGE
	Alder Wood	50	Western region of Oros.	Build village huts, craft weapons and items in the Crafting menu.
	Slate	50	Western region of Oros.	Build village huts, craft weapons and items in the Crafting menu.
	Reeds	50	Western region of Oros, near water.	Build village huts, craft weapons and items in the Crafting menu.
	Rare Reeds	10	Small chance to receive it when collecting reeds.	Upgrade weapons and items in the Crafting menu.
	North Cedar	16	Northern region of Oros.	Build village huts, craft weapons and items in the Crafting menu.
	Rare North Cedar	10	Small chance to receive it when collecting north cedar.	Upgrade weapons and items in the Crafting menu.
	North Black Rock	50	Northern region of Oros.	Build village huts, craft weapons and items in the Crafting menu.
	Blood of Oros (Rare Resource)	10	Complete Blood of Oros mission to unlock this resource. Small chance to receive when collecting north black rock.	Upgrade weapons and items in the Crafting menu.
	North Clay	50	Northern region of Oros, mostly near water.	Build village huts, craft weapons and items in the Crafting menu.
	South Maple	50	Southern region of Oros.	Build village huts, craft weapons and items in the Crafting menu.
	Rare South Maple	10	Random chance to receive it when collecting south maple.	Build huts, upgrade weapons.
	South Stone	50	Southern region of Oros.	Build village huts, craft weapons and items in the Crafting menu.
	Rare South Stone	10	Small chance to receive it when collecting south stone.	Upgrade weapons and items in the Crafting menu.
	South Rock Dust	50	Southern region of Oros, mostly near water.	Build village huts, craft weapons and items in the Crafting menu.

ANIMAL SKINS

After killing an animal, walk up to the carcass and hold the Interact button to skin it. This gives you a skin of the animal, a possible rare version if it exists, animal hide, meat, and animal fat. A tamed Dhole does the skinning for you, which is really convenient. Upgrading the huts to level two requires rare skins. Collect the resources from dead game, whether your kill or not. Complete the Wogah's Claw mission to unlock Rare Feathers when collecting feathers from any bird.

ICONS	RESOURCE	INITIAL CAPACITY	LOCATION FOUND	USAGE
	Goat Skin	10	Goats are found all across Oros.	Build village huts, upgrade items in the Crafting menu.
	Deer Skin	10	Deer are found all across Oros.	Build village huts, upgrade items in the Crafting menu.
	Rare White Deer Skin	5	White Deer can be spotted sometimes among other Deer.	Build huts.
	Wolf Skin	10	Wolves are found all across Oros.	Build village huts, upgrade items in the Crafting menu.
	Rare White Wolf Skin	10	White Wolves can be spotted sometimes among other Wolves.	Upgrade items in the Crafting menu.
	Rare Stripe Wolf Skin	5	Stripe Wolves can be spotted sometimes among other Wolves.	Build village huts.
	Dhole Skin	10	Dholes are found in the western region of Oros.	Upgrade items in the Crafting menu.
	Rare Black Dhole Skin	5	Black Dholes can be spotted sometimes among other dholes.	Build village huts, upgrade items in the Crafting menu.
	Brown Bear Skin	10	Brown Bears are found all across Oros.	Build village huts, upgrade items in the Crafting menu.
	Cave Bear Skin	10	Cave Bears are found in the Northern region of Oros.	Upgrade items in the Crafting menu.
	Sabretooth Tiger Skin	10	Sabretooth Tigers are found all across Oros.	Upgrade items in the Crafting menu.
	Cave Lion Skin	10	Cave Lions are found all across Oros.	Upgrade items in the Crafting menu.
	Rare Black Lion Skin	5	Black Lions can be spotted sometimes among other Cave Lions.	Build village huts.
	Tapir Skin	10	Tapirs are found all across Oros, only at night.	Upgrade items in the Crafting menu.

ICONS	RESOURCE	INITIAL CAPACITY	LOCATION FOUND	USAGE
	Tall Elk Skin	10	Tall Elk are found all across Oros.	Upgrade items in the Crafting menu.
	Rare Red Elk Skin	10	Red Elk can be spotted sometimes among other tall Elk.	Build village huts.
	Yak Skin	10	Yaks are found in the Northern region of Oros.	Upgrade the Guts Bag in the Crafting menu.
	Rare White Yak Skin	5	White Yaks can be spotted sometimes among other Yaks.	Upgrade Winter Clothing in the Crafting menu.
	Boar Skin	10	Boars are found in the Western region of Oros.	Upgrade items in the Crafting menu.
	Badger Skin	10	Badgers are found between the western and southern forests of Oros.	Build village huts, upgrade items in the Crafting menu.
	Jaguar Skin	10	Jaguars are found in the western and southern regions of Oros.	Build village huts, upgrade items in the Crafting menu.
	Rare Black Jaguar Skin	5	Black Jaguars can be spotted sometimes among other Jaguars.	Upgrade items in the Crafting menu.
	Leopard Skin	10	Leopards are found in the northern region of Oros.	Upgrade items in the Crafting menu.
	Mammoth Skin	10	Mammoths are found all across Oros.	Build village huts, upgrade items in the Crafting menu.
	Woolly Rhino Skin	10	Rhinos are found in the Southern region of Oros.	Upgrade the Spear Belt in the Crafting menu.
	Rare Two Horn Rhino Skin	5	Two Horn Rhinos can be spotted sometimes among other Woolly Rhinos.	Build Huts.
	Monkey Skin	10	Monkeys are found in the southern region of Oros.	Upgrade items in the Crafting menu.
	Bitefish Skin	10	Bitefish are found in water all across Oros.	Upgrade items in the Crafting menu.
	Rare Red Bitefish Skin	5	Red Bitefish can be spotted sometimes among other bitefish.	Build village huts.
	Feathers	4	All across Oros, on any bird.	Upgrade the Quiver in the Crafting menu.
	Rare Feathers	4	Complete Wogah's Claw mission to unlock this resource. Small chance to receive it when collecting Feathers from any bird.	Upgrade the Quiver in the Crafting menu.

My favorite beast companion is the Cave Lion, because I had the same stuffed animal when I was young.

— *Mickael Labat, Art Director*

COLLECTIBLES

Five types of collectibles are hidden throughout Oros, resting on high cliffs, deep inside caves, underwater, or behind weak walls. Keep an eye out for these items as you explore the environment. When you get within range of a collectible, the blue icon appears on the mini-map. A small triangle above or below means the item is higher or lower respectively. These pieces give you various XP when collected, except for Spirit Totems that add a +2% XP bonus for each one. Check the Collectible Cave Wall on the left side of the cavern just behind Takkar's bed to see how many of each you have found.

CAVE PAINTINGS

NUMBER	22	
AWARD	XP	
STORIES OF SURVIVAL, SHARED BY WENJA ACROSS OROS.		

Find Cave Paintings on well-hidden walls inside the Lost Caves. Often found deep inside, enabling Hunter Vision causes them to glow a bright yellow. Sometimes, thorns must be burnt down to get at the paintings. Once you find one, study the painting to receive credit for finding it. Refer to our Lost Caves chapter for details on how to find them all.

DAYSHA HANDS

NUMBER   100
AWARD   XP
GLOWING HANDPRINTS SHOW SITES OF SPIRIT ENERGY.

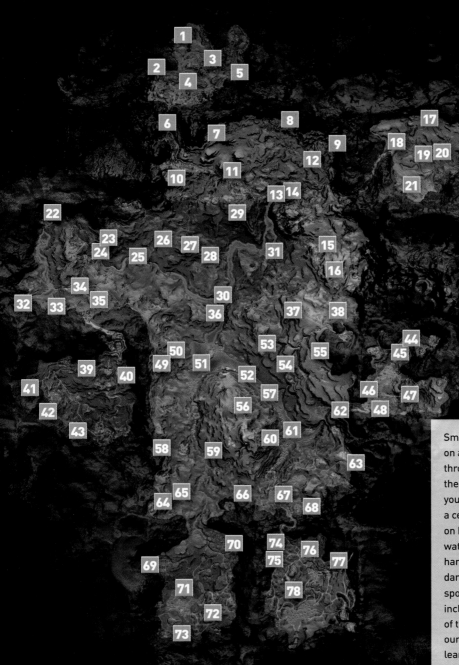

Small handprints, stamped on a rock, are found throughout Oros. Look for the blue icon to appear on your mini-map when within a certain range. Often found on high outcrops, under water, or inside caves, the handprint glows bright in the dark, making them easier to spot at nighttime. Here we include the 78 found outside of the Lost Caves. Refer to our Lost Caves chapter to learn how to find the other 22 Daysha Hands.

1

In the far northern reaches of Oros, look for water just below an Udam camp, next to the cliffs. A Daysha Hand sits on the west side.

2

Just south of Cave of Bones, a Daysha Hand sits behind a big boulder.

3

East of the second handprint look for a shallow pond. Resting in the middle of the water is the third Daysha Hand.

4

Southwest of Mamaf Graveyard, look for grappling points on the north side of a plateau.

5

Use a grappling point on the east cliffs to reach the higher level. Run directly east to find Mammoth tusks just inside a small opening in the rocks. Tucked in behind the left boulder is a Daysha Hand.

6

A Daysha Hand rests on a rock outcropping above the trees. You can reach it from the main path that leads to the northern area of Oros. From the route, find the grappling point on the southwest side. Jump across the rocks to reach the collectible.

7

South of the Cave of the Drowned, a Daysha Hand rests on a rock high on the cliffs. Follow the snowy path to a grappling point. Climb up, head west, and then drop down.

8

Find this on the way to the Hagwi Drink Lost Cave. Use a grappling point to reach the north ledge high on the cliff and follow a path of grapples and a log bridge.

9

North of Big Darwa Fort, follow the snowy path along the mountains until you find a couple of grappling points above, leading you to the cliff where the Daysha Hand sits.

10

A Daysha Hand rests on a cliff high above the western edge of northern Oros. From Charnga Cave, follow the path down the mountain to find a grappling point. Lower yourself to find the collectible.

11

Sitting atop Twarsha Den Outpost, the next handprint rests on another pointy rock. Follow the path to the top of the cave and find the sharp outcrop. Walk to the end to collect the prize.

12

Northwest of Big Darwa Fort, three grappling points sit on the southwest side of a cliff. Take them up to reach the higher level. Walk out along the flatter section of the outcrop to reach the Daysha Hand.

13 Above the river, a Daysha Hand rests on a rock. Reachable from inland by moving around the cliff or from the grappling points along the water.

14 This Daysha Hand is found on another rock protrusion just east of the previous one. Walk up the path and out onto the rock to collect the handprint.

15 East of Gwarashnar Bonfire, a Daysha Hand sits on the side of a plateau. If you are having trouble spotting this one, use Hunter Vision as it is hiding in a bush.

16 West of Cold Swim Cave, look for a couple of big rocks jutting out of the ground next to a hunter's shelter. Jump onto the western one to find a Daysha Hand.

17 In Udam homeland, well north of Ull's cave, look for Mi-Mamsa Falls. Use the two grappling points to the west to find a shelter. Sitting southeast, at the top of the falls, is a Daysha Hand.

18 In the western section of The Hunting Valley, a Daysha Hand sits inside the Raider Camp, behind a couple of bone trees.

19 In the middle of Udam homeland, north of the river, a watchtower sits just west of the main path. Underneath, a Daysha Hand waits to be collected.

20 A small island sits in a body of water north of Ull's cave. Just northeast of the island, a Daysha Hand rests at the bottom of the lake. Use Hunter Vision to spot it.

21 In the southern region of the Udam homeland, south of the Bone Finder Camp, move south up the hill to find the Daysha Hand sitting in front of a big boulder.

22 It is worthwhile to collect this Daysha Hand during The Peak of Oros mission. As you climb the cliffs, a grappling point to the east takes you to a grassy area. Move up the hill to find a big boulder with the collectible sitting on top.

23 Just outside the cave where you find Tensay, a Daysha Hand rests on a rock just south of a small waterfall.

24 South of Tensay's cave, look for the Wenja ring next to the water. Move south through the wreath to spot the Daysha Hand on the edge of the cliff.

25 Just north of Shayu's Cave and south of a big tree, a Daysha Hand rests next to a sunken canoe at the bottom of the river.

26 Look for stacks of rocks northwest of Roaring Falls Bonfire. A Daysha Hand sits on a rock ledge nearby.

27 At the base of the cliff that holds Roaring Falls Bonfire, a Daysha Hand rests next to the water.

28 Follow the stream east from Roaring Falls Bonfire to a small pond. At the bottom is another Hand. Be careful not to provoke the Mammoths that swim in the water.

29 Northeast of Marsa Cave, south of snowy Oros, a Hand sits on the side of a cliff. Use the upper grappling point to lower yourself onto the small ledge and collect the prize.

30 Find the cave you spent time in during Wogah's Trapped mission. A rock arch spans a gap between two cliffs above. Lying on top is a Daysha Hand.

31 West of Gwarashnar Bonfire, in the middle of the water, a Daysha Hand sits at the bottom of the lake.

32 Head south from your village until you find a waterfall. The nearest Daysha Hand sits in the rocks below.

33 Directly east of the previous Daysha Hand, another one sits at the base of a waterfall.

34 South of Stones of the Lost, a Daysha Hand is ready to be plucked from the bottom of a pond, but a Crocodile lies in wait. Take care of it before collecting the reward.

35 West of Stone Watch Bonfire, another Daysha Hand rests at the bottom of a pond. Dive in to collect it.

36 At Forgotten Crater, dive into the water to find a Daysha Hand sitting next to a dolmen.

Go to the campsite next to Pardaku Lookout and move over to the grappling point. Use it to swing over to a ledge to the west. Climb up to get the Daysha Hand.

North of Mash Baya Rocks, a Daysha Hand rests on a narrow ridge at the top of a waterfall. You can drop from above or climb the ledges to collect it.

Southwest of the Ring Wall Outpost, look for a Daysha Hand near Kashatigri's Home. North of the path this item sits around the cliff from a hunter's camp.

South of Ring Wall Outpost, find a small pond. A Daysha Hand sits next to a rock on the east side.

Directly south of your village find a lake on the west side of the region. Sitting on the southwest bank, collect the Daysha Hand next to the boulder. Beware of the Crocodile who stalks in the water nearby.

South of Bloodfang Den, look for a tall tree on the south side of the rocks. A Daysha Hand hides just behind it.

Dive into the water east of the Dangu Cave. This Daysha Hand rests at the bottom of the lake just in front of the waterfall.

Search in the water west of Great Scar Bear Den to find a Daysha Hand sitting on the bottom, just below the waterfall.

Look for the taller waterfall directly east of High Cliff Bonfire. Climb onto the ledge at its base and continue up the ivy to find a Hand sitting on a platform behind the waterfall.

46 East of Great Prashrawa, just inside the eastern region of Oros, look for a stone shelter providing protection for a couple of Boars. Grab the Hand from inside, keeping an eye out for nearby Izila Hunters.

47 Northeast of Fallen Tashla Outpost and directly north of The Gathering Tree, a Daysha Hand rests on the bank of a stream that flows into a waterfall to the west. This one is easiest to reach from the south.

48 In between Great Prashrawa and Fallen Tashla Outpost, look for a boulder south of the water. A Daysha Hand rests on the ground on its west side.

49 North of Night Watch Bonfire, a Daysha Hand lies on a rock outcrop. It is easily accessed from the north or south.

50 Directly west of Payska River Outpost, look for the plateau where you placed the Spirit Totem during the Village Mission. Below, a Daysha Hand rests at the bottom of a small pond.

51 A Daysha Hand lies at the bottom of the big lake, just southwest of Payska River Outpost. Be sure to check for predators in the water before diving in.

52 Northwest of Great Prashrawa, a small cave hides behind a small waterfall. Follow the rock path southwest into the waterway and look to the right, where a Daysha Hand lies underwater.

53 West of Burning Spear Bonfire, a narrow passage cuts through the cliffs, southeast of the Wenja rings in the Rings of Fire Village Mission. On the east side of this path, high on the plateau, a Daysha Hand rests next to a standing rock.

54 Southwest of the Twarshi Basin standing stones, just down the hill, a Daysha Hand sits upon a boulder.

55 Look for a pile of rocks and logs at the base of the cliff, southwest of Mash Baya Rocks. Sitting on the upper rock is another Daysha Hand. Drop from the plateau above or climb the debris to collect it.

56 South of Burning Sun Circle, Use the grappling point on the side of the cliff to reach the plateau above. Move along the edge to the east to find a Daysha Hand sitting between a rock and a tree.

57 A Daysha Hand hides among the flora on the long, narrow island west of Great Prashrawa.

58 Directly west of Rotten Lake Outpost, a Daysha Hand rests at the base of a high cliff. Climb the ledge from the east to reach the item.

59 East of Rotten Lake Outpost, look for a log leaning against a big boulder. Walk up the tree to reach the top of the rock where a Daysha Hand awaits.

60 Use the grappling claw to climb the mountain west of Nada Swamp Outpoost and then look for a narrow ledge, accessible from the north. Sitting next to a tree is another Daysha Hand.

61 Another Daysha Hand rests at the bottom of the river. This time find it northeast of Nada Swamp outpost.

62 At The Great Prashrawa falls, a Hand rests on a rock ledge in the middle of the second waterfall from the bottom. Access it from the north by hopping across the rocks.

63 Just south of Kaba Blade Outpost, a much tamer waterfall brings water to the river. A Daysha Hand rests on a rock on its north side.

64 The Izila's Stone Shadow Camp sits on a plateau in the far southwest corner of the region. A Daysha Hand lies on a rock at the edge of the cliff to the northeast.

65 A short distance northeast from the previous Daysha Hand, another one sits on a rock outcrop above a small waterfall. Access it from the west.

66 A campfire located on the path west of Fire Screamer Fort offers Fast Travel. A Daysha Hand sits out in the open nearby.

67 Run up the hill located northwest of Fire Screamer Fort. At the very top, on the west side, a Daysha Hand is ready to be grabbed.

68 High on the cliff directly east of Fire Screamer Fort, a Daysha Hand overlooks the Izila stronghold.

69 In the far southwest region of Oros, move to the west side of Kwacha Stone Outpost. Find the opening to the rock shelf and search the flora to the left.

70 Find the small waterfall near Walkwa Den. Enter a tunnel to the north, follow it to an opening, and grab the Daysha Hand that lies on the ground. You can also access this one by dropping in from the north side.

71 On the north side of the swamp that holds the Praying Stones, spot a big boulder protruding out of the ground. Resting next to its south face is another Daysha Hand.

72 Follow the narrow passageway south from Digway Camp until you spot a grappling point high on the right cliff. Use it to reach the peak and search behind the nearby rock to find a Daysha Hand.

73 Southeast of Stone Damshi Island find a Daysha Hand resting next to a tree, behind a bush. It sits just outside of the lake.

74 Just inside Izila homeland, follow the western path south until you reach two standing stones on the right. Lying next to them, between a few pots, is a Daysha Hand.

75 On the northwest side of Izila homeland, just west of the Forsaken Altar, move up the embankment from the western path. Run around the rocks on the left to find a little nook. Just in front of it is a Daysha Hand.

76 Northeast of Kala Island, this Daysha Hand sits among two standing stones, between the water and dirt trail.

77 Several standing stones have been placed in a pond in the northeast corner of the Izila homeland. Northwest of there, just off the trail, a Daysha Hand sits behind three small tree stumps.

78 A tall hill sits in the middle of the Izila homeland, just northwest of Izila village. Access the incline from the north path and climb most of the way up to find a Daysha Hand next to a couple of rocks on the left.

IZILA MASKS

NUMBER	25	
AWARD	XP	
ONCE WORN BY SUXLI'S SACRIFICES; THEY MARK IZILA LAND.		

Izila Masks, only found in Izila territories, mostly hang on cliff faces—though they can also be found on trees, or even on the ground. Shoot the item with your bow or hit it to add it to your collection. Some of these masks must be shot from far away, so equip the Long Bow and account for arrow drop by aiming a little above the target.

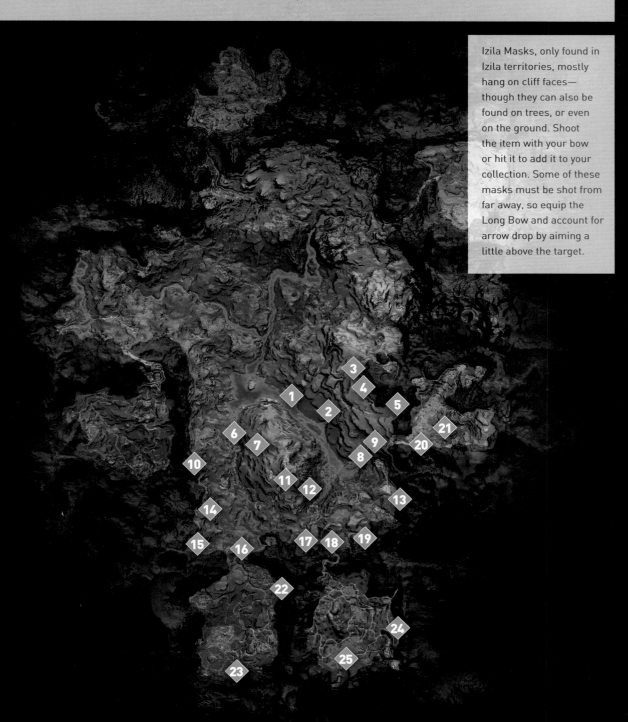

1. East of Payska River Outpost, a campfire offers a Fast Travel point. Hanging on the cliff directly west of the fire is an Izila Mask.

2. A Mask dangles from the cliff on the west edge of Tushwarha Outpost, just left of an entrance to the outpost's underground lair.

3. Situated in between Burning Spear Bonfire and Mash Baya Rocks, an Izila Mask hangs just left of a grappling point and waterfall.

4. Southwest of Mash Baya Rocks, find a pile of boulders and logs. The Mask hangs on the cliff above a little to the south.

5. This Mask hangs on the side of the mountain, just north of Bandu Blood Stone. It is above the trees, so find an opening to shoot through. It can also be targeted from the southern shelf with the standing stones.

6. Head to the rock bridge east of Chishta Cave and find the Izila Mask that has been pinned to the south side, sitting above the arch.

7. Northwest of The Tall Watchers, the side of the mountain is tiered. Look for the tall west cliff facing just south of the standing stones. A Mask faces south high above.

8. Northeast of Drowning Huts, this Mask hangs just left of a waterfall. Climb the cliff to get a closer shot.

9. From Great Prashrawa, look at the big waterfall to the east. An Izila Mask hangs high on the rock between the rushing water.

10. A small, shallow pond sits on a plateau northwest of Rotten Lake Outpost. Dangling to the west, on the relatively short cliff face, is an Izila Mask.

11. Northwest of Blajiman Stones, this Mask is left of a southeast-facing waterfall. Shoot this one from a platform right of the water or from above. Drop down to the ledge that holds an eagle's nest for the easiest shot.

12. Move northeast up the grassy path that is located just east of Blajiman Stones. At the end, stop next to the grappling point and look up. Dangling from a rock outcrop is another Izila Mask.

Follow the small stream south of Kaba Blade Outpost until it runs into the eastern mountain. This Izila Mask hangs on the rocks left of the waterfall.

Southwest of Rotten Lake Outpost, a waterfall flows into a small pond. An Izila Mask has been placed on the middle ledge in the middle of the rushing water.

In the southeast corner of the region, the Sisters of Fire reside at Stone Shadow Camp. On your way to the village, a Mask hangs on the left side of the path.

North of the Great Scar Bear hunting grounds and east of Kalni Grave, move to the right side of the stream. The Izila Mask dangles over the water from an outcropping.

West of Fire Screamer Fort, a campfire gives you another Fast Travel point. Southeast of there, a big rock juts out of the ground. Shoot the Izila Mask that hangs on the east side.

Just west of Fire Screamer Fort, an Izila Mask has been placed on the east cliff face. Watch out for patrolling Izila if the command post has not been captured.

Head east from Fire Screamer Fort to find another waterfall. An Izila Mask dangles from a rock high above and to the left. The cliff face can be climbed to get a better shot, but it is reachable from the ground.

East of Great Prashrawa, just inside the Snowblood Wolf hunting grounds, find a pile of offerings for Suxli. Setting in the middle is the next Izila Mask.

Move to the base of the waterfall located north of Fallen Tashla Outpost. Use the grappling point on the left to climb to the top. This Izila Mask sits on the ground among gifts for their god, Suxli.

On the northeast side of the Great Scar Bear hunting grounds, look for a den at Tomb of Teeth. A log leans against a rock ledge at the entrance. Enter the cave and make a right turn to find the Izila Mask.

At the far south end of Oros, past the Praying Stones, find a standing stone in the middle of a small body of water just west of Split Rock Cave. An Izila Mask dangles from the rock wall behind it.

South of the Altar of Suxli, deep inside Izila homeland, find a lone hut. Another Izila Mask hangs above the entrance.

Southwest of Izila Village, spot the broken tree on the south side of the water. It is located just northeast of a small waterfall at the southern tip of the lake. Shoot the Izila Mask that hangs from the tree.

SPIRIT TOTEMS

	NUMBER	12
	AWARD	+2% XP Boost

TOTEMS ASK SPIRITS FOR SAFE AND SUCCESSFUL HUNTS.

Twelve altars around Oros stand empty, but you can remedy that by placing a small totem on each one. Step up to the pedestal and hold the interact button to make it complete. Each one gives a +2% XP boost, so be sure to get these done early.

1 One Spirit Totem is placed during the Spirit Totem Village Mission. (Not shown on map.)

2 In the mountains east of Stone Beak Bonfire, there are two bodies of water. Northwest of the right one, use the grappling point to reach the pedestal.

3 At Blood Snow Totem, west of Cut Mamaf Lost Cave, an altar is found just west of an Udam camp.

4 From Snow Shwalda Outpost, move through the valley and then north until you reach a rock hanging over the path. Head east to find several protruding rocks along with a quest giver. An altar sits next to the southern rocks.

5 At Bayabar Hunter Totem, located at the southeastern tip of the snowy region, a cave opening is found on the northeast side of the camp. The pedestal sits on the right side of the cavern.

6 Not far from your village, north of the Stone Watch Bonfire, stop at the small village that sits on the main path. Sitting next to a tree, near the huts, is another pedestal that waits for a Spirit Totem.

7 West of Burning Spear Bonfire, look for a group of standing stones just north of a circular waterway. An altar is found on the south side of one of these stones.

8 Head to Blajiman Stones to find a pedestal just northwest of the Izila's sacrificial altar. Place the totem to bring safe and successful hunts to the Wenja.

9 Northeast of Stone Shadow Camp, look for the small pond that sits on the main path. An altar has been built atop a rock platform just behind a small waterfall.

10 Find this pedestal just outside a cave opening deep inside Bloodfang Sabretooth Hunting Grounds, near the unknown location, Hiding Hole.

11 Directly west of Chanting Cave, this altar sits at the base of a misty waterfall. Look for it on the right as you move up a grassy path, east of the waterway.

12 The final Spirit Totem must be placed just east of Hold Rock Bonfire. Sneak through the camp or capture it and look for a water hole in the back. Dive in and follow the tunnel back to a small chamber.

WENJA BRACELETS

NUMBER	25	
AWARD	XP	
WORN FOR LIFE, THEY REPRESENT THE TRIBE'S ETERNAL BOND.		

Much like the bracelet that Takkar received from Dalso at the beginning of the game, lost Wenja Bracelets hide throughout north and central Oros. As you approach one, a green circle appears on the mini-map showing you the vicinity of the bracelet. Search this area for the tiny collectible. Enable Hunter Vision to make it glow, but it can still be tough to spot from a distance.

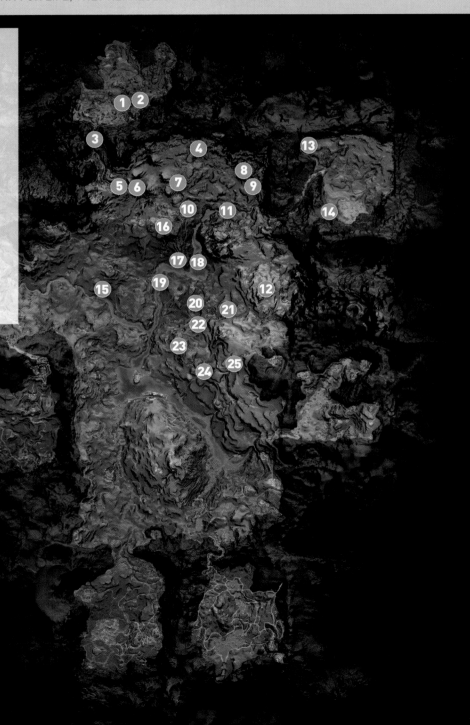

1 In the most northern region of Oros, head northeast from Stone Beak Bonfire to a grappling point and drop to the intersection below. Continue straight to another grapple and climb to the top of the plateau. At the base of a bone tree is a Bracelet.

2 Move to the plateau directly southeast from Mamaf Graveyard and use the southwest grappling point to get on top. Look for a pile of small rocks straight ahead. A Wenja Bracelet lies on the right side.

3 As you move north through the valley connecting the northern region with the rest of Oros, notice a group of three bone trees. Cut in front of them to the left and drop down. Hug the cliff on the right to find a Bracelet in a crevice.

4 Follow the path northwest of Platu Cave Outpost until you reach a frozen pond. Spot a pointy rock right of a big tree at the back of the ice. A Wenja Bracelet rests at the base of this rock, next to a skeleton.

5 Go north from Yagi Arrow Bonfire until you reach water. Move around the rocks on the left to the top of the small waterfall. A Wenja Bracelet sits in the middle of the water, next to some bones.

6 Follow the stream east until another circle appears on the mini-map. Drop down the next waterfall and search the bank on the left to find the Bracelet.

7 Follow the trail east from Twarsha Cave Outpost until you reach a rocky area, shaped like a horseshoe on the left. A Wenja Bracelet lies on the right side next to a sack.

8 East of Platu Cave Outpost, move northeast into the valley, climb the grappling point on the right, and continue up the hill to activate the vicinity circle. Grapple up another level and search near the dead Wolf on the right to find the Bracelet.

9 Follow the trail northwest of Big Darwa Fort, taking the right path at the split. At the first sharp rock on the left, step out onto the ledge and walk under a second pointy rock. Drop down to find a spear and Bracelet resting next to an old campfire.

10 Northwest of Cut Mamaf Cave, move around the left side of the cliff and use the grappling point on the right to reach the plateau above. Go northeast to find a skeleton with an arrow sticking out of its ribcage. The Bracelet is still on its left wrist.

11 Go to the far east side of the lake, opposite Cut Mamaf Cave, and search at the foot of the waterfall. The Bracelet is next to a skeleton.

12 In the southeastern corner of snowy Oros, directly west of Cold Swim Cave, look for a hut next to a lit fire. Find a Bracelet resting on a rock inside.

13 Explore into the Udam homeland and head to the northwest corner, north of a waterfall. A Bracelet lies next to the mountain, near a pile of sticks.

14 South of Mamsa Saja Bonfire, in the southwest corner of the Udam homeland, run up the hill past the watchtower. Grab the Bracelet that sits next to a pile of rocks, near a couple of Mammoth skulls.

15 South of Roaring Falls Bonfire, move southeast along a ridge until you find an opening on the right that has been filled in with small rocks. Bust down the weak wall to find a Bracelet hiding inside.

16 South of the snow line, between Marsa and Cut Mamaf Caves, run northeast up the hill toward the cliff. A skeleton lies next to two small rocks, just left of some ivy that leads to a rock platform above. It hides behind a boulder until you get close. Grab the Bracelet next to the bones.

17 From the campfire, east of Marsa Cave, run southeast down the hill. Follow the ridge until you enter the green circle, turning left at the big tree. A spear stuck in the ground marks the spot.

18 From the previous Wenja Bracelet, move around the southern tip of the mountain and onto the island. At the top of the hill, find a spear sticking out of a skeleton and collect the Bracelet.

19

Cross the river east of the Swaras Outpost and find the weak section of the rock face. Bust it open to collect a Wenja Bracelet from inside.

20

Head downhill northwest of Piki Meat Outpost until you find a human skeleton sitting next to a Sabretooth Tiger skull. Resting between the bones is a Wenja Bracelet.

21

Follow the path directly east of Piki Meat Outpost until you reach a big puddle of mud. A Wenja Bracelet rests on the north side next to a rib cage.

22

Southwest of Piki Meat Outpost find another mud pot. A Bracelet sits behind a sharp rock outcrop on the south side.

23

Discover the campfire northeast of Cave of Sun Walkers. Drop off the cliff to the southwest to find a Wenja Bracelet resting on a rock next to a spear.

24

Find the island west of Burning Spear Bonfire and south of the standing stones. On the north end, a Bracelet still hangs around the wrist of a dislocated arm.

25

East of Burning Spear Bonfire, dive into the water below the waterfall. A Wenja Bracelet rests at the bottom; use Hunter Vision to find it in the cloudy water.

How did the decision to use PIE as the spoken language in the game come about?

Being set in 10,000 BCE, it was immediately apparent that any modern language would feel out of place. The world, the materials, and the predators were all grounded in the Stone Age. We couldn't drop the ball when it came to language. So we teamed up with expert linguists who helped us craft a language appropriate to the Mesolithic Age.

— *Kevin Shortt, Lead Writer*

TROPHIES AND ACHIEVEMENTS

GAME PROGRESSION

Complete the missions and secondary quests to earn the following awards.

TITLE	DESCRIPTION	GAMER SCORE	TROPHY	UPLAY
This Way To Oros	Survive the Mammoth hunt by completing the intro. Your first Trophy or Achievement is earned as soon as you are alone.	20	Silver	10
Spearproof	Repel the Udam attack by completing the Attack of the Udam mission—revealing more specialists around Oros.	20	Silver	—
Liberator	Rescue a Wenja captive from the Izila in The Taken Wenja mission. This unlocks Fire Screamer Fort which is your gateway to Batari.	20	Silver	—
Uncaged	Escape the Udam caverns by completing the Into Udam Land mission. With the Antidote, you are now able to invade the Udam homeland and find Ull.	20	Silver	—
Krati, Krati, Krati!	Steal the Izila mask of Krati by completing The Mask of Krati mission and unlocking the Izila homeland. Be sure to grab the Mammoth Rider skill to proceed inside.	100	Gold	40
Deadeye	Karoosh joins the Wenja village. Complete the Brother in Need mission and gain access to the some great Warrior Skills including the Heavy Takedown.	10	Bronze	—
Spiritual Advisor	Tensay joins the Wenja village. Find Tensay and complete the Vision of Beasts mission. This gives you the ability to tame beasts and unlocks the Shaman Skills.	10	Bronze	—
Mister Fix-It	Wogah joins the Wenja village. Complete the Trapped and Blood of Oros missions to gain access to Crafter Skills and some great gear.	10	Bronze	—
Gray Huntress	Jayma joins the Wenja village. Complete the On the Hunt mission to unlock Hunting Skills.	10	Bronze	—
Twelve Labors	Complete any 12 Specialist missions. This includes any mission given by the seven specialists. Several are required to complete the story, so that is a good start.	20	Silver	20
Evolution in Action	Complete the mission, The Hunt for Ull by defeating Udam leader, Ull. You must obtain the Antidote by completing Into Udam Land before accessing Ull.	20	Bronze	—
To Ash	Complete the mission, The Fall of Batari by defeating the Izila leader, Batari. You must purchase the Mammoth Rider skill to access Izila homeland and reach Batari.	20	Bronze	—
Here Kitty	Track, defeat, and tame the Bloodfang Sabretooth. Complete Jayma's The Tall Elk mission to unlock the Beast Master Hunts.	20	Bronze	—
Big Teddy	Track, defeat, and tame the Great Scar Bear. Complete Jayma's The Tall Elk mission to unlock the Beast Master Hunts.	20	Bronze	—

TITLE	DESCRIPTION	GAMER SCORE	TROPHY	UPLAY
Endangered	Track and defeat the Bloodtusk Mammoth. Complete Jayma's The Tall Elk mission to unlock the Beast Master Hunts.	20	Silver	—
Good Boy	Track, defeat, and tame the Snowblood Wolf. Complete Jayma's The Tall Elk mission to unlock the Beast Master Hunts.	20	Bronze	—
Conquest	Capture all forts by defeating Dah at Big Darwa Fort and Roshani at Fire Screamer Fort.	20	Bronze	—
Good Neighbor	Complete 15 "Help Wenja" quests. Look for Wenja around Oros in need of help, noted by a circular orange icon displaying a hand.	20	Bronze	—
Crush Your Enemies	Complete 10 "Tribal Clash" quests. These fights against the Udam or Izila are shown on the map with a circular, orange icon with a black skull.	20	Bronze	—
Master Tracker	Complete 5 "Beast Kill" quests. A quest giver asks you to defeat a certain beast in Beast Kill quests, which are signified by an orange icon with a paw print.	20	Bronze	—

KILL AWARDS

Killing enemies in a variety of ways earns you a whole lot of awards.

TITLE	DESCRIPTION	GAMER SCORE	TROPHY	UPLAY
Tears of Shame	That is cold, but in order to get this award, you must kill your own companion and then skin it. Perform this on a lower level beast to save on the revive.	20	Silver	—
Killer's Belief	Eliminate 25 enemies using any takedown. Takedowns are a great way to decrease enemy numbers without being detected. Purchase the takedown skills from Karoosh for a variety of options.	15	Bronze	—
And Stay Down	Eliminate 100 enemies using a club. The weapon of choice in close combat, the club is especially effective against smaller animals. Be sure to upgrade the club when you get the chance.	20	Bronze	—
Skewered	Eliminate 100 enemies using a spear. Spears are very effective when thrown. Use them to take down the bigger wildlife and tougher enemies.	20	Bronze	—
Sharpshooter	Eliminate 100 enemies using a bow. The bow and its various iterations are best from a distance before being detected. Get headshots to finish off weaker enemies with one shot.	20	Bronze	—
Inflammable	Eliminate 50 enemies with fire. This includes any attack with fire; light a weapon or toss a Fire Bomb.	10	Bronze	—
David And Goliath	Eliminate 10 enemies using a sling. Great for headshots and unlimited ammo, what else could you ask for? Grab the Precision Sling skill from Wogah to pierce elite enemy headgear.	10	Bronze	—

TITLE	DESCRIPTION	GAMER SCORE	TROPHY	UPLAY
Outta My Way	Eliminate 25 enemies while riding a Mammoth. Purchase the Mammoth Rider skill from Karoosh to gain the ability to mount young Mammoth. Ride it through a few villages to quickly rack up 25 kills.	10	Bronze	—
Bad Trip	Influence 25 enemies using poison. Confuse hostiles with Berserk Bombs or Shards. Toss a bomb into a group of human foes and watch them fight amongst themselves.	10	Bronze	—
BEES!	Eliminate 10 enemies using sting bags. Toss these bombs into crowds to cause total chaos. Be sure to keep your distance or face the wrath of the angry bees.	10	Bronze	—
Quickdraw	Eliminate 15 enemies using throwing shards. Grab the Shard Takedown to add a quick shard attack after a normal takedown.	10	Bronze	—
Right On Target	Kill a target 50m away or more using a spear. Find a weak enemy such as an Udam Slinger at a camp. Take him out with a long-distance spear throw. Be sure to account for a lot of drop from that far away.	15	Bronze	—
Bullseye	Kill a target 70m away or more using an arrow. You must have a long line of sight on an enemy to score a kill from 70m away. Flat areas around the river in central Oros give plenty of opportunity to kill from distance. This can also be achieved from a high cliff. Equip the Long Bow and account for arrow drop when aiming.	15	Bronze	—
Gotcha	Eliminate 10 enemies using hunting traps. Use traps whenever capturing bonfires and outposts. Study patrol patterns and place them in the enemies' path.	10	Bronze	—
Sic 'Em	Eliminate 50 enemies using a tamed beast. Grab a Sabretooth Tiger or Cave Bear and you will have this number in no time.	20	Bronze	—
Feathered Friend	Eliminate 15 enemies using your Owl. Attacks and dropped bombs from your Owl are a great surprise for unsuspecting enemies. Purchase the Owl: Weapon Drop and Owl: Attack I skills from Tensay.	20	Bronze	—

YOUR VILLAGE

Building, improving, and growing your village earns three awards. This requires a lot of resources, including rare skins, but it is well worth the time.

TITLE	DESCRIPTION	GAMER SCORE	TROPHY	UPLAY
Home Improvement	Perform two upgrades on any village huts. Build Sayla and Tensay's huts.	10	Bronze	—
Subdivisions	Your Wenja tribe reaches a population of 20. Complete quests and capture landmarks to increase your village population. Access the Village tab in your menu to check the current number.	20	Bronze	—

TITLE	DESCRIPTION	GAMER SCORE	TROPHY	UPLAY
Real Estate Baron	Complete all hut upgrades. Build and upgrade the cave and all seven huts. This requires a lot of resources, including several different rare skins. Check the Village tab to find out what is still needed.	50	Silver	—

COMPLETIONIST

These accomplishments are for those who go beyond the story missions.

TITLE	DESCRIPTION	GAMER SCORE	TROPHY	UPLAY
Expert Wenja	Learn all skills. Complete missions and secondary quests to earn the XP necessary to afford all skills.	50	Silver	—
Armorer	Craft 100 weapons of any kind: clubs, spears, arrows, bombs, or shards. It doesn't take too long before racking up this many weapons. Crafting arrows gains a good amount on its own.	20	Silver	—
Skirmish	Capture 10 outposts. Look for the red fire icons on the map and kill the Udam or Izila that guard it.	20	Bronze	—
Expansion	Capture all outposts. Outposts, signified by a red hut icon, are usually tougher than bonfires. Watch out for alarms and Elite Slingers. If you are detected the enemy can call in reinforcements, making your job that much tougher.	50	Gold	30
Menagerie	Tame seven beasts. You must purchase Beast Master Skills to tame many of the beasts. Completing three of the Beast Master Hunts give you a tamed beast.	15	Bronze	20
Fancy Friend	Tame 1 rare beast. Rare beasts are found at the same locations as the regular animals, but at a much lower rate. For example, look for a Black Lion where you find Cave Lions.	10	Bronze	—
Veterinarian	Heal a tamed beast 25 times. Beasts often get in trouble, running off and taking on enemies on their own. Be sure to keep them healthy by feeding them meat.	15	Bronze	—
Cave Hoarder	Pickup 80 collectibles. This includes Daysha Hands, Izila Masks, Wenja Bracelets, Cave Paintings, and Spirit Totems. There are 184 in all, so you need less than half to score this award.	20	Bronze	—
Mapmaker	Discover 15 hidden locations. Hidden locations are signified by a white question mark on the map. There are a lot, so it doesn't take long to get this one.	20	Bronze	—

MARK 4 WENJA

Find a cave at the top of a waterfall just northwest of Big Darwa Fort. Follow the path to the back and peek through the hole.

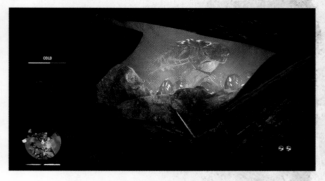

TITLE	DESCRIPTION	GAMER SCORE	TROPHY	UPLAY
Mark 4 Wenja	Discover the future past.	15	Bronze	10

KANDA OF FAITH

Find the campfire located high on a hill, northwest of Mash Baya Rocks. With that spawn point established, climb south and east to find the highest rock outcrop. Being careful not to fall to your death, slide out to the edge and spot the pool of water below. Jump out from the cliff to dive in. You earn the award on the way down, not on entry, so it is possible to get it and die. You will reset at the campfire above.

TITLE	DESCRIPTION	GAMER SCORE	TROPHY	UPLAY
Kanda of Faith	Climb to the peak of Pardaku Lookout and leap off.	10	Bronze	—

PLAYSTATION PLATINUM

TITLE	DESCRIPTION	GAMER SCORE	TROPHY	UPLAY
Apex Predator	Obtain all the Trophies.	N/A	Platinum	N/A

WELCOME

SURVIVING
THE WILD

LAND OF OROS

TAKKAR'S JOURNEY

MAJOR LANDMARKS

LOCATIONS

VILLAGE
CONSTRUCTION

ENEMY TRIBES

WILDLIFE

GEAR

SKILLS

FOOD RECIPES

RESOURCES

COLLECTIBLES

TROPHIES/
ACHIEVEMENTS

THE ART OF OROS

THE ART OF OROS

 The land of Oros is based around our research into the central and Eastern regions of Europe of the time. The Danube River was often followed by primitive humans as they migrated from Africa, and then you have the Carpathian Mountains further north, which at the time were covered by a glacier. That gives us a great space to create a believable world where you'll see a mix of forests, icy landscapes, and other locations.

— *Clark Davies, Lead Game Designer*

The Mesolithic period is an age where communities began to form. Tribes moved away from nomadic lifestyles and started gathering around villages. This meant tribes were settled in the same regions and drawing on the same resources. That created conflict within tribes and that led to fights to the death. Our adventure needed to reflect that reality and so we crafted a story about a wounded tribe that must reunite to survive against fierce enemies. Takkar is a Wenja cousin returning to his tribe and faced with a splintered people that he must rally.

— *Kevin Shortt, Lead Writer*

What location draws me the most? The forest of giant cedar trees. I grew up a little north of Montreal, in an isolated house near a forest. I've always envied the forests of the west coast; ours don't even come close here.

— *Vincent Pontbriand, Senior Producer*

Players shouldn't miss seeing the Izila quarry. It is a place with a lot of history because this is the place the monoliths were created.

— *Fabien Govini, Level Design Director*

You are ripped from your everyday life and plunked down in the land of Oros. What becomes of you?

I would scream, run and find the nearest bush.

— Fabien Govini, Level Design Director

I lie down and go into fetal position until I freeze to death or something comes to kill me.

— Jean-Sébastien Decant, Narrative Director

I would try to make a fire for the whole first week and then finally die because I would eat a poisonous plant
by mistake.

— Jean-Christophe Guyot, Creative Director

I think I would become a berries gatherer. I wouldn't stand a chance as a warrior.

— Vincent Pontbriand, Senior Producer

I don't survive the first five minutes. If I survive, I would find the biggest and strongest Wenja and stick with him.

— Mickael Labat, Art Director

CREDITS

SENIOR DEVELOPMENT EDITOR
Jennifer Sims

SENIOR GRAPHIC DESIGNER
Carol Stamile

PRODUCTION DESIGNERS
Justin Lucas
Julie Clark

PRODUCTION
Tom Leddy

MAP ILLUSTRATOR
Darren Strecker

PRIMA GAMES STAFF

VP & PUBLISHER
Mike Degler

EDITORIAL MANAGER
Tim Fitzpatrick

DESIGN AND LAYOUT MANAGER
Tracy Wehmeyer

LICENSING
Christian Sumner
Paul Giacomotto

MARKETING
Katie Hemlock

DIGITAL PUBLISHING
Julie Asbury
Tim Cox
Shaida Boroumand

OPERATIONS MANAGER
Stacey Beheler

ACKNOWLEDGMENTS

Prima would like to thank Marie-Jeanne Sauvé, Roy Del Valle, Vincenzo Spina, Jean-Philippe Rajotte, Trey Williamson, Nolan Ellis, Matthew Scriver and their QC teams, and the rest of the amazing team at Ubisoft for their help and support on this project.

Written by Michael Owen and Will Murray.

The Prima Games logo and Primagames.com are registered trademarks of Penguin Random House LLC, registered in the United States. Prima Games is an imprint of DK, a division of Penguin Random House LLC, New York.

DK/Prima Games, a division of Penguin Random House LLC
6081 East 82nd Street, Suite #400
Indianapolis, IN 46250

ISBN: 978-0-7440-1698-7

Printing Code: The rightmost double-digit number is the year of the book's printing; the rightmost single-digit number is the number of the book's printing. For example, 16-1 shows that the first printing of the book occurred in 2016.

19 18 17 16   4 3 2 1

Printed in the USA.